The Sopranos

spin offs

A production of the Console-ing Passions books series
Edited by Lynn Spigel

Duke University Press   Durham and London   2009

The Sopranos

DANA POLAN

© 2009 Duke University Press

All rights reserved

Printed in the United States of America

on acid-free paper ∞

Designed by C. H. Westmoreland

Typeset in Warnock by Tseng Information Systems, Inc.

Library of Congress Cataloging-in-Publication Data appear

on the last printed page of this book.

FOR DOUG AND ANN

—*who first introduced me to a certain New Jersey family*

Contents

Acknowledgments

Any resonant work of television becomes part of a broad cultural conversation, and, in my own case, I benefited immeasurably from the rich dialogue that *The Sopranos* has encouraged among viewers. For their rewarding reflections (and with special thanks to those who came to Sunday-night *Sopranos* fests), I offer much gratitude to Barbara Peterson, Bill Peterson, Kara Kirk, Doug Thomas, Ann Chisholm, Marianne Hirsch, Leo Spitzer, Kristin Ross, Harry Harootunian, Nick Mirzoeff, Kathleen Wilson, Nick Couldry, Louise Edwards, Noah Isenberg, Melanie Rehak, Tom Kemper, Alison Trope, Lesley Stern, Jeffrey Minson, Toby Miller, Andrew Sheppard, Jeff Sconce, Cynthia Chris, Scott Bukatman, and Chris Anderson. Chris, Nick M., Ann, and Noah also read the manuscript and offered supportive comment. Maurice Yacowar graciously gave me information on his *Sopranos* course, one of the—if not *the*—first! My own undergraduates in a University of Southern California *Sopranos* class willingly and energetically participated in the experiment of reflecting on a television series that was still in its first years of broadcast.

A few lines or passages here or there are adapted from my essay, "Cable Watching: HBO, *The Sopranos* and Discourses of Distinction," published in *Cable Visions: Television Beyond Broadcasting*, ed. Sarah Banet-Weiser, Cynthia Chris, and Anthony Freitas (New York University Press, 2007).

Special gratitude to Allen Rucker for talking to me about his *Sopranos* tie-ins and to Matt Weiner for recounting his experiences as writer for the show. And big thanks go out to Zarah and the team at the Rhinebeck Smoke Shoppe.

Lynn Spigel is a great friend and a wonderful series editor. Her sharpness as an analyst of television in its myriad forms constituted an invaluable support for this project.

Ken Wissoker at Duke University Press has been a model of professionalism and editorial rigor. Likewise, Courtney Berger at the Press has been a great supporter and brought immeasurable aid at each stage of the process.

Also at Duke University Press, Neal McTighe ushered the manuscript through its final production phases with efficiency and commitment: thank you. And deep gratitude to my graduate assistants, Dan Gao and Alex Kupfer, who aided with proofing and indexing.

The intrepid Marie Sturken was the perfect companion for the *Sopranos* bus tour.

Marita Sturken gave so much—in time, support, love, and patience—to this project. This is definitely a case where it is not an idle cliché to say that words can't convey everything I owe her, everything I feel for her.

Little Leo-Andres Polan came into our lives as this book was nearing its final stages. He has been a joy and I am so happy to tie the completion of this scholarly project to the beginning of our new family life together.

At the end of a story, you'll find it's all been told.
—Earl Grant, "The End," 1958

Prologue

THE NON-SENSE OF AN ENDING

In the days immediately following June 10, 2007, the date on which the last episode of HBO's hit show *The Sopranos* was aired, the word "Sopranos" itself was the most frequent search term on Internet search engines.[1] And in the first few minutes after the episode finished, the HBO Web site crashed and remained down for several hours due to the volume of people trying to log into it.

There are several lessons to be drawn from this. One is about the increased role of new media—such as the Web—in extending and amplifying the life cycle of any particular cultural product, of which this television series is an example. Even as it finished out its first run on HBO, the *Sopranos* phenomenon would spill beyond the discrete object that was the show itself and find additional vitality in multiple sites of media and of everyday culture. Later, in Part II, this book will deal with the ways *The Sopranos* came to be appropriated and reappropriated to diverse ends in the larger context of media entertainment and salesmanship. This increasingly can be the fate of any cultural work today: its meanings and its effects go beyond its initial manifestation to be reworked and repurposed for new audiences and new profit elsewhere in the social landscape.

But there is also a lesson here about *The Sopranos* in particular, and my goal in Part I will be to describe and analyze those specific and even unique features of the series that both fostered intense audience involvement in its original unfolding, episode after episode, *and*, by those means, contributed to the series' extended role in a vaster media landscape. There is something particularly apt about the ways *The Sopranos* has been picked over for new profits and pleasures and been granted ancillary afterlives, since its own story world (the lives of New Jersey mobsters and the people in their orbit) chronicles an exploitative economics of creative destruction that seeks profit wherever it can and is driven to eke every last bit of value from any object, including the scraps that remain when products are sent to the junk pile.

In its original run on HBO, *The Sopranos* mattered, and it matters still. The furor over the show's controversial "ending" confirmed how it resonated famously—or infamously, depending on one's point of view—in ways that demonstrate just how fixated the fans had become on the ending's expected role in rounding out the series. Revealingly, HBO's hope for a show to replace *The Sopranos*, *John from Cincinnati*, which debuted just after the final episode of *The Sopranos* with the clear expectation that viewers could now—and would now—transfer their affection to another HBO offering, exhibited a seventy-five percent drop from the viewership that *The Sopranos* finale had enjoyed just a few moments earlier. (Two months later, HBO announced cancellation of *John*.) *The Sopranos* had played a key role in giving HBO distinction, within the field of popular culture and popular media, as a venue for hip, innovative television fare, but that distinctiveness was not necessarily transferable to other HBO shows.

With electronic rapidity, the sign-off of *The Sopranos* achieved notoriety. As is now well known, *The Sopranos* ended by not ending its fictional narrative: in a diner with his wife, Carmela (Edie Falco), and son, A. J. (Robert Iler), New Jersey Mafia capo Tony Soprano (James Gandolfini) waits for his daughter, Meadow (Jamie-Lynn Sigler), to show up so that they all can have dinner together. Tony and his crew had been at war with the New York mob; some of his gang have died, and his consigliere Silvio Dante (Steve Van Zandt) remains in a coma. But Tony had managed to locate the head of the New York mob, Phil Leotardo (Frank Vincent), and have him killed, and there is now a negotiated peace among the survivors. Tony's dinner with his family is intended to serve as a moment of respite. Yet an air of menace hangs over the scene. Is the furtive guy who's gone into the bathroom going to come out with a gun and kill Tony or his family (à la Michael Corleone's shooting of

Sollozzo in *The Godfather* [1972])? Is that other guy with the Boy Scouts in the corner booth really as innocent as he appears? Does one figure seem to be the avenging brother of a truck driver who was shot dead years ago in a heist gone bad, back in Season 1? What about those two black men who come in and are made to play into the show's convention of pairing African Americans hired as hit men, as well as into a general racist stereotype of black men as threatening? And even if none of these men turn out to be assassins, might there not still be something portentous in Meadow's running across the road toward the diner as cars zoom around her? (In an earlier season finale, Meadow had almost gotten run over as she crossed a busy street, and the memory of that would be operative here for the regular viewer of the series.)

Meadow approaches the diner. Tony glances up, just as he has been doing for each customer to come into the establishment. And as he looks up—and as the Journey song he has picked out on the jukebox comes to the line "Don't Stop"—the show stops. The scene cuts to black and, after what seems like an eternity (during which numerous viewers with digital recording systems thought something had gone wrong with the timing they had set to record the episode), the credits roll.[2]

As a television series, *The Sopranos* had ended. What hadn't ended at that moment was the narrative of the characters within the fictional world of the series, and this had an explosive effect on the viewership. Many audience members vociferously condemned the non-ending ending as a cheat. To take just one example, the London *Times* online edition reported on one of the several hundred or so fans who viewed the finale at a goodbye bash at the Satin Dolls gentlemen's club in Lodi, New Jersey, which had served as the fictional strip joint Bada Bing in the show and at which "out of respect, the dancers took an hour off and joined the customers . . . marking a moment of television history." The interviewed fan, Joseph Manuella, was miffed: 'It was a big dud. People were getting ready for the big bang, like maybe the whole family was going to get whacked in the restaurant. But it was like a fireworks show without the finale."[3]

Quickly, those viewers who really needed narrative closure began to pore over their just-terminated recordings of the episode to find clues

Alternate endings?

that ostensibly could explain what would happen in the Sopranos' fictional world after that cut to black. Like the medieval exegetes of religious allegories who would devise ever more complex systems of interpretation to make their meanings fit the ambiguous texts they were confronting, the desperate fans took any and every detail of the final sequence of *The Sopranos* as potentially revelatory of narrative things to come. (Strikingly, though, their need to establish a definite ending was so strong that they sometimes got this or that detail wrong and let the tenacity of interpretation override accuracy.) Might the fact that the diner's doorbell tinkles each time it is opened, except for the last time, indicate that Tony is about to be shot and move into the silence of the grave? (This was a theory told to me by a neighbor. In fact, it is not an accurate recollection of how and when the bell tinkles.) Might the fact that the shifty guy who goes to the bathroom is listed in the credits as "Man in Members Only jacket" be a clue to his role as an angel of death, since the first episode of the season was titled "Members Only" and therefore could have made this guy part of the mob? Does an obscure figure in one booth look like Davie, a gambler from a much earlier season who had been ruined by Tony and who might now be coming back for revenge? Might not the two black guys be the same ones who had tried to kill Tony in a previous season, now back to finish the job? (This hypothesis, posed by several fans, ignores the fact that one of those two earlier assassins had been killed by Tony.)

There's an interesting paradox here. The fans wanted to know what happened to fictional characters they were treating as if real, but they were accepting that revelations about that reality could come from outside: from the creative artists who had made the fiction. This was a confusion of narrative levels—the fiction versus its fabrication and its narration—that are actually separate. To put it bluntly, Tony Soprano and the *Sopranos* creators exist in different worlds, with different claims on reality. If viewers want Tony to be a real person to whom real things can happen, they can't ask the show's creators, in the narrational frame around Tony's universe, to magically put revelatory clues about Tony's fate into that universe, since by taking Tony to be real, viewers are, in fact, denying that he exists inside a fictional context that has creators behind it.

Perhaps part of the problem for *Sopranos* fans was not only that the finale provided no end to the fiction, but that the show itself had already made clear that no such end could probably be fully satisfying within its framework. Might Tony go into a witness protection program? Not likely, after he had talked so much in a previous season about the horrors of having to accept a life of middle-class blandness if he did so. He also knew firsthand—when he himself strangled one informant, shot another, and had had another killed by Silvio—what often happened to snitches. And, in any case, Martin Scorsese's *Goodfellas* had already followed that route. Through its seasons, *The Sopranos* had taken as a theme its somewhat ersatz relation to prior gangster stories—especially classic, resonant gangster films—and this self-conscious awareness of the generic tradition it had come out of made it less probable that it would or could opt for any ending similar to the ones gangster narratives had enacted before. This meant then that it was also not likely that other family members would get a stray bullet meant for Tony—*The Godfather III* had already gone down that road with the shooting of Michael's daughter—or even that if Tony died, Meadow or A. J. might take up a weapon to avenge their dad: the first *Godfather* had already been there, done that, with Michael turning away from the path of non-violence when another gang did a hit on his dad. In fact, in season 6, when A. J. had declared his desire to avenge the wounding of his dad by his demented Uncle Junior (Dominic Chianese), he had himself cited the precedent of *The Godfather*, only to be admonished by Tony that "it's a movie"—i.e., a fiction not to be taken as a model. It was unlikely, too, that the series would adopt the wistful ending of *The Godfather III* where, at some unspecified time after the killing of his daughter, the emotionally broken Don Michael Corleone simply fades away into death. In any case, another HBO show, *Six Feet Under*, had gone that route in its own finale by tracing out the last moments, often far in the future, of its many characters. Although, as I'll argue later, aging and the succumbing of the body to the wearying ravages of time are constant images and themes in *The Sopranos*, there would not be, for Tony, an onscreen rendition of the inevitable, natural giving up of the ghost.

And it was likewise not very probable that Tony would die gloriously in a hail of bullets from a rival mob family or from the cops, since the classic gangster films of the 1930s—one of which, *Public Enemy*, Tony pointedly had been shown watching in season 2—had specifically taken that destiny as the culmination of their investment in "the gangster as tragic hero," to cite critic Robert Warshow's famous phrase about the classic films and their concern for a resonantly meaningful tale of rise and fall, with deep lessons.[4]

To be sure, bookies in Las Vegas and Atlantic City (two cities of illicit activity that Tony Soprano himself visited in various episodes of the show) were giving odds that Tony would indeed die. Likewise, the attempt by fans to imagine that this or that quickly glimpsed figure in the diner might be out to avenge some wrong committed by Tony in *Sopranos* episodes far past at least had a logic of irony to it: Tony would have survived the war with the New York gang and gone to his moment of respite with his family, only to be brought down for something from long ago that came back to punish him just when he thought all the danger was over. But this sort of ironic ending could run the risk of seeming gimmicky and far-fetched. For instance, is it plausible that the brother of the dead truck driver really would have waited close to a decade to go after Tony?

There could be no satisfaction in *any* ending to the fictional story. Instead of choosing, then, a narrative ending, ironic or not, the creators behind *The Sopranos* opted, instead, for a greater irony: admitting that the show was just a constructed bit of entertainment and not giving in to the audience's desire to imagine that its fictions could have a real-life closure to them. The abrupt cut to black that looked like the TiVo timer running out before the show ended was a reminder that the show, finally, was just a show. And the refusal to satisfy the viewer's easy expectations was in keeping with the overall trajectory of *The Sopranos* across its seasons. Over the years of *The Sopranos*, all narrative bets had been off, as contingency, accidents, and twists of fate, surprise, story detours, and so on worked to create an atmosphere of instability and unpredictability. To the end, the show kept one guessing.

One of the aesthetic traditions that *Sopranos* creator David Chase has declared had strongly influenced the series in its narrative structuring (or more precisely, de-structuring) and in its tone of undecidability is the European art cinema of the 1960s, which trafficked heavily

Art cinema freeze-frame: *The 400 Blows*.

in ambiguities of plot and person alike. Like the foreign art movies, *The Sopranos* worked with a seemingly popular form of media—in this case, narrative-based television—but opened it up to modes of veritably modernist experimentation. In this respect, the cut to black that concluded the adventures of *The Sopranos* is like the freeze-frame that ended François Truffaut's *The 400 Blows* (1959) and left the future of its own delinquent protagonist open-ended.

Like those films, *The Sopranos* is a show that often didn't go where one had anticipated—that didn't make things simple and that didn't always take the easiest paths. The non-ending ending is, in many ways, a culmination of the series' constant toying with viewers, challenging them by not making it easy for them but also delighting them with that very challenge. Perhaps the outcry at the finale suggests that the show's defiance of audience expectations had gone a bit too far, and that not all experimentation was tolerated. But the experiment itself was well in keeping with a show that, from start to finish, reveled in the quirky and the unconventional and that suggests a form of palpable, popular modernism.

The formal adventurousness of *The Sopranos* takes shape as, among other traits, a concern with the episodic and even the fragmentary; a meandering of plot that leads to mini-tales that go nowhere or, at the very least, nowhere expected; a constant shifting of tone from, say, the downbeat and morbid to the comic and farcical and back again; a multiplicity of perspectives and points of view; a blurring of the boundaries of dream or fantasy and everyday reality; and a rendering of narrative as a permutational flux in which characters come and go and bear between them endless new possibilities for interaction, even as they never seem to progress or grow in any substantial way.

I pointedly call *The Sopranos* a practice of *popular* modernism, since treating the series as an experiment perhaps risks making its plays with television narrative form seem exceptional, rather than integral to what the television experience often is about. Mass culture works necessarily by blending the comforts of the already known with the challenges of the boldly new—challenges which themselves comfort by confirming how mass society seemingly has space for innovation, renovation, fresh starts. Mass culture is itself, in many ways, a site of experimentation, and in that may lie its popular appeal.

Indeed, it will be a central argument of the pages to follow that *The Sopranos* is a work of popular culture deeply invested in irony, but an often playful one caught up in the undoing of each and every certainty we try to formulate about the show—certainties about the stories it tells but also about the values and viewing skills its audience might want to bring to it. Every time you think you've grasped *The Sopranos* and either figured out its story or its ethical point of view, it veers off in some unexpected direction and encourages a revision of everything you've brought to the viewing experience.

It is, then, an additional ironic twist that if *The Sopranos'* debt to modernist European art cinema might provide one answer to its complexities—namely, it's complex because it is a work of artistic superiority from a tradition devoted to ambiguity—other viewers were able to write away the non-ending ending in a very different fashion. Here, instead of seeing *The Sopranos* as a work of experimental artistry superior to the populist needs for narrative closure on the part of average viewers, the hypothesis now is that the *Sopranos* creators, and HBO more broadly, didn't end the television series because they have a movie sequel in mind. In other words, in this view the non-ending was a calculated bit of commercialism. If the European artsy nonclosure explanation invests in mythologies of art's specialness and of the artist's refusal to give in to the market, the "there'll be a movie coming out" argument opts for the opposite equation and sees *The Sopranos* as fully caught up in the webs of business decision, its non-ending now viewed as a marketing ploy. But perhaps in a further irony, even this twist has been anticipated by the show itself, which so frequently depicts how almost everyone in its story world, from gangsters to legitimate citizens who imagine themselves above criminality, is invested crassly in worlds of exploitation and maximum extraction of value. No one escapes the market. Everything is up for grabs in the *Sopranos* universe and, as we'll see especially in the latter pages of this study, that includes *The Sopranos* itself as a saleable work of popular culture.

It is one marker of the show's own ironic stance about the marketplace that when one *Sopranos* character explicitly laments, "Is it all just about money?" (when an affront to his wife is excused by his associates because harping on it would be bad for business), it happens to be New York mob boss Johnny Sacrimoni, a.k.a. Johnny "Sack" (Vince Curatola), who is shown elsewhere in the series to generally believe it is indeed all about the money. The irony of *The Sopranos* frequently tips into a cynical belief that there is no higher moral or aesthetic ground that is free of money connections and that could in purity judge the pecuniary depredations of the world. Perhaps, then, a movie version of *The Sopranos* is in order.[5]

It's significant that so many people were willing—if only up to a point in the case of those who felt betrayed by the non-ending ending—to play *The Sopranos'* game and invest in its cynical, albeit comical, outlook about human interactions in an essentially venal world. *The Sopranos* could certainly be appreciated as a form of engrossing everyday popular entertainment: it often provided action and glimpses of tantalizing and titillating lifestyles. But as often, its experimentation with storytelling meant that it would not offer narrative pleasures in simple form. For some viewers, this was a good thing. For others, not so: in the dour evaluation of the two Italian brothers who are my local butchers, who felt the last season was going too far, "Not enough action," "Not enough Bada Bing."

The controversy over the ending signals yet one more way in which *The Sopranos* has taken up a resonant place within its historical moment and achieved notoriety. The series became a signpost for the times. Minimally, the show would be alluded to in ways that were relatively benign and lighthearted, as if driven by the recognition that a series that itself had something jokey about it merited jokey response. For example, the inspired advertising campaign for the Animal Planet's popular show *Meerkat Manor* borrowed typography and iconography from *The Sopranos* to confirm how animal shows typically anthropomorphize their cast of characters. Given that Tony Soprano was shown, over the course of the seasons of his series, to have a special soft spot for denizens of the animal kingdom, the idea that the meerkats themselves were a Soprano-like family had a wacky, but fitting, irony to it.

Other citations of *The Sopranos* move past recognition of the series as a bit of postmodern television ripe for postmodern allusion to find in its narratives allegories of morality and misdoing that reflect back on real life. Within the story world of *The Sopranos*, money circulates, and any number of people from all walks of life and all social classes want some of it to flow their way. Not surprisingly, then, the show has come to function as a general symbol for corruption in contemporary culture. That is, beyond its specific stories, *The Sopranos* serves as a cultural shorthand for economic perfidy and corruption. Take, for instance, "The Rise of the Digital Thugs," a front-page article from the Sunday business section of the *New York Times*. The article deals with criminals who hack into the data banks and Internet services of large companies and then use the sensitive, stolen information in attempts to extort money from the companies. The article is accompanied by a very large photo of Tony Soprano and his mob standing in tailored suits before a computer terminal and looking straight at the reader; one of the gang, Paulie Walnuts (Tony Sirico), even holds up a drink glass as if he were sardonically toasting the *Times* consumer who is thus imaged as a potential target of the cyber-scam and asked thereby to participate in a new cyberspace moral panic.[6] It is revealing, though, that the article itself makes no mention at all of *The Sopranos* television show, and the image bears no caption (just a copyright acknowledgment to HBO), as if to confirm that there is no need for further explanation. It's as if the mere image of these bad men from this notorious series is enough to signal the dangers of a new world of quotidian criminality that is omnivorous and omnipresent. Likewise, an article on the ugliness of dealings in the Hollywood entertainment industries at the time when shareholders sued the Disney corporation for ostensibly giving former president Mike Ovitz a golden-parachute deal worth $109 million finds it logical to make reference to the immoral universe of *The Sopranos* as an analogy for Hollywood malfeasance and backstabbing. In his court testimony, the article explains, "Mr. Ovitz described a place where agents and executives traffic in gossip, adeptly manipulating the press and opinion makers . . . and intimidation and threats are the cornerstones of deal making. It is, as some noted, a world where the fictional family the Sopranos would be at home, and probably do well in."[7]

In other instances, *The Sopranos* can come to serve as metaphor not just for industry venality and for unethical behavior in the corporate realm but for a corruption that is so endemic a part of American life that it is now logically and inevitably a part of governmental politics as well. Thus, for instance, an article in the British newspaper *The Guardian* reports on a fight between New Jersey poet laureate Amiri Baraka and the state governor, who tried to oust him after Baraka wrote a poem that supported the wild idea that Zionists themselves had orchestrated the 9/11 attacks on the World Trade Center. Refusing to step down from his post, Baraka lashed out at opponents with a not-so-veiled comment on the governance of the state of New Jersey: "You want 'real' antisemites, then go look at the poems your schoolkids are reading: Ezra Pound and T. S. Eliot. . . . Hell, this is New Jersey. You fear poetry and you don't fear gangsters? This state is run by Tony Soprano. You don't think that he's dangerous?"[8]

During its H B O run, perhaps the most striking shorthand utilization of *The Sopranos* as cultural sign came in the presidential debates of 2004, when Democratic Party candidate John Kerry admonished that "being lectured by the president on fiscal responsibility is a little bit like Tony Soprano talking to me about law and order." Here Kerry played on and played into cultural hierarchies in America. This was the East Coast liberal intellectual distancing himself from redneck (or red state) lowlifes and associating his opponent, the ostensible cowboy man-of-the-people, with failure in law, leadership, and economic wisdom alike. In today's complicated media landscape, *The Sopranos* had been striving for distinction among cable offerings by targeting a specific taste comunity—urban sophisticates who, by watching the series, could go slumming in a world of kitsch, tastelessness, political incorrectness, taboo breaking, and so on. Kerry could use reference to the show to confirm both the right-wing propensity for immoral behavior, as well as his (and his social class's) easy superiority to such an endemically un-ethical way of life. Tony Soprano might have things to say about law and order (and President Bush might have things to say about fiscal respon-sibility), but their "lessons" would have no real pedagogical value: they needed themselves to be schooled in proper behavior by intellectually inclined, cultured mediators who had the sophistication to know right from wrong.

Logically, then, the flip side of easy allusion to *The Sopranos* as auto-matic sign for corruption is the way in which knowing reference to it also establishes one as member of a cultured urban elite that is suppos-edly above the venality the series depicts. Despite the fact that the story world of the show luxuriates in crime, violence, raw sexuality, and in-vective and insult of the most politically incorrect sort, the very ways in which *The Sopranos* increasingly came to be framed as aesthetically and morally valuable by makers and markers of high cultural distinction, from the Emmy awards to scholarly books to the effusive columns of the *New York Times*, mean that the act of watching it serves as an entitle-ment for viewers, announcing their membership in a cultural vanguard. If the above-mentioned cases employ *The Sopranos* as a shorthand ref-erence to illegal or immoral activity—for example, sophisticated crimi-nality in the case of the *New York Times* depiction of cybercrime using elegantly suited Soprano mobsters who seem at home in the world of computers, crude redneck venality in the case of John Kerry's imputa-tion of low-life ethics to George Bush—other articles or ads refer less to the show's content than to the fact of the show itself as cultural product that fits in well with an upscale urban professional lifestyle. Thus, a *Wall Street Journal* article on recordable DVD machines sports the headline "A New Way to Record 'The Sopranos'" but, like the *New York Times* piece on the cyber-blackmailers, makes no reference to the show in the body of the text. Here, the association is between a highly anticipated consumer technology (the new generation of DVD players described in lovingly detailed technical terms) and a lifestyle for which this particu-lar show can stand as an easy and easily understandable prime example of the sort of cultural artifact that potential users would most want to capture with such technology.[9]

Everyone, it seems, wants a piece of the *Sopranos* action. From the

New York Times and the *Wall Street Journal* to John Kerry, the short-hand reference to the show as a marker of tenacious, widespread criminality has, in its own way, been a means of glomming onto the show for one's own purposes to pull profit from it. That *The Sopranos* itself is about the multifarious ways one can exploit and draw benefit from the commodities that circulate through the world is one irony in this appropriation of the show. That the series itself often depicts precisely those sorts of urban sophisticates who would imagine themselves to be morally superior as, in fact, implicated themselves in the world of sleaze and venality is another.

During its run, *The Sopranos* served amply as an example of what has come to be called a "water cooler" show—a referenced bit of the culture that is talked about in the workplace (where the boundaries of leisure time and labor time are not always clear, and where not getting a cultural reference might rebound on one's professional reputation). Revealingly, with more than a bit of that savvy awareness of cultural trends that seems so much part of today's postmodern popular culture, HBO ran self-reflexive spots about the very ability of its shows to elicit conversation around the workplace water cooler. In these ads, managers and employees supposedly from the water cooler industry would speak to the camera to thank viewers for making their business so profitable, while a series of sketches showed such viewers offering pithy interpretative comments about various series, delivered in deadpan monotone. The comments were all about the shows' engagement with big questions of the human condition and thereby mocked the very way HBO shows might be talked about as deeply meaningful by urban professionals. HBO's own marketing of its shows suggests then that the channel also cultivates audience relationships that are not inevitably about morality, profundity, depth of meaning, and so on. High seriousness is overlaid smugly with a knowing wink, a putting of "deep purpose" into quotations. Today's urban professional requires not only meaningfulness and substance but also hipness, newness, and cutting-edge innovation. Not only should cultural offerings be meaningful or useful; they should also be forms of fun, a luxuriating in game playing.

This tells us something about our society and what it's become, but also about the specific functioning in it of ironic works of popular culture. An analysis of *The Sopranos* needs, then, to talk about the world at large within which the series plays its part, but it needs also to examine how the series itself incorporates awareness of the values of that world all the better to weave ironic play around them. This means looking closely at *The Sopranos* and trying to understand the particular kind of cultural experience it offers.

1

The Sopranos on Screen

We will have these moments to remember

—The Four Lads, 1955

1 Watching *The Sopranos*

Over a period of a month and a half, in final preparation for this volume, I watched all the seasons of *The Sopranos* in order from start to finish. I'd seen all the episodes numerous times over the years since the show began in 1999, but I'd never viewed them this close together, as a veritable single entity. In fact, I could have watched the seasons at a faster pace (10 or so hours a day would have got me through it all in a week!), but I had other things I also wanted to do with my time, and this balancing of entertainment and life seems itself to hold a lesson about fandom, about what it takes to be committed to a popular long-term television series, and about the ways we work to find spaces for our chosen cultural pleasures in our everyday schedules.

In any case, by compacting the viewing of the series as best I could into my own schedule, I wanted to see, in fact, if the many episodes of the show (86 altogether) formed a coherent totality: that is, if they created that organic unity so beloved of classic commentators on aesthetics. Indeed, many influential critics of *The Sopranos* specifically compare it to great novelistic works of nineteenth-century fiction, with the implication that the show indeed finds a unifying coherence and specifically does so at the level *of narrative*. For them, it is the logical unfolding of a story and the taking up by its characters of assigned places in that story that tightens the individual episodes of *The Sopranos* into a large-scale saga.

I wouldn't take my own experiment to be definitive, but what struck me, in contrast, was that the compression of the episodes into a relatively short viewing period actually seemed to lessen the impression of an overall narrative arc more than strengthen it. True, as the series winds down toward the final season and as important characters die and some important issues get resolved, there is sometimes the sense of a governing narrative logic that has taken over individual actions and given them meaning as integral parts of a whole. As noted in my prologue, by season 7 (the last), war had developed between the New Jersey gang of Tony Soprano and the New York gang of Phil Leotardo. Things had sort of been building toward an ultimate confrontation, and there certainly was some impression of narrative purpose and destiny here. With the piling up of deaths in the episodes of the last season, the fictional universe within the show became less peopled with key players in the plot, and this itself no doubt leads to a logical compression in which one plot line, one interaction of characters (the two important, last-standing gangsters, Tony and Phil), gains priority.

That should not be underestimated. Clearly, the degree of audience outcry over the final episode's ultimate lack of complete resolution, even with the killing of Phil earlier in that episode, says something about viewers' investment in hoped-for closure.

But neither should the role of narrative in the pleasures of *The Sopranos* be overestimated. To my mind, it's revealing that so many different endings were guessed at by the fans of the show in the days leading up to the finale: Tony would go into witness protection, Tony would be shot dead, Tony would go to prison, one of his children would die, one of his children would inherit the life of violence, and on and on. Each of these might have closed the narrative, but their sheer multiplicity and diversity suggests that none necessarily was the dramatically *logical* ending, the one that structurally would close the show in a way that seemed rightly meaningful and would cast its significance over all that had come before.

A quick contrast with one of *The Sopranos'* acknowledged antecedents, Francis Ford Coppola's *The Godfather*, might be instructive here. In *The Sopranos*, Mafia members venerate *The Godfather*, not so much as a guide to their own behavior as, rather, a bit of popular culture, however close to home, that they quote from and analyze (for example, Soprano lieutenant Paulie Walnuts explained how "Francis" framed this or that shot for maximum dramatic effect). In fact, *The Godfather* exhibits a tightness of narrative logic that gives it a sense of the tragic unavailable to the epigone gangsters of *The Sopranos*, who live in a more farcical, more undisciplined, much more fallen and confused world than that of the Coppola film. The distance from *The Godfather* to *The Sopranos* is both that distance, that Tony explains in episode 1 of the very first season, from an older conception of the Mafia as dignified and high class, and that distance between a cinematic work that still offers belief in tragedy and a more recent, postmodern bit of television that sees everyday life as so permeated by popular culture that its characters become pale imitators of the prior model and everything takes on the quality of a wink-wink knowingness.[1]

A small detail—the scene where *The Sopranos* perhaps comes closest to having characters in its fictional world relive a situation from *The Godfather*'s antecedent fictional world—is telling. While in a dramatic turning point from the film, Godfather Vito Corleone was gunned down as he bought oranges from a fruit stand in Little Italy, Tony Soprano is almost gunned down (in season 1) as he buys commercially packaged orange juice on a street in New Jersey. Appearing early in the run of the television show, this latter assassination attempt is much less consequential than the one in *The Godfather* (where Vito eventually dies of his wounds), is much less about ties to the romance of the old ways of life (tacky, mass-mediated New Jersey now is substituted for Little Italy), and is much more about the replacement of tradition-bound lifestyle by ersatz popular culture. Processed juice replaces real oranges, a television show replaces an epic film, a then relatively unknown actor (Gandolfini) replaces screen great Marlon Brando: in sum, postmodern allusion replaces a scene of tragic, dramatic originality.

There is a meaningfulness, a narrative rightness, to the trajectory in *The Godfather*, in which the cocky gangster son dies and the morally upright son who wanted nothing to do with the criminal world decides to take up the mantle and become the successor godfather to his imposing figure of a father. In contrast, *The Sopranos* is a structurally more sprawling work which flirts with narrative logic—for example, in season 6, the gangster's son A. J., like Michael Corleone, also tries to avenge his father (wounded by a senile uncle) but immediately screws up as he has always done—only to suggest that no path toward resolution

Don Corleone buys oranges.

Tony Soprano buys orange juice.

is especially resonant and that little sense of meaningful tragedy can be wrought from its farcical, trivial, confused characters and the fallen world they inhabit.

Even as it comes, in the end, to tell its tale of ultimate battle (Tony versus Phil), *The Sopranos* emphatically does not conform to a model of tight and meaningful narrative coherence. Even the last episodes of the last season, where the homing in on the final confrontation of Tony and Phil should logically have led to narrative concentration and compression, exhibit many of the traits of narrative dispersion that had characterized *The Sopranos* across its many seasons. For instance, season 7 gave time, just a few episodes before the finale, to an inconsequential plot line about a minor character who at best had had a couple lines of dialogue in previous episodes and had never really mattered to any important primary narrative thread: Vito Jr., the son of Vito Spatafore (Joseph Gannascoli), a gangster in the Soprano Mob who had been killed because he was gay, had been reacting badly to the death of his father and eventually had to be carted off to an attitude-reprogramming camp in the West. Precious moments that might have been devoted to the battle of Tony and Phil were given over to this story, which added nothing narratively. But this was typical of the show: even as it should have been hurtling toward a startling narrative conclusion, *The Sopranos* took its leisurely time and went off into a discrete, disconnected subplot about this youthful character who mattered to no one.

Moreover, the Vito Jr. subplot, which came from nowhere and went nowhere, was itself derivative of another subplot—the story, in season 6, of how the recently outed Vito Sr. had tried to flee to the quiet of country life in New Hampshire when his gayness made him persona non grata in the Mob and then had been killed when he returned to New Jersey to see his family. Vito Sr.'s story was no doubt quite fascinating, but he himself had been a fairly minor player in the Soprano gang in previous seasons; as the show was winding down and the big question had to do with the overall survival of the Soprano gang in its rivalry with the New York Mob, the tale of Vito was an interruptive detour. In fact, much of the Vito Sr. story was presented as a veritable interlude—a time-out from the seemingly consequential big narrative questions that hung over the final seasons—with Vito exploring nature in New England, touring small-town Americana, and finding temporary romance with a gay New Hampshire firefighter (one series of shots of the two of them picnicking in the grass, the chubby Vito now a beaming cherub, seemed a comic version of pastoral painting). At the same time, this country interlude would itself be subject to disruption as the next few episodes of season 6 dropped the Vito narrative completely and kept it in fraught abeyance until its bloody resolution later on. It is, then, an additional confirmation of the ways *The Sopranos* incessantly gives itself over to detour and distension of narrative progression—even as the series would move into seasons that were supposed to be bringing things to an end—that the stories that thereby interrupted the Vito narrative themselves only vaguely returned to the supposedly overriding Tony/Phil rivalry and instead went off into new, digressive mininarratives of their own.

For example, in one episode, one plot detour involved Tony's restaurateur friend Artie Bucco (John Ventimiglia) finding his business falling apart around him; this subplot became a veritable character study in its own right. Another detour in the episode gave time over to a short tale about how Paulie Walnuts had tried to skimp on a religious street festival he handled the finances and operations for in the local parish and then had had a vision of a chastising Virgin Mary (on the dance floor of the Bada Bing strip joint no less!). Neither tale did much to advance major plot lines even though they might be fun and fascinating in their own right. Moreover, it is a further sign of *The Sopranos'* unremitting breakdown of narrative logic that this episode, so given over to digressions about Artie and Paulie had itself, teasingly, begun with a moment of seemingly major narrative import: Tony's nephew Christopher, who had always had his ups and downs about his commitment to his longtime girlfriend, Adriana (Drea de Matteo), before finally setting her up to be killed when he discovered she was an FBI informant, now asked his current, pregnant girlfriend, Kelli (Cara Buono), to marry him. The problem was that Kelli had figured in no previous scenes and her very existence had never been brought up, so that the revelation that Christopher was now ready to commit to a woman and build a family had no context to it and seemed less a solid narrative line than the mock performance of story. Either *The Sopranos* would go off into irrelevant digression or jump into a major, new plot thread in a fashion so perfunctory that the narrative came undone.

When the last season of *The Sopranos* sort of got past all these detours, delays, and narrative decoys and did finally, in the very last episode, resolve the rivalry of Phil and Tony, this itself was stripped of epic resonances and could come to seem relatively inconsequential. Behind Phil's back, Tony brokered a truce with the rest of the New York gang so that the larger war simply ended. This negotiation of peace to avoid bloody action is in keeping with a show that, while often violent, is also about a belated, information-society version of the Mafia, where physical force is often replaced by the power of words: a well-placed whisper in the ear or well-timed cell-phone call. *The Sopranos* is oftentimes dramatic and exciting, but it also has frequently to do with a flattening of visceral excitement into chit-chat. The thrill of violent battle is emptied out.

Part of Tony's negotiation with New York involved his getting permission to have Phil killed ("whacked," in the show's parlance), but even the whacking that ensues in the last episode seems strangely anticlimactic. First, it is presented in a veritably low-comic manner: shot at a gas pump, Phil falls to the ground, and his own car comes out of gear and runs over his head while a bystander pukes from the shock of it. The very grotesqueness and weirdness of it all remove from the scene much of the monumental epicness that this final confrontation had promised to deliver. Second, the scene itself is literally anticlimatic, since it isn't, in fact, what ends the final episode of *The Sopranos*. As noted, *The Sopranos* would end by not ending: after Phil's death, Tony seeks a moment of calm with his family while a series of individuals in that diner may or may not bode ill for the future. This is an ending that combines the non-narrative regularity of anodyne family activity with the non-narrative singularity of a non-ending that ties nothing up.

Throughout its seasons, *The Sopranos* offered episodes that only minimally provided a story (for example, a notorious 23-minute dream sequence in season 5) or that told a story with no end (the infamous tale from season 3 of a Russian who escaped from the gang and whose fate remained unknown) or presented multiple stories that would move at various paces to their noninterlocking individual resolutions (which might exceed the boundaries of the single episode) or introduced new stories that had not been part of the original promise of the narrative logic and now sent that logic in unexpected directions, or even broke out of its narrative space to go into alternate universes (in season 6, Tony, having been shot and in critical condition, imagines for several episodes that he is a salesman who has lost his wallet and is stuck in a convention hotel in Orange County, California).

My compressed viewing of the seasons of *The Sopranos* suggests that the show is not so much governed by any overarching narrative logic as it is given over to the force of individual, resonant vignettes. No doubt, these can sometimes take on narrative form, and even extend beyond individual episodes or span seasons, but they operate, still, as discrete units that may contribute vaguely to a larger narrative trajectory but more centrally serve as moments of interest and delectation in their own right. In fact, the vignette can be as short as the furtive moment that flits up for an instant, pleases the viewer for this or that reason (for example, a striking composition, an absurd situation, a funny line of dialogue), and then fades as the next passing moment is offered up. Yet the moment can extend over time and still be experienced as a single, and singular, resonant unit. For example, it is certainly possible to come up with a symbol-by-symbol interpretative translation of the famous 23-minute dream sequence from season 5 into a list of themes and meanings,[2] but it is as tempting to treat the whole dream as a single, extended moment of bravura experiment, one in which this cutting-edge television series luxuriates in the suspension of its narrative(s) for the sake of sheer weirdness.

Such moments in *The Sopranos* have many functions and resonances. There are moments of comic shtick: for example, this or that gangster will act out some scene from the popular culture he's grown up with: Silvio doing Al Pacino impersonations, Tony Blundetto (Steve Buscemi) doing Jackie Gleason. There are moments of comic deflation of human pretension: for example, male FBI agents primping in veritable unison when a pretty female agent is called in to be coached by them on going undercover into the Mob. There are many moments that seem to move beyond comedy into some sort of realm of the weird or absurd: for example (a minor but telling one), when Paulie, out of anger at a relative,

A passing moment.

throws a flat-screen television out of her room at a retirement home, there is a throwaway shot at ground level, as the screen comes crashing down in the background, of an elderly person tooling by unawares in a motorized wheelchair. The vignette is curious and fleeting, and all the more funny for that. It doesn't advance the narrative and seems to have no point other than to add weird levity to the instant.

Conversely, along with comedy, there are moments of high seriousness which seem geared to show off a bravura of dramatic acting as much as to actually contribute narratively to the forward movement of story. For example, in season 6, as Tony lies in a coma after he has been shot by his demented uncle, there is a long sequence in which Carmela soliloquizes over him in his bed. The scene no doubt matters because of its story role: Carmela and Tony had broken up but now have gotten back together and are beginning to rebuild their shared life. But it resonates all the more as a sheer moment of performative display by actress Edie Falco in which we get to see an intensity of emotional acting with all its gradations of anguish and hope. And lest we give too much narrative import to the scene and try to think of it as consequential beyond its dramatic resonance for us *at the moment it plays out*, a later episode alludes to the sequence, but in comic fashion, as if to deflate its earlier pretension: as she prepares for her first long trip away from Tony (a week's vacation in France that she won at a charity auction), Carmela tells Tony she wishes she told him more often she loves him and asks if he remembered that she did tell him that while he was in his coma. Tony's bemused "no" clarifies that he had no awareness of anything at the time and serves, for the show, as a self-reflexive assertion that Carmela's soliloquy existed only for its momentary, sheer quality of performance by the actress playing her and for the delight of the spectator watching her.

And, in between comedy and drama, there are moments that themselves serve as veritable switching points between tones and emotional registers, either comic intrusions into a scene of gravity or the reverse. For example, in the second-to-last episode of the series, whatever reaction we want to have to the shooting of Silvio Dante at the Bada Bing by gunmen from Phil's gang (and I think for most viewers, Silvio is a character we'd come to care about despite the fact that in a previous season he killed Adriana, whom we had also come very much to care about) is confused by the comic image of strippers running out of the club, which is then itself interrupted by the horrific sight of a passing motorcyclist run over by the hit men's getaway car. Even this one quick scene, then, offers a roller coaster of emotions and toys with straightforward viewer response.

There are moments in which story development is suspended and a non-narrative experiment with temporality takes over. On the one hand, for instance, there are lyrical interludes—frequently set to music—that become free-form displays of visuality in their own right: for example, in season 6, one of Christopher's backslides into heroin abuse stands as a veritable music video in which a series of vignettes, accompanied by a plaintive tune, show him getting increasingly wasted against the backdrop of a street fair filmed slightly out of focus with the blinking neon of carnival rides and attractions offering a poetic counterpoint to his fall.

Likewise, although it tends to maintain a bare style geared to showing off acting and writing, the series sometimes engages in a flashy display of medium-specific techniques: complex camera movements, some of

The visual fuzziness of the drug trip.

which appear to defy gravity and render the filmed reality seemingly vertiginous, as when, for example, one shot of Tony in his bed has the camera weave around him in ways that make him look like he is floating in space; striking camera angles (the most extreme of which may be an overhead shot that looks down on the Mafiosi from the vantage point of the pig statue that adorns Satriale's Meats, one of their meeting places); slow motion and freeze frame; and even reverse motion.

On the other hand, the show frequently opts for a relative effacing of demonstrative cinematic style to give representation to the weighty duration of everyday reality, in which not much seems to go on. The series here empties the story out by depicting a paused temporality in which nothing happens. Most striking to my mind is the opening of an episode in the middle of season 6—which, I remind the reader, is a season that is supposed breathlessly to be moving things toward their end—in which Tony, fresh out of the hospital after his wounding by Uncle Junior, sits by the pool for a moment of calm, only to have an electric filter start making annoying grinding sounds that continue and continue, for close to two minutes. From its very first episode in its very first season, with Tony silent for a long while as he observes a statue outside the office of psychiatrist Jennifer Melfi and remains silent even when he enters the office and sits facing Melfi, *The Sopranos* takes its time, literally so, as it explores the sheer unfolding of duration. Here, again, narrative will be held in abeyance for a luxuriating in the moment—even if a distended and anodyne one. This seems far from the frenetic pacing of much television in the post-MTV video age. For example, *The West Wing* became noted for beginning its episodes with a staging technique known as walk-and-talk, in which the scene started with characters in mid-motion as they moved through the White House (or elsewhere) and fired fast bursts of dialogue at each other.[3] This would offer a strong contrast to *The Sopranos*' opening sequence, and many other scenes, which slow things down, impart minimal information, and set up a situation in which the spectator waits at leisure for something to happen.

And yet, in that very first scene of the very first season, after the ice is broken and Tony begins to recount to Melfi his day leading up to his panic attack, one of the flashbacks of his day's events is strikingly offered up in vibrantly frenetic fashion. Tony has been explaining to Melfi that earlier in the day he had needed to see someone who owed him money, and when Melfi stops his tale to clarify that she as a therapist can't be privy to knowledge of any criminal activity, Tony asserts that nothing of that sort transpired—that he just had had coffee with the debtor. Cut to Styrofoam cups of coffee splashing violently to the ground as the debtor realizes Tony and nephew Christopher are out to run him down in Chris's car. The scene is distinguished by rapid cutting, fast movement within the frame, and fast movement of the camera, all of this set to the pulsing beat of a quickly paced doo-wop song. When Christopher and Tony catch up to the debtor and the car smashes into him, the perspective shifts into the inside of an office, through the window of which we can see the man's body fly up into the air and come crashing down. The scene is both violent and exaggeratedly slapstick (the man seems to flop up and down), and the effect is amplified by the fact that the cut to the office interior moves into silence (we don't hear the car hit flesh) as if to use the absence of noise as comic counterpoint to the freneticness. Silence, in other words, is used here not for durational contemplativeness, as it had been employed a few moments earlier to show the pauses between Tony and Melfi, but as part of an effect of action, energy, wacky blends of violence and vitality. As much as a slow, patient, and even brooding uneventfulness that approximates the art film in its emptying out of high sensation, the moments of *The Sopranos* can also offer directly sensational, vibrant, and visceral engagements with action, mayhem, strong sexuality, anger, and obscenity, all thrown hurly-burly at the spectator in fever-pitch style.

Starting from its very first episode, then, *The Sopranos* demonstrates a mixing of tones that will extend over the seasons of the show. And this complex interweaving of styles from scene to scene will intersect with a complexity of storytelling modes in the overall narrative structure of the series. In its largest moments as well as its smallest, *The Sopranos* adheres to no simple logic or look in the chronicling of its curious fictions.

2 Eight Million Stories in the Naked City

The Sopranos weaves its spell in large part by taking two basic structures of narrative television—namely, series composed of stand-alone episodes that individually recount full-fledged stories, and series of a more serial form in which each episode contributes to an ongoing narrative unfolding—and creating a complex interplay between them. The tension between individual episodes and larger narrative arcs comes from the building up of a complex fictional universe peopled with a diversity of characters, each with their own tales and each generating ever more tales in their interactions with others. While it is clear that the makers of *The Sopranos* always intended for it to cease production at some point, and while it is evident that in its final episodes the series does lead to a compression of its fictional universe (if only through the killing off or wounding of key characters), the course of the show has to do with sustaining the existence of its fiction by the endless generation of new characters, the endless revelation of new aspects to characters we thought we already knew, the endless permutations of interrelationships between characters, and so on. All of this distends narrative into something that at times only vaguely resembles epic storytelling.

As the last season or two especially bear out, there are opposing pulls in *The Sopranos* between compression and contraction *and* potentially endless expansion and proliferation of narratives. The risk of the term *modernism*, especially in its historical reference, is that it can imply an art primarily of the fragment and of the piling up, in random form, of discrete bits with no narrative logic to them. In fact, *The Sopranos* does have its fragmentary side—for instance, some of its subplots are discrete enough to potentially have taken place anywhere in the series' many seasons—but temporal randomness is always held in place, however loosely, by an essentially chronological framework. There are narrative boundaries to experimentalism in the series.

But within the overall chronology, the fictional space of *The Sopranos* is one that can endlessly generate new situations, new plot lines, new permutations of character and interpersonal interaction. It is revealing that early on series creator David Chase had momentarily thought to write his series around characters in the Hollywood entertainment business, and not the Mafia. It is revealing, too, that Chase brought Matt Weiner in as a *Sopranos* writer (and eventually executive producer) on the basis of a script he wrote about advertising agents on Madison Avenue (which Weiner eventually returned to and released, after the final airing of *The Sopranos*, as the AMC show *Mad Men*). Furthermore, as I write these lines, it's being announced that another *Sopranos* writer, Terence Winter, has been signed by Martin Scorsese to adapt a memoir about high-level scams in the boiler rooms of stock-market investing. On the one hand, in terms of resonant content, all of these fictional settings thematically represent worlds of venality, competitiveness, backstabbing, and masculine privilege and bravado. On the other hand, formally, they all are about worlds of people who come and go, people in new encounters (all four—the Mafia, Hollywood, Wall Street, and Madison Avenue—are all about the art of the deal), people who rise and people who fall, people who are replaceable by the next in line. Formally, these are worlds that can endlessly generate new situations and new narrative lines.

In passing, it's worth noting how *The Sopranos* uses yet another of its ways of life as an example of potential narrative expansiveness: psychotherapy. Clearly, for the structure of the series, Tony's encounters with Jennifer Melfi (Lorraine Bracco) work as both narrative and antinarrative device: the therapy sessions enable Tony to have moments of clarity and provide him with guidance (not all of which he interprets as Melfi would like), but the sessions also constitute a site of stuckness and silence, a rehashing of the same old arguments, an inability to move forward, a fading of ambition into self-doubt. At the same time, it's also interesting to note how the glimpse of therapy expands beyond the one figure of Melfi to take in a veritable totality of the therapeutic profession: the therapist that Tony goes to when things aren't working out with Melfi, the one Carmela goes to when she begins to have moral doubts about being married to a Mafioso, the one their daughter goes to after her boyfriend's killing, the ones A. J. starts seeing when he becomes depressed and then suicidal, but also, importantly, Melfi's own shrink Elliot Kupferberg (Peter Bogdanovich) and the larger cohort of therapists whose dinner parties both Melfi and Kupferberg frequent. A gathering of the therapists late in season 7 reveals them to be as duplicitous and sneaky, and as unethical, as many of the other figures encountered in the morally dubious world of *The Sopranos*. The venal Mafia world has its potential for endless expansion and permutation, but so does the venal psychotherapeutic world. Behind each therapist is another with another story to tell.

In a useful analysis of the broad industrial context for the role of sameness and innovation in television, media scholar Jeffrey Sconce argues that central to the narrative structure of today's television dramatic series is a combination of older formats of episodic series and ongoing serial form, and he sees this as a tactic of commodity differentiation. In Sconce's words, "In the 'postnetwork' era of increased competition for viewing audiences, 'cumulative' narration provides distinct programming and demographic advantages. By combining the strengths of both the episodic and serial formats, this narrative mode allows new and/or sporadic viewers to enjoy the stand-alone story of a particular episode while also rewarding more dedicated, long-term viewers for their sustained interest in the overall series."[1]

The Sopranos, for instance, offers veritably self-contained mininarratives like that of the Emmy-winning episode "College," in which the three narrative strands—Tony taking Meadow to visit college campuses in New England, Tony discovering an FBI informant hiding out in one of the New England villages and setting out to kill him, and Carmela engaging in an ill-fated flirtation with the priest Father Phil—all pretty much begin and end within the space of the one episode. But individual episodes of the series also introduce narrative arcs that extend over a season or beyond (for example, Tony's tensions with Richie Aprile, a key antagonist who dies by the end of season 2, or the ongoing expectation that some day Tony will come to loggerheads with Johnny Sack, a big-wig in a rival Mafia family). The sheer multiplicity of narratives enabled by all these permutations of characters, both old and new, allows for a proliferation of plots that may run parallel to each other and even have overlapping or intersecting actions, but it also means that the series contains discrete narratives of divergent lengths and divergent pacing.

Moreover, we might note that another tactic of *The Sopranos* has to do with blurring the boundaries between full narrative closure and a simple disappearance or temporary suspension of a narrative line. Some stories end; others just peter out and vanish. Episodes and seasons may resolve certain narrative points, but other such points simply are not returned to. In some cases, there lingers the possibility that the suspended narrative could revive at some later date. Probably the most famous case of such suspension is the "Pine Barrens" episode, which left viewers wondering if a tough and seemingly invincible Russian, a Chechen war veteran, that Christopher and Paulie set out to kill is in fact alive and could return; David Chase himself evidently never intended to bring the Russian back and was surprised that audiences made his possible reappearance a topic of discussion. When, in a much later episode from another season, Paulie and Chris debate whether the Russian is alive and conclude "Who the fuck knows? Who the fuck cares?" it is easy to see the scene as a self-reflexive commentary on viewers' exaggerated concern with narrative closure. The dropped narrative line such as this one both builds suspense that sustains audience fidelity *and* requires the audience to hone viewing skills around narrative memory (what happened when, what might still happen later on).

As Jeff Sconce notes, there are a number of specific strategies that television programs employ in the expansion of their narrative universe. These can involve spin-offs of characters into new narrative worlds (so that, for example, *Friends* generates *Joey* or, perhaps, the *Sopranos* television series may generate a feature film that extends the narrative beyond the series' own closure), amnesia plots that mean that a narrative virtually needs to be started again, "evil twin" plots that create new dramatic resonances among characters who already have been fixed in place, "what if?" plots by which characters move into alternate universes that generate new narrative possibilities, "it was all a dream" plots that erase established narratives and start things from scratch, "fish out of water" plots (the characters move to a new narrative world where interest is generated from the contrast between what they were and what they are now forced to be), and what Sconce terms the "meat locker" plot in which the characters are cut off from their typical narrative universe and new narrative interest is generated from their interiorized interactions with each other.

The Sopranos employs many of these tactics. For example, the trip that Tony and his gang take to Italy in season 2 obliges them to be "fish out of water," as all the home-turf coordinates that typically help them orient themselves and master situations seem lacking. Paulie basically fails the test, discovering Italy to represent an alien and alienating context despite his attempts to find traces of his heritage there, while Chris survives the experience by drugging himself into virtual oblivion and being mentally absent to everything going on. It is then a mark of Tony's skills as Mob boss that although he initially finds some of the elements of the Italian experience disconcerting—especially the discovery that a woman and not a man is running the local Mob—he soon regains control of the situation and comes away triumphant. In other words, the "fish out of water" plot allows the generation of new story permutations, but it also in this case enables characters to be tested in ways that distinguish them and perhaps prepare them for new narrative lines.

Similarly, the famous "Pine Barrens" episode is a veritable "meat locker" narrative in which two characters (Paulie and Christopher) are cut off from civilization and where drama is generated from the unforeseen conflict that develops between them (and that then generates suspense for the next season: will Paulie and Christopher come to blows?).

The Sopranos even makes use of the "evil twin" premise to a certain degree in the plot line of gang member Patsy Parisi (played by Dan Grimaldi), whose identical twin Philly is killed on Tony's orders, and who seems, in some seasons, not fully satisfied with his role in the Family under Tony's tutelage. And it might even be argued that the way in which in early seasons Soprano sister Janice keeps hooking up with dysfunctional and violent heads of Mafia crews within Tony's jurisdiction but bridling against his power is a type of amnesia plot. While other

What if? An alternate Tony in Convention-Land.

characters in the series often have a long-term memory that enables them to connect incidents across long stretches of time (for example, many episodes after Bada Bing dancer Tracee is killed, Tony has a quick flashback of her), Janice appears to forget the lesson to learn about abusive lovers. To bring home the point, we are even given a scene of her with her therapist who basically tells her that she doesn't seem ever to learn. Tony endlessly has to remind Janice of things she has done—of a syndrome she is locked into—that she would rather forget. Here is an amnesia of a metaphoric sort, but one that is no less productive of alternate narrative lines (the plots that come from Janice's new romantic entanglements).

Strikingly, though the setting of *The Sopranos* in a somewhat realist narrative universe governed by rules of ordinary logic means that the show wouldn't take on more science-fictional directions in its search of narrative expansion, the series even flirts with alternate universes through dream sequences and, more importantly, the long subplot of an unconscious Tony going off, in season 6, as a salesman into an Orange County of the mind.

The Sopranos thus has a variety of strategies at hand for expanding its narrative universe through the generation of new tales. From the start, for instance, there is potential for endless subplots in the sheer number of characters in the basic cast. There are pictures of thirty-six different characters on the HBO page for the cast of *The Sopranos*, although some of these admittedly turn out to be of less importance over the course of the seasons (for example, the very menacing hood Feech La Manna [Robert Loggia], who disappears after a few episodes). Characters may have relatively fixed personality traits that lead them inevitably into certain types of plot: for example, restaurateur Artie Bucco is henpecked by his wife and often allows himself to be entranced and sometimes even conned by the succession of women he hires as hostesses for his restaurant. At the same time, revelations from the past can come to disturb a character's stability of personality and require a revision of the beliefs and values they have made part of their very being (and that we've come to associate them with), and this can create new story potentials for them. For example, Paulie will discover that his "aunt" is his mother, and not the reverse, as he had always been told; this leads to new narratives about his relationship to both his elders. And such revelations can even span the generations: one subplot begins, for instance, when Tony meets his father's mistress, Fran Felstein (Polly Bergen), and spends an episode gaining new insights about the past from her. This, then, leads to a complex narrative structure for this one subplot: there are the stories of the past that Tony learns about from Fran, but there is also the story of Tony's present interaction with Fran which both involves him going to the Mob for money she has been owed *and* flirts scarily with the possibility that something sexual may happen between Tony and this woman who had "belonged" to his father.

Finally, there is also the possibility that a character can try to change some aspect of their lives and, with a new set of personality traits, enter into new types of stories. Most importantly, much of season 5 chronicles Carmela's attempts to be her own person and make it on her own (romantically and otherwise) during a separation from Tony. By the end of the season, Carmela comes back to Tony and reaffirms her basic character traits in ways that make her somewhat predictable again (Tony can thereby manipulate her fidelity by carefully choosing words in keeping with her personality), but the episodes of separation from

Tony allow furtive glimpses of a potentially different Carmela, one with a different life to live.

And beyond each of the stories that individual characters enter into or bring from their past, there is also the potential for stories to be generated from new and unexpected interactions among the set of basic characters. Characters are fairly fixed in personality and fairly fixed in their place within the Soprano work world and domestic world, but there always can be new ways for them to interrelate. For example, might Silvio be itching to become a Don and not just a consigliere? Might Paulie be turning traitor and dangerously switching his allegiance to New York? The extreme perhaps of such permutations in a character's basic relation to others is an episode from season 5 entitled "Irregular around the Margins," in which, with Christopher away on a job, his girlfriend Adriana enters into a flirtation with Tony that has the potential to tear apart both Tony's work life and home life. Over the previous seasons, Tony's relationship to Adriana had been fairly respectful of her connection to Chris, befitting the place and placement of everyone concerned in the fictional universe of the show. But now the characters threaten to move into new narrative possibilities. The fraught plot that ensues is an emotional roller coaster of narrative reversals: (1) Tony tells his therapist, Melfi, he wants to do the right thing and not go after Adriana, but he then agrees to go off with her late at night to score drugs, and it is an open question if this might lead to something between them. (2) But they have an accident in Tony's SUV, and it will never be known if something would indeed have happened. (3) Rumors start flying that the accident happened because there was indeed something sexual going on between Adriana and Tony in the SUV, and Christopher hears the innuendoes and goes hunting after Tony. (4) But Tony and his henchmen drag Christopher to the countryside to kill him for his disrespect to a boss like Tony. (5) But then Tony's cousin convinces him to spare Christopher. (6) Tony offers to do so, but only if Christopher agrees to rid himself of all suspicion and pledge his fealty to Tony. (7) The episode ends with Carmela, Tony, Adriana, and Christopher all out in public together, showing off to suspicious minds around them that the original relationships have been restabilized. The episode shakes up a set of fixed connections, generates new story and suspense from that, and then basically terminates the new plot line to return to business as usual (although, it must be admitted, emotional fallout from the subplot would have vague effects later on in an antagonism between Tony and Christopher that culminates in Tony's cold-blooded killing of his nephew in season 7).

Obviously, beyond its initial set of characters, *The Sopranos* also can expand its narrative potential by bringing in new characters with their own narrative implications and story-generating potentials. Here, again, the setting in the Mafia world matters. First, it is considered a given of this world that the men will have a series of mistresses, and, in Tony's case, this enables a variety of subplots about the women in his life. Second, although generally confined to one territory, the Soprano gang engages in its criminal activities with a venal voraciousness that means it always is expanding into new spaces and new situations. Each of these can introduce new characters and new plots as the gangsters find new worlds to exploit. To take a minor example, "Denial, Anger, Acceptance," an episode from the first season, involves the gang putting the pressure on a Hasidic motel manager—and learning that he doesn't respond to threat or torture as other victims have. The gang members have to adapt to a new situation created by contact with an attitude and a way of life unfamiliar to them.

As an additional contribution of the Mafia setting to narrative permutation, there is always the implication that even though Mafia life is structured and hierarchical, any slot in the structure can be filled by a new character with a new set of character traits. Thus, for instance, each new captain that comes to work under Tony brings along with him new plot lines and new situations to resolve. If classic soap opera introduces new characters by the conceit of the person who moves into the town or of the long-lost relative who returns to the fold, *The Sopranos* finds its Mafia equivalent in the narrative ploy of the criminal who is let out of jail and returns to the old neighborhood (and, in one case, the narrative in season 5 of Tony's cousin Tony Blundetto [Steve Buscemi], the ex-con is, in fact, also a long-lost relative). That the ex-prisoner premise is indeed a ploy for generating possible new narratives is borne out by the subplot in season 5, where Feech La Manna, an old Mafioso in the Soprano crew recently released from prison, wants a piece of the action and is ready to use all manners of violence to get it. Feech seems to portend that he will serve as that season's example of the recurrent upstart figure in Tony's crew—someone who wants too much too fast and seems destined to come to loggerheads with Tony (equivalents are Richie Aprile in season 2 and Ralph Cifaretto in seasons 3 and 4). But, asking himself if he hasn't learned anything from those past cases, Tony realizes the danger that Feech's continued presence poses to him and sets Feech up to be arrested and sent back to jail. Here, again, the series generates a new plot line with a great deal of suspense and expectation around it, only to let it dissipate and disappear before any violent payoff.

Throughout the seasons of *The Sopranos*, there are scenes of law enforcement officials pinning up pictures and organizational charts of Mob power structure, and these function as markers for the viewers to keep track of the fate of some of the characters in this endlessly permutational fictional space. (A comparable function in HBO's *Sex and the City* might be Carrie Bradshaw's voice-over narration, which interconnects the various exploits of the four women but also clues the spectator in on where each woman is at with various lovers, past, present, and potential.) Such scenes of reminding and remembrance have their functions within the narrative (the FBI needs these charts), but they are also part of the play between show and spectator: they are themselves allegories of reading that remind the viewer of how things go together, how the permutations of the multiple narrative elements are articulated.

This then is the challenge of the multiseason show—a challenge for the show but also for spectators, who enter into a complex game and make of it what they can. At the extreme, *The Sopranos* can demand that its viewers expend a great deal of effort at interconnecting the characters and narratives. To take just one example, the very first episode of the first season has Carmela telling Tony as he undergoes an MRI that if he dies he will probably end up in hell; this condemnation is something that he will quote back to Carmela in season 5, revealing that he's been brooding over it as an unresolved tension within the marriage. The reference across seasons says something about Tony in his narrative world—he has not forgotten this, it has been eating at him—but it also says something about the show's courting of viewers' fidelity and attentiveness to detail. The series sets out to train its spectators, through rule making and rule breaking, just how to expand their skills in the reading of this complex proliferation of tales and situations.

It is revealing that many of these formal traits and strategies for story generation and permutation in *The Sopranos*, which high-culture critics praise as marks of what has come to be called "quality TV," appear also in genres of television that frequently are disdained by the very same critics. For example, the daytime soap opera operates, as does *The Sopranos*, with complexity and multiplicity of narrative lines, slowness of development, painful extension of duration, and an uneventful everydayness punctuated and punctured by moments of crisis or triumph, repetition, and a general resistance to easy, forward progression of a singular story.

The Sopranos even directly acts like a traditional soap in those consequential, but unanticipated, moments where someone receives a phone call that brings earth-shattering news that sends the plot (or, rather, a set of overlapping and interweaving plots) in new directions. For instance, the death of the relatively minor character Karen Baccalieri (Christine Pedi) in a car accident early in season 4 had narrative convulsions that would play through later seasons, including freeing up her husband Bobby (Steve Schirripa), also a somewhat minor character up to then, to become a target for Janice Soprano's predatory skills in turning men in Tony's gang into her lovers (and, in Bobby's case, into her husband).

True, within the story world of *The Sopranos*, there might be moments that mock the soap opera, in keeping with that genre's widespread reputation as a low, kitsch form: for example, when Uncle Junior is put under house arrest in the second season and has to find ways to occupy himself, it is considered one mark of how this once-violent Mafia bigwig has fallen when he becomes glued to his television set and, in particular, shows himself to be obsessed by daytime soap operas. However, whatever local jokes it may make at the expense of an ostensibly superficial television low culture (thereby seeming to proclaim its superiority over it), *The Sopranos* adopts many of the conventions of the soap opera. For example, the soap opera offers *The Sopranos* a tempering of its gangster stories of men out in the world doing violence to other men by means of the genre's attention to the domestic sphere, to family and familial conflict and affirmation, to interpersonal interaction that occurs as much in the realm of the unsaid as the said (hence, the use of pregnant pauses, blank stares, coded communication which ends up at times with the interlocutors at cross-purposes with each other), to an emphasis on the reverberation of events within extended networks of family and community, to emotion as an integral part of human psychology and response to circumstance, to the centrality of affective response as key component of human interaction (as much as cold calculation and pragmatic reason), and so on.

Perhaps the distinction between *The Sopranos* and the traditional soap opera is not so much formal, residing in the quality or aesthetic values of specific traits in one or the other, as cultural. *The Sopranos* benefits from a television phenomenon that TV scholar Rachel Moseley refers to as the "daytime-ization" of nighttime television, by which she means that evening shows can adopt the style and subject matter of daytime television, yet garner attention as somehow distinctive, somehow more consequential, and somehow of higher quality than daytime fare.[2] One context for this differential attribution of aesthetic value to nighttime and daytime programming, even as they often resemble one another, might have something to do with practices of masculinity and their redefinition and re-evaluation in a postfeminist age. On the one hand, men move into realms traditionally associated with femininity and try to appropriate them, asserting a tough, no-nonsense control over them: thus, for instance, the television run of *The Sopranos* overlaps with that of the Food Network, where Iron Chefs and burly macho men like Emeril Lagasse or Bobby Flay assume roles in the seemingly domestic space of the kitchen and "kick it up a notch" with their "bam" style of cooking. On the other hand, in a historical moment that needs to coin the term "metrosexual" to describe a new maleness that combines strength with sensitivity, machismo with caring and softness, men invest in cultural forms that allow a play of emotions, the power of confession, and a getting in touch with feelings. Thus, the run of *The Sopranos* also overlaps with that of Bravo TV's *Queer Eye for the Straight Guy* where each week gay men teach a straight man how to dress, decorate, cook, and eat like them, all the better to enable him to have heterosexual romantic success (with a jaded spouse or girlfriend) as a now-hipper straight man.

The gangsters of *The Sopranos* may find risible—and feel themselves superior to—what they see as the womanly, whining teariness of Kay (Diane Keaton) when gangster Michael closes off his Mafia life to her in the first *Godfather*. But they can betray themselves as no less prone to complaint, tremulous quivering, and emotional vulnerability.

In saying this, I am not trying to argue that *The Sopranos* somehow becomes simply a nighttime soap opera. Its identity is complex and its resonances come from its investment in a variety of cultural forms, high and low. The debt to soap opera provides one more way in which the series can open itself up to new narrative experiences and new tonal possibilities.

No doubt, *The Sopranos* is not saying one simple thing, then, about masculinity today or endorsing one position about it. When in one particularly emotional visit to his therapist, Tony feels the tears welling up and laments, "Jesus, fuck, now he's gonna cry," the third person may signal his attempt to gain a distance from himself, but it also speaks of an ironic perspective which runs through the show and insinuates itself into all simplistic attitudes and interpretations. Let us now follow some of the meanderings of this play and display of irony.

3 Food for Thought

The first episode for season 6 of *The Sopranos*—the second-to-last season—had Tony and Carmela obsessed with sushi. They devoured it greedily, spoke of little else, and, when Tony snuck out surreptitiously to ingest more of it, it almost aroused as much jealousy in Carmela as had Tony's various mistresses. Where, the spectator could well wonder, might this be going? As an example of serial television, the first installment of season 6 might be expected to pick up the memories of narratives long in abeyance and reveal new, satisfying developments out of them. As an instance of episodic television, the first show of the new season could teasingly have stand-alone elements that might turn out to connect up to nothing before or after. In the immediate unfolding of the moment, it would be hard to say what was what.

In fact, as a blend of episodic and serial forms of television, *The Sopranos* delivers a complex, if not weird, version of historical memory for its spectators. On the one hand, there are some details that the show "remembers" across vast expanses of time, and the spectator is encouraged to keep up with the references and the returns to previous narrative motifs. For example, when, in season 3, Tony's mistress Gloria Trillo (Annabella Sciorra) responds to his expressions of dismay at the difficulties of his life with an unsympathetic "Poor you," it matters that this was the exact phrase Tony's cold and callous mother had been saying to him throughout his life (and up to her death earlier in the season), and it matters that Tony winces when Gloria says it, showing us that he well remembers the original sting. On the other hand, over the course of the seasons, the viewer may build up knowledge about the narrative world of *The Sopranos* that the show then doesn't logically follow up on, either by contradicting it in some respect (to cite a minor version of this, both Drea de Matteo and Joseph Gannascoli were each cast across episodes as two different characters, while a different actor plays Father Phil in the pilot than in later episodes) or by simply abandoning one of its narratives or dropping a character one assumed was being prepped for a major plot line. In this vein, the sushi obsession, as it unfolded, could have gone in any number of directions, narrative and not.

In this respect, the opening episode for season 6 serves as an ironic commentary on the very role of memory across the seasons of a show where the hiatus between those seasons had gotten bigger and bigger.

Perhaps, the viewer might assume, there was something resonant in Tony and Carmela's newfound passion for sushi, a raw food embued, in season 1, with *negative* associations of potentially pungent impropriety when Tony wanted to assail his Uncle Junior's masculinity by referencing his famed skills at cunnilingus. Sushi would contrast then with rich Italian food, so beloved in earlier seasons but now itself given less than positive connotations. Indeed, in this first episode of season 6, the newfound affirmation of sushi ran alongside skepticism about Italian cuisine: Artie Bucco's restaurant, Vesuvio, which Tony and his family or his minions had often consumed memorable meals at in the past, was now said to lack excitement and innovation (with ennui, the mobsters declared they could recite the menu by heart), and the only figure who lusted after saucy Italian fare was the less-than-respected representative of law and order, FBI Agent Harris (Matt Servitto), who had come back from the Middle East with a parasite and was obsessed with thick hoagies from Satriale's Pork Store restaurant. Maybe, then, the show was saying something about the loss of a cuisine tied to tradition in a new America increasingly open—at the culinary level at the very least—to multicultural experience.

Or maybe the show was just playing at meanings, all the better to play with its regular viewers.

For all the consequential narrative threads that the viewer knew were hanging over from the previous season—and even from earlier ones—the opening episode's own obsession with depicting an obsession with sushi seemed perversely antinarrative, an irrelevant and perhaps irreverent distraction by the little things of everyday life. Season 6 had been announced as the penultimate season for the hit show; given the big narrative questions that the expectant fan would be posing as the program began inexorably to wind down—such as Tony's very fate as his New Jersey crew prepared for war with their counterparts across the river in New York—the concern with what the narrative's characters were eating as they moved toward the (their?) end might not perhaps have seemed that important. Indeed, by the last scene of that first episode from season 6, Tony was close to dead after being shot unexpectedly by his seemingly senile uncle. This in itself was a very big surprise: it had seemed from the previous season that the big question would now be the war with New York and how Tony would (or wouldn't) survive that, and now that plot line was being put on hold for a wounding that seemed to come out of nowhere. But even as it played with expectations about where season 6 might be going, the shooting of Tony by his uncle also had the effect of disrupting the everydayness of life on the show (which itself had disrupted what the viewer assumed would be the more monumental concerns of this new season).

With the shooting, a narrative occurrence of major import had intervened into the daily routines of consumption and into the apparently endless discussions of those acts of consumption. The shooting interrupted the seeming inconsequentiality of the scenes around food. Soon, in critical condition in his hospital bed, Tony would go off in his imagination into the alternate universe of a conference hotel in Orange County, California, where he had a different identity and where the only sustenance seemed to be the endless freebie drinks offered him by a bartender sympathetic to his dilemma. Sushi dropped away and was not mentioned thereafter. It appeared to be one more blind alley that the series threw in the path of the spectator eager to resolve the show's narrative points but finding that in bold defiance of expectations the show would, in fact, go where it wanted: whether into a nonplot about sushi, or into an unexpected new narrative line about Tony's shooting by his uncle, or even into an alternate universe in which Tony became someone else. With such a topsy-turvy challenge to expectation and narrative logic, it was ultimately both surprising and not so surprising, then, that the show soon dropped the alternate-universe subplot and never returned to it, but for a rare mention here or there, just as it dropped so many other tantalizing threads.

The extent to which the sushi motif disappeared so quickly (though who knew at the time if it would figure in the narrative later on? After all, there was still that unresolved question from season 3 of the wounded but resilient Russian last seen in the Pine Barrens) could seem a confirmation of its relative triviality, one more comic element thrown up for quick delectation along the path of the show's breathless move toward its finale. But, conversely, the very fact that it came up so pointedly in the first episode might also indicate its importance as both narrative and antinarrative device. Maybe the sushi motif had its job to perform for the season opener; having performed it, it could retire from the scene.

I watched this opening episode for season 6 at a friend's house in Los Angeles, one of the world capitals of a rarified cuisine in which sushi has been a key player. For upscale urbanites, L.A. is very much the site for the meal as aesthetic tableau marked by the separation of delicate items and often laced by light traces of sauces that interweave on the plate like so many dainty brush strokes. But this night, in honor of the show and in keeping with long-running ritual, we were going for classic, rich Italian food: pasta with bolognese sauce, rounds of buffalo mozzarella, thick slices of salami and prosciutto, and so on. Like many other faithful viewers, I suppose, I and my friends would celebrate each new season by the self-consciously corny consumption of precisely the sort of hearty food that we associated with the *Sopranos* world, and in this we could find inspiration in such commodity tie-ins as the best seller, *The Sopranos Family Cookbook*.

But our playing with *The Sopranos* didn't anticipate all the ways it could play with us. In this respect, then, while the season 6 opener's emphasis on sushi may have had something to do with a theme of tradition versus modernity, it also took on the quality of a joke—one that moved outward from the fictional world within the series itself, as when Tony referenced sushi to mock Uncle Junior, to take in the show's viewers as themselves targets of a comic setup. As the urban and suburban professionals who form HBO's privileged audience base gave up their typical and often Asian-inflected takeout or delivery food and opted instead for the downscale cheesy richness of the heavy Mediterranean cuisine they would cook and consume in ironic honor of season debuts, *The Sopranos* itself in the season 6 opener had its characters turning their backs on Italian comfort food and preferring precisely the sort of exotic fare that typical viewers might have renounced for the night. Over the course of its run, *The Sopranos* received endless accolades for its innovativeness, and here a seemingly throwaway plot thread reiterates just how the show's inventiveness is one that directly incorporated awareness of the audience into its very structure. The joke on Japanese/Italian cuisines, then, is only one exemplary moment from a duel/duet between a channel and series looking for distinction *and* spectators who are themselves looking for distinction in their lifestyle choices, one sign of which included subscribing to HBO and watching, and talking about, *The Sopranos*.

Willingness to play along and participate in the meanderings of the moments accounts for much of the inventive pleasure of *The Sopranos*, but it is a pleasure in which the viewer's own values and expectations are played with. *The Sopranos* is an endlessly citable work, and each of the moments from it can open up multiple avenues of resonant thematics and sumptuous delight.

Take, for example, another complicated food reference from the show, a passing moment—virtually a throwaway one—from the third season of the show: Tony has been explaining to Jennifer Melfi how he's had some memories of an early childhood antecedence to the panic attacks and fainting spells he's been experiencing from time to time as an adult. In particular, while looking at some old, wrapped-up cold cuts still in the refrigerator of his recently deceased mother, Livia, Tony flashed back to the time his small-time gangster dad used a meat cleaver to chop a finger off of the local butcher, Mr. Satriale, who was behind on his protection-money payments. As the flashback went on to reveal, young Tony had had his first fainting spell a little later when his mom put out for her family a roast that Mr. Satriale provided as a tribute offering to Tony's dad.

Working with Tony to get him to understand how his panic attacks tie in to a quite fraught family dynamic (to say the least!), Melfi makes an allusion that falls flat: meats, she tries to explain to Tony, are for him what the eating of a madeleine meant to Proust. When that name garners no recognition from Tony, she explains that he was a French author who wrote a multivolume classic centered on the ways (in Melfi's words) "that one bite unleashed a tide of memories of his childhood and ultimately of his entire life." Tony's reply: "This sounds very gay."

As I say, this is just a passing moment pulled from the many episodes that make up the experience of *The Sopranos*. It's even a relatively minor one. Elsewhere, Tony somehow stores up other bits of higher knowledge that Melfi imparts to him in order to employ them tactically, if somewhat distortedly, in other contexts of his daily life (as when he turned Melfi's mention of Cap d'Antibes into a reference to "Captain Teebs"), but the Proust reference is never touched on again. True, Mafia homophobia becomes a central motif in season 6 when one underling, the aforementioned Vito, is discovered to be gay and eventually is killed brutally for that seeming affront to Mafia codes. But while Tony's response to Melfi is in keeping with a distrust of supposedly aberrant masculinities expressed across the show's seasons by the macho men of the Mafia, it doesn't contribute in any stated way to a further articulation of that distrust. Melfi's learned allusion and Tony's disdainful response flit up and float away in relative insignificance, and the show moves on.

Even if the interchange in Melfi's office doesn't do anything for the show's narratives, it is in keeping with motifs that float through *The Sopranos*, season after season. For example, the very fact that Tony's panic attacks are linked to meat fits with the series' constant concern with food and acts of eating. For all its emphasis on men going about their cold business of crime and killing, *The Sopranos* is also very much about the moments when even hardened tough guys (as well as others in their world) pause for consumption of comestibles and frequently comment at length on their gustatory likes and dislikes. The gang members of *The Sopranos* eat meals together *a lot*. *The Godfather* famously includes a scene where, with the Corleone family at war, one Mafia soldier, Clemenza, showed his confreres the best way to make a pasta sauce; the implication was that this was a special occurrence, and that the man's presence in the kitchen was legitimated by the particular fact of the family being at war. In *The Sopranos*, in contrast, food is everywhere, and even the nastiest of tough guys can find time to enjoy culinary delights from preparation to consumption. Thus, in season 3, it seems a

Masculine metrosexuality? Aprons, pasta, and a good gun.

veritable comment on the ways cooking has been naturalized as a man's activity in our metrosexual times when the unbelievably vicious Ralph Cifaretto (Joe Pantoliano) is seen in an apron in the kitchen making pasta. The comic incongruity of the scene is all the more intensified when a young would-be hood, Jackie Aprile Jr. (Jason Cerbone), comes to ask Ralph (who is dating Jackie's mom) for a gun, and the two men discuss the relative merit of various pistols while Ralph, in apron, continues preparing the evening's dinner.

Even as it doesn't make a major contribution to the ongoing progression of the show's narrative (or multiplicity of narratives), the Proust moment qua moment does seem representative of the particular experience of *The Sopranos* as a television show. At the very least, we might want to note how the scene embodies many of the aesthetic virtues on display through the many seasons of the series. In fact, my quoting of the dialogue can't convey the qualities of acting, pacing, and composition that pervade this scene, like others from the show, but which are difficult to distill using our available vocabularies of aesthetic discernment. There is, for instance, a seeming rightness of acting style of a sort that makes *The Sopranos* stand out—a rightness in timing, in emotional control and range, in the way one actor plays off against another, and so on. Interestingly, while the acting on *The Sopranos* probably most approximates what we might think of as a realist mode, with some debt to the repressed emotionalism and stumbling expressiveness of method acting (a debt referred to explicitly in an episode in season 2 when Christopher takes an acting class and performs the final scene from James Dean's *Rebel Without a Cause*), the acting styles in *The Sopranos* can be broader than that and include performances at the limit of caricature and the grotesque. For example, Silvio Dante and Paulie Walnuts are played as cartoon figures almost, joke versions of the gangster cliché. Revealingly, though, the intrusions of unrealism that these characters bring to the show never seem damaging and themselves become delectable moments, throwaway bits that bob up in the course of the show and are absorbed with the rest.

In fact, it may be an inconsistency—in acting but also in visual style, in subject, in morality, in meaning—that is more defining of the experience of *The Sopranos* than its adherence to any one particular set of virtues in these areas. Thus, as with the acting styles, we might note the show's stylistically skillful navigation of a range of temporalities in its unfolding of scenes; this is a series that cannot just luxuriate in longueurs of pacing (as in the pauses and unspoken moments of reflection and hesitation in Melfi's office) but can also master the freshness of quick repartee, the striking comeback. The Proust scene is about snappy dialogue, but at the same time it is also about the ironies of a gangster show, filled with brutal killings, taking time to have its own Proustian moment.

For some viewers, those ironies can include the fact that Tony, who's never heard of Proust, still guesses correctly at his sexuality: Marcel Proust indeed *was* gay, and maybe liking little tea cookies and then spending a lifetime to write about the delectation of them does, in fact, fit a certain gay lifestyle. The sometimes intellectually superior Melfi name-drops a reference that goes by the brutish Tony, but he, in his naiveté, still cuts through the high-culture fancy and grabs the truth of the matter. But the ironies then would include the fact that the viewer who gets the reference—and clearly the makers of the show hoped there would be many such viewers—can both feel superior to Tony *and* be impressed by his talent at clearing away the verbiage and getting to the core of the situation. The target viewer for *The Sopranos* is probably more like Jennifer Melfi than Tony Soprano (and like her, probably hasn't so much actually read Proust as learned the madeleine reference in passing and internalized it as cultural capital), yet this scene—like many others—shifts our admiration from the pretentious upscale urban professional to the street-smart tough guy. Like the sushi motif that opens season 6, the Proust exchange is not only about the characters in the fiction but about us as viewers—what we expect of this gangster story and what it expects of us.

Again, this scene is a minor one. But *The Sopranos* is adept at making even the most throwaway moment seem all-consuming and all-important as it passes over the television screen. In fact, the world of *The Sopranos* is one in which the ostensibly minor can turn out to be major, or vice versa. At the broadest level, the overall structure of the show, with Tony's constant moving back and forth between the consequential issues of gangster life and the fraught problems of domesticity, raises the questions of significance and insignificance. To cite two of the dilemmas from an episode in season 6, which matters more: that one of your capos has been killed by a rival, or that your son has gotten fired from his job at Blockbuster Video? But, at a more local level, individual moments of the show are themselves often about little things that turn out to be quite consequential (and vice versa). This is a world where, to take another example, a seemingly forgettable joke, made in the hazy booziness of the moment, can sink into the consciousness of an injured party and almost lead to the whacking of the jokester gangster. Likewise, this is a world in which a glance, a twitch of the eye, a turning of the corner of the mouth can seal an entire fate. And the show self-reflexively comments on this: in an episode from season 4, one of Christopher's underlings thinks he has gotten a subtle look from Chris authorizing him to steal materials from a construction site, only to be admonished by Christopher: "A look? So now you're a fucking mind reader now?" In her work as a therapist, Jennifer Melfi serves as a professional reader of people's personalities, but the gangster world of the show also asks its mobsters to be readers who pore attentively over each little gesture and look to discern the motives and meanings of others. It likewise asks that of the viewer.

And if the show is so often about little things that turn out to have big consequences, the reverse can also be the case: something that appears initially to matter a lot can turn out to be irrelevant. In addition to plot lines that disappear (when, for instance, does Meadow actually break up with her cloying boyfriend Finn?), there are others that peter out in clearly calculated fashion. Most famously, season 3 begins with, and then devotes parts of subsequent episodes to, the FBI's attempt to install a bugged lamp in Tony Soprano's home. There are long sequences devoted to the planning of the intrusion into the house (which involves, through sequences presented by cross-cutting, the FBI's making sure that each and every member of the Soprano household is away and accounted for), to an aborted first attempt, to a successful second entry, and to the firing up of the surveillance equipment as it is put into regular operation. Along the way, it could be noted, the bugging subplot includes a strong example of something seemingly insignificant turning out to be significant: as they prepare the first time around to figure out where they will install the bugging device, the FBI agents study footage of the Soprano house that was shot clandestinely, and they laugh derisively when they notice that the water heater is rusting out and about to break down, little knowing that when this soon happens, it will cause a household emergency that will require the first attempted surveillance mission to be aborted.

But the subplot also dramatizes how the significant can turn insignificant. Suddenly, several episodes into the season, Meadow decides to take the lamp with her to her dorm room at Columbia. As the FBI buggers listen helplessly into their headphones, her seemingly innocent action terminates their surveillance. Abruptly, a narrative line that opened the season, and that has had a lot of time devoted to it, dies. Vaguely, to be sure, it feeds into a new narrative line—in which the FBI now decide to get insider information by having an FBI agent infiltrate the gangster milieu by befriending Christopher's girlfriend, Adriana—but in itself it has the quality of a prank perpetrated on viewers' investment in narrative buildup and suspense.

The joke here is both on the FBI and on viewers, who eagerly have gotten into the new season through the surveillance plot line. And, no doubt, for the time that plot line endures, it is delectable. It has humor (the FBI comes up with funny code names for each of the Soprano family members, such as "Baby Bing" for A. J. and "Princess Bing" for Meadow), it has titillation (we, along with the FBI, spy through binoculars on the comely Adriana in a skimpy tennis outfit), it has suspense, it has a seductive pacing and tonal weirdness (the intrusion and the installation of the device are scored to the "Peter Gunn" theme and the song by the Police, "Every Breath You Take"). Even as it extends over time and constitutes a self-contained comic mini-narrative with setup and punch line, a subplot such as this stands as one more discrete moment from the show, enjoyable in its own right and only moving the story forward in the most minimal of ways.

4 Living in the Moment

No doubt, much of our experience, and our memory, of our popular culture revolve around resonant moments: the unforgettable lyric or the striking musical riff, the memorable line of film dialogue, the endearing comic routine, the bravura moment in which style is shown off for its own sake, and so on. Think, for instance, of the fascination that the Academy Awards show has with montages of great moments from great movies. But if one way we use our popular culture is to pick and poach momentary pleasures from it, it is also the case that some cultural works themselves appear to take the fascination with the moment as a structuring principle. In a 1960s essay influential in literary theory, "The Reality Effect," critic Roland Barthes had argued how details mentioned in a literary work frequently serve as a realist veneer to foster additional interest and reader investment in narrative development.[1] In a sense, much of today's postmodern popular culture reverses the relationship, so that it is the narrative which now serves as a mere alibi to a variety of plays with form and style. Think, for instance, of special effects-driven spectacular cinema, which often combines the emptiest of plots and the flattest of characters with striking spectacle. Think, more generally, of the fascination with look and design over narrative substance and meaning in so many films, television shows, advertisements, and other works of visual popular culture. In its own fashion, *The Sopranos* tells a series of great stories, but it also uses those stories self-reflexively to insist on its own virtuosity in weaving complex performances—of acting, of visual display, of experiments with temporality and multiplicity of characters and character situations—around its varied narrative premises.

The series' impulse to live in the present and its dispersion of a single and singular narrative coherence into a multiplicity of shifting ways of telling a series of stories are frequently and, in their own way, logically accompanied by a sort of narrative forgetfulness. Plot lines may simply disappear and characters may not always seem to learn the lessons of the moment and carry them on into their narrative future. Undoubtedly, a kind of "forgetting" has always been central to episodic television, where each week a fixed set of characters enters into adventures similar to ones they have been involved with in previous weeks and for which they seem to have gained no new insight: Lucy Ricardo, for instance, endlessly tries to get onto her husband's show (and thereby spice up her bounded domesticity), and the Clampetts endlessly confront an urban modernity that they never appear to get the hang of. Growing up, my own favorite was *The Wild, Wild West*, where each week assistant Artemis Gordon would fabricate some clever gadget for spy James West, and that very gadget would turn out to be needed in that episode *but* would never show up again in any subsequent one. Watching the show, I could well get into the various stories, but I also began to sense—as I think many consumers of popular culture do—how conventions of the form and of the individual work could often override any "reality effect."

In terms of this fundamental forgetting endemic to the episodic series, a 2004 *Saturday Night Live* parody of an advertising campaign for the then upcoming fifth season of *The Sopranos* is singularly perceptive. The hiatus between seasons had started to get very long, and this might well test the viewers' memory skills over the years. As the SNL narrator announces that the fifteen-month wait for the new season of the series has ended, the screen shows Tony coming into the kitchen of his house and facing hostility from Carmela. When he asks her what he's done to incur her anger, she replies that she can't remember, and this launches the entire cast of *The Sopranos* into an attempt to recollect what happened in previous seasons and episodes (the only thing they all recollect well is that Janice and Ralphie had had weird sex together). Stevie Van Zandt (played by Jimmy Fallon) shows up in E Street Band clothes to say that it has been so long he's forgotten his character's name and has gone back to performing with Bruce Springsteen. The narrator intones, "*The Sopranos*. The show everyone is talking about, because they're trying to remember just what happened last season."

In *The Sopranos*, such "forgetting" is both structural and thematic. That is, some of the effect derives from the nature of episodic television and its concern for relatively self-contained offerings that tell full, if miniature, stories in their own right, only to start the process all again with the next installment. Some, though, comes from the particular story world *The Sopranos* traffics in. On the one hand, the Mafia operates in the television series as a veritable army, where those sacrificed on the field of battle are always able to be replaced by the next soldier in line and where there will, in any case, be new battles to be fought (and new stories to be told of them). On the other hand, many of the men and women in this particular world are presented as figures of somewhat stunted personality and ambition, fixed in their personality traits, and given over to desires of the moment which take priority over any long-term vision or concern with growth. In some cases, characters rely on the others around them to forget past insults, to overlook the consequences of change and accept it as merely an extension of the present, or to bury the hatchet and proceed as if it were all business as usual. The show, and also the characters in it, frequently work in a sort of iterative mode where they submit to the same behavior again and again. Carmela, for instance, may bridle at Tony's infidelities, but she also constantly retreats to a position where she accepts these as coming with the territory when you're married to a Mafioso. Perhaps no scene captures this sense of a willed repetitiveness on the part of the characters so well as one from the very first episode: in succession, we see Tony take his mistress to a restaurant and then cut to a scene of him taking his wife to the same restaurant, the maitre d' now greeting Tony with the declaration that he hasn't seen him in a long time. The implication is that the maitre d' is playing along with Tony's infidelity and covering up for it, just as Carmela herself has learned a kind of forgetting around Tony's sins of the flesh. In the story world of *The Sopranos*, characters will often try, through compromise, to live life as they always have, and this entails a willful forgetting of change; at the level of the show's temporal structuring, this entails scenes that frequently appear as repetitions of earlier ones, that leave out information about any change that has transpired between one repetition and the next (for example, it's unclear how much time has transpired between Tony's taking his mistress and his taking his wife to the same restaurant), and that substitute a slow unfolding of plotless duration for eventful narrative.

In this respect, it is tempting to read the non-ending ending of the series in season 7 as, in fact, offering a closure of sorts, even if no end to the narrative was shown. In this view, there is no need to show what might happen next, since in a sense we know already what life had been like, is like, and will be like, for each character: Tony thus will always be seeking quiet moments with his family, even as he knows that menace could come from anywhere and at any time; Carmela may try to find furtive moments of independence, but ultimately she will always be there to stand by her man; Meadow will always be a bit unskilled at things like parallel parking and will always be coming to family events from her own life elsewhere; A. J. will always have limited career ambitions (or, rather, he will have ambition but not the follow-through) and will settle for whatever brings him immediate material comfort (like onion rings).

In the show, living in the present moment goes along with a concomitant structure of stasis, repetition, and cyclicity, where characters seem to replay certain types of behavior again and again rather than move forward. *The Sopranos* tells tales, and certainly by season 7, it has gotten somewhere that it hadn't been before (if only because certain key characters have died), but it also keeps telling versions of the same stories as its characters compulsively repeat the behavior ingrained in them.

Take, for example, the fraught, even perverse, relationship between Tony Soprano's drama-queen sister Janice (Aida Turturro) and Soprano gang member Richie Aprile (David Proval) in season 3 of the series. That season, like the final season, has its own promise of violent and ultimately consequential confrontation between Tony and a rival—in this case the very psychopathic Richie, who, although a member of Tony's gang, is increasingly going his own way and provoking Tony. But suddenly the logical drive of that narrative and the viewer's expectation of a bloody confrontation is fully disrupted when Janice shoots Richie dead in a domestic squabble. While Janice's killing of Richie comes as a great shock, and not only for what it means in itself but for what it does to the viewer's strong narrative expectation of a final, violent confrontation of Richie and Tony (rather than Janice), the very fact of Janice's taking up with Richie in the first place comes soon to fit a pattern by which in various seasons she becomes involved with members of Tony's crew, often with disastrous results. The surprise of Janice's first dispatching of a lover becomes naturalized into cycles in which she will do terrible things, each unbearable in its own way but all of them becoming predictable markers of her monstrous nature. Over the seasons, as she moves in and out of amorous relationships, Janice will disappear and then reappear, and entirely new narrative situations will develop, but they all seem to come back to this one narcissistic woman who never will change, no matter how many Eastern philosophies she studies or how many revelations of new paths she claims to have had. Perhaps over the years there is some slight intimation of narrative progression (Janice's last relationship in the series, her husband and gang member Bobby Bacala, might have been a keeper—at least until Bobby gets killed by Phil's guys). However, the greater logic is one governed by the impossibility of progress and by the entrapment of characters in modes of behavior and attitude they can never really get out of. Revealingly, in season 5 Janice—irascible and quick to flare up and pick a fight—tries to change her violent ways (or, rather, is ordered by Bobby to do so) by taking an anger-management class. But whatever progress she makes there is quickly undone when Tony (who alone was privy to her killing of Richie) baits her into new outbursts of anger and thereby confirms that she will always be who she is. As Janice bears out to the extreme, characters in the series may show promise of progress, but it is as often the case that their "stories" are non-narrative ones of regression, in which they fall back on attitudes and modes of behavior they always have displayed.

Perhaps, if we want to play the game of comparing *The Sopranos* to a literary genre, it should not be so much to the story-centered, character-driven form of the nineteenth-century novel—for example, Dickens's *David Copperfield*, whose famous opening line establishes its strong investment in overarching narrativity: "Whether I shall turn out to be the hero of my own life, or whether that station will be held by anybody else, these pages must show." Perhaps a better reference might be the literature of the picaresque, that genre in which a character of relatively fixed identity and minimum psychological development over time goes through an episodic series of adventures that come to him (or, more rarely, her) as discrete events and that never coalesce into a single story, never add up to constitute a progress of any sort, and maintain the central character as fairly unchanged from one episode to the next. Think of Voltaire's Candide, who unflinchingly wanders from one situation to another, learning only what he implicitly knew all along—that this is the best of all possible worlds and that he must cultivate his own garden. This could be Tony's lesson too, one that he also has always known, except that his garden is the erstwhile "Garden State" known as New Jersey, and it is not so much to be cultivated as exploited and picked over.

But even more than the picaresque, which still attends to one primary character even though it surrounds him or her with a larger cast of colorful figures to interact with, *The Sopranos* is, as its title reminds us, not the story of one protagonist but an adventure in the plural. To be sure, Tony Soprano is certainly the central pivot of the story, but *The Sopranos* shows itself adept at multiplying its focus across diverse characters. Across the ebb and flow of the episodes, the story of this or that person—and not just immediate Soprano family members—will flare up for a moment, only to fade as another story comes to the fore. For example, diverse characters are granted dream or fantasy sequences in which their hopes and fears are given visualization. And at the very local level of individual shots, any number of characters—important and not so important—can suddenly be provided with strong representation of their subjectivity through vivid point-of-view shots (for example, in season 2, Tony's bedridden mother Livia awakes in a daze to a blurry shot of flowers that the always-calculating Janice has brought to her bedside). Even as it concentrates nominally on Tony, point of view in *The Sopranos* floats among the characters as a corollary to the way its narrative lines float from episode to episode, fading, modulating, disappearing, reappearing in new guises and with new consequences for further narrative development.

The series' diverse characters wander from event to event in a "move-ment" that ultimately is a stasis and repetitiveness of its own. Motion and motionlessness work together in this regard. Typical in this respect is an episode from season 6 entitled "The Fleshy Part of the Thigh." Tony is in the hospital recovering from the near-fatal wounding by his senile Uncle Junior and finds himself vulnerable to musings about the mean-ing of life. Various versions of such meaning present themselves in the form of visitors and patients that come into his hospital room or that he meets as he wanders the halls and who offer him diverse philosophies of existence. Thus, an evangelical preacher shows up to proselytize for the need to come to Christ, and Tony likewise encounters a patient, a Bell Labs engineer named John Schwinn (Hal Holbrook), who speaks to him of a belief that the universe is composed of an essential oneness. With each case, with each philosophy, Tony seems to be listening and mulling his options, even though his gangster identity might make any conver-sion to a higher belief system unlikely. At the same time, Tony has sev-eral encounters with yet another patient, a wounded rap star, and gives him insider advice on high-level sports betting. In other words, Tony continues to engage in the illicit business typical of his way of life even as he seems to be contemplating some sort of spiritual or cosmic alter-native to it. The hospital, then, serves structurally for the episode as a resource for various narrative lines, each of which brings with it its own form of suspense—for example, might Tony become born again?—and each of which participates in the episode's overall delaying and seeming forgetting of ostensibly major plot lines that had been set in place before the detour of Tony's wounding by his uncle. Importantly, then, when Tony does choose a course of action, it is to go back to the life of the mobster: wheeled out in his wheelchair by his family and Mafia associ-ates, he demurs at saying a last goodbye to John Schwinn, and it is clear that Tony is returning to business as usual. In other words, when Tony does opt for a path, it is one that cycles him back to what he's always been. He begins again, just as the narrative begins again, now having brought him out of the wounding subplot and back into the workaday world of Mafia business.

5 The Late Style of *The Sopranos*

I've found it useful in reflecting on non-narratives of stasis and cyclicity in *The Sopranos* to reference a concept first articulated by the philosopher Theodor Adorno and then given book-length elaboration in a posthumous analysis by the literary and cultural critic Edward Said: what they term "late style."[1] Adorno, and Said after him, argue that some artists toward the end of their careers, instead of looking benignly on the world from a perspective of wizened maturity, adopt a position of jaded, even weary, cynicism that is embodied then in artworks whose subject matter is the failure of human progress and whose style is given over to fragmentation, silence and noncommunicability, lack of narrative accomplishment, nonprogressing cyclicity, repetition, irony toward affirmative forms of aesthetic expression, and what Said refers to as "intransigence, difficulty, and unresolved contradiction . . . a nonharmonious, nonserene tension" (7). Works of late style refuse easy pleasures and comforting evasions. In Said's words, "lateness includes the idea that one cannot really go beyond lateness at all, cannot transcend or lift oneself out of lateness. There is no transcendence or unity" (13). At the level of form, late works seem willfully stuck in place and offer little belief in narrative movement; at the level of content, late works depict, at best, an experience that is depressive, claustrophobic, repetitive, and uneventfully downbeat to the point of deadness.

Adorno's description of the breakdown of expressiveness in artworks of late style could well apply to the controversial non-ending ending of *The Sopranos*: "It leaves only fragments behind, and communicates itself, like a cipher, only through the blank spaces from which it has disengaged itself" (566). Or, as Said says of the nonresolution in the late plays of Henrik Ibsen, they "stir up more anxiety, tamper irrevocably with the possibility of closure, and leave the audience more perplexed and unsettled than before" (7).

If *The Sopranos* meanders formally and breaks narrative coherence into a series of moments of shifting value that render ironic each attempt to find sure footing, perhaps this has something to do with a time (our historical present) in which it is easy to feel cynical about the idea or ideal of a higher authority that would legitimate our actions, that would grant moral purpose, and that would enable us to imagine that the flow of time coalesces into a narrative that we could call "progress."

Hence, the fascination in *The Sopranos* with cyclicity and repetition: even as episodes may move forward and narrative arcs form over the seasons, there is also the sense of a world in which little is learned, in which the same rituals and routines—both good and bad—are endlessly being played out time and time again. For example (and chosen somewhat at random): Soprano sister Janice will continually be a narcissist, Tony will go from one mistress to the next, henchman Paulie Walnuts will always be vain about his looks (the very last shot of him in the series shows him suntanning with reflectors outside Satriale's as if nothing ever changes and life will just go on), son A. J. will never be mature enough to not be seduced by flashy commodities like the high-end vehicle his father gets him at the end of the series. And on and on. True, some characters will come and some will go (a number of them violently), but at its core, *The Sopranos* depicts a world of unchanged people stuck in a place and time where sameness is substituted for difference and where progress gives way to repetition.

Might this not have something to do with the larger historical moment in which *The Sopranos* appears and in which it, too, is easy to feel ironic or cynical about progress? Politics, for instance, seems wearily cyclical: the run of *The Sopranos* coincided with a new Middle Eastern war for an older one, a new George Bush for an older one, a new Clinton presidential hopeful for an older one, and on and on. Turns of centuries (and turns of millennia especially) are, as historian Norman Cohn famously argued, fraught moments in which it is possible to wonder just how far we've come, how far we can go,[2] and *The Sopranos*, debuting in 1999, can seem very much of its time in its posing of questions about narrative and progress. Predictably, though, the show itself cannily and humorously cautions us to not go too far in messianic interpretation of this sort. Thus, in an episode from season 4 (which aired in 2002), Tony tells his nephew Christopher that he wants Chris to take more and more responsibility for the Soprano gang as they move into the twenty-first century, only to have the frequently oafish and literal-minded Christopher remind him that it's been two years since the start of the new century so that they're already behind on that project.

Late style has to do with artworks that express the sentiment that they've literally arrived late on the scene of history and that there's nothing affirmative left to be said. The great sustaining myths have become exhausted, and there's worry that no new affirmations of purpose can take their place. The upward progress of human adventure has been replaced by decadence and decline. *The Sopranos*, for instance, is filled with scenes and discussions both about the wearing down of the human body as it ages and about a general potential the body has for incontinence and failure even in moments of seeming youthful vigor. The series is insistent on showing bodies that turn ill, that decompose, that lack control and grotesquely expel the substances of the interior (blood and brains, vomit, urine, and feces) into the world, that buckle under pressure, that give into bloated excess, and so on. There is no dignity of the human here, just a sense of the body's inevitable betrayal and breakdown. The individual body itself participates in that general turning of everything to waste that is central to the economic operation of the show's Mafia family.

Edward Said opens his book on late style with a discussion of the biological temporality of the individual body in relation to larger temporalities of history and society, and *The Sopranos*, it could be said, is about a belatedness in both these realms. For the latter, there is the sense, as Tony outlines in the very first episode, that he—and those around him, along with the series itself—have arrived late on the scene of history; in Tony's terms, the moral certainties that allowed a Gary Cooper to stride boldly toward his destiny have been replaced by a culture of complaint, of victimization, and of waffling around proper courses of action. For the former, there is the sense of a biological oldness—of a waning of strength and acuteness. In an episode from season 2, the son of a black activist who has passed away warns Tony that the death of each elder means that the generation of those in middle age has gotten the first signal of its own decline and mortality, and an air of fatality—not just from violent death, but from the mortal destiny that awaits everyone—hovers over the show, especially in its last seasons. Both individually and collectively, *The Sopranos* is peopled with characters who seem out of sync, stuck in a time out of joint.

I've already noted that the show combines seriousness of acting style with caricature, and that is appropriate, since one of the themes of belatedness is that one comes onto the scene of history too late and in ways that threaten to make one's actions appear caricatures of the accomplishments of the past. *The Sopranos* offers ersatz figures who increasingly all appear simultaneously as jokes or like mere spectral versions of full-bodied humans. As critic Geoffrey O'Brien puts it in his excellent postmortem appreciation of the series, "The whole family seemed increasingly like the ghosts of people who hadn't quite died. . . . After years of reveling in the uncannily life-like counterreality of *The Sopranos*, we found ourselves washed up at last in a domain of zombies. . . . The images themselves darkened, as if the sun were removing itself permanently from northern New Jersey."[3]

Edward Said notes that in a more affirmative art about old age, there is frequently the optimistic comedy of elders who respectfully, from their position of deep wisdom and insight, realize the need to pass the mantle of romance and adventure to a younger generation. As Said clarifies, classic comedy often concludes with an elder giving his full and unreserved blessing to the marriage of younger suitors. In contrast, especially in its last seasons, *The Sopranos* could only look upon the romantic comedy of a younger generation as a depressing farce. Specifically, if an older generation—Uncle Junior but soon Tony himself—is feeling the physical ravages of time (by season 7, even Tony is saying he feels old), there is little cheerfulness to the idea that a younger generation will replace them. In particular, the last season includes the relatively downbeat subplot of daughter Meadow giving up her medical career to go into law and settling down for marriage with the son of one of her father's lesser henchmen. There is the sense here of compromise, of potentials not realized, of a fading of dreams (not only Meadow's but her parents'). Only the fact that Meadow might be making a lot of money at the law firm helps Carmela and Tony adjust to the idea of her compromised career and her compromised love life.

Not everything, it must be admitted, that Adorno and Said offer in their analysis of late style applies to the case of a late work *of popular culture* from the end of the twentieth century. Adorno and Said were both fairly, if not to say virulently, negative toward popular culture, and their insights were directed most toward high-culture efforts in European art. Critics have noted, with some amusement, that when Said claims, in *On Late Style*, to test the idea of late style in the arena of popular culture, he does so with Luchino Visconti's film *The Leopard*, an example of European high-culture pretension if there ever was one. At the same time, a comparison of this work of Italian culture with the Italian American *Sopranos* could be productive: Visconti's film and the television series both are large-scale, time-spanning works that range over various strata of social life to center eventually on a world of privilege and power worried about its ability to endure the modern age and hiding its vulnerability beneath surface displays of pomp and ostentatious consumption. Both are about a belated power that is entering into a phase of decadence and exhaustion and giving itself over to backstage scheming and furtive conspiracy.

A corollary of Adorno's and Said's disdain for popular culture is their emphasis on the individual artist, and here again the notion of late style would have to be employed with caution in the case of a mass-media form such as television. True, one might be tempted to attribute the sense of belatedness and the exhaustion of uplifting mythologies in *The Sopranos* to David Chase's own biography in television and the evident jaded stance he now frequently adopts as his public persona. Indeed, in interviews and public appearances, Chase can come off as a wryly cynical figure who seems disenchanted and emotionally distant. He talks frequently in interviews of a career of suffering through mainstream television's compromises and of fatigue with the empty conventions of commercialized entertainment.

But it seems to me as useful to move the concept of "late style" beyond individual artists and thereby see it as a way to pinpoint some of the shared cultural tendencies in particular historical periods. Said, and Adorno before him, imagine the individual artists of late style as outsider figures whose bitterness and cynicism about dominant ideologies isolated them from the public at large and turned them into veritable exiles. Yet so much of today's popular culture traffics in—and makes highly marketable—the very sort of intransigent experiment and the very sort of ironic posture that Said and Adorno hope would be an alternative to the market. Moreover, in an inflection that Said only hints at, the ironic art of today often takes on a tone less of downbeat bitterness than of humor and levity. The world may stink, it may all be turning to shit, but at least we can laugh at that, find fun in it.

For example, in depicting the ravages of the body and the gush of fluids that can erupt from it, *The Sopranos* is perhaps offering a dour image of every human's fate: so many scenes in hospitals, hospices, doctors' offices, and, ultimately, funeral parlors. But the series is also about a *comedy* of the body, and it finds hilarity even in the very grotesqueness of decay and decline. Not for nothing does the series have one character die on a toilet when, wracked by constipation, he tries to force himself to shit and has a heart attack from the effort. The show taps into vulgar traditions of physical and corporeal comedy. It even directly acknowledges such tradition when Tony Soprano's cousin Tony B acts out a bit of buffoonery from the Three Stooges. As television scholar John Caughie suggests, when dealing with the persistence of bodily comedy in supposedly high-quality British TV of a sort that one wouldn't have imagined to be "vulgar," the "cheap laugh on the way up meeting the tears on the way down" that characterizes the postmodern comic undoing of high seriousness in contemporary television drama is, in fact, not that far from a modernist experimentation which had its own moments of comic deflation. In this comparison, Caughie cites the moment in *Waiting for Godot* where a character who intends to hang himself whips the belt off his trousers, only to have them fall down around his ankles.[4]

The Sopranos often takes characters who aspire to financial and cultural ascendancy and displays both the veritable revenge of lower bodily functions on their claims to dignity and their inability to escape from a lowly world of mud and muck that keeps messing things up for them. Probably most noteworthy is the famous "Pine Barrens" episode, which takes Paulie Walnuts from the beauty salon of the first scene to the mire of the desolate woods, where all his ostensible fineries of look and style are stripped away from him. More generally, *The Sopranos* wallows, almost literally one might say, in images (and sounds) of vomit, of flatulence and diarrheic release, of trails of urine (intended, as when Johnny Sacks pees on someone he thinks [wrongfully, it turns out] had insulted his wife; unintended, as when Matt Bevilacqua pees on himself when he fears [rightfully, it turns out] Tony is going to kill him). This can lead to moments where the proper reaction is horror but also to ones where only broad, derisive, carnivalesque humor seems appropriate.

It matters that the character who comes most, at the end of the series, to utter endless lament at the rot and rut of existence and at the sorry capacity of human beings to hide themselves from the ills of the world is A. J., Tony's son. To the extent that *The Sopranos* takes seriously its own concern with belatedness, with failure, and with empty cyclicity, it also simultaneously qualifies that seriousness by having it voiced by a character who is whiny and immature, capricious in his commitment, and flighty in his depth of purpose. By the show's end, A. J. is easily enticed to discard his dismay at the bad things of life by a job in the film industry, a cool car, and eating onion rings with his dad and mom at a diner.

It's important to insist on the broadly comic side of *The Sopranos*, since it cautions us to take an ironic view of our own desires to make too much of the series' seeming display of deep meaning. It well reminds us of the show's participation in a social climate of irony and distrust that takes on the form of comic derision of deeper values and higher meanings. If *The Sopranos* is an example of what has been called "quality TV," it allows quality to include a great deal that is sleazy, decadent, disgusting even. Whatever the seriousness of the themes it raises, *The Sopranos* plays an often funny, even grotesque, game, one in which the aspiration of humanity to higher realms of culture and spirit is frequently mocked and its pretense and pretension zanily debased.

In one of his writings, a study of Richard Wagner, Theodor Adorno had noted how that artist's temptation toward the silence of noncom-

The modernist mystery of waves.

The postmodernist punch line.

munication and his rebellious bridling at presenting his art in an easy public idiom found enticing symbolism in the naturalistic image of waves: waves offer the ultimate in ineffable nonmeaning, in a rush of noise that has nothing to say, in a cyclicity that overwhelms all individual stories of the humans who confront it, in what Adorno terms "a state of immutability that refutes all history by confronting it with the silence of nature."[5] But if *The Sopranos* can likewise seem tempted by this sort of modernist symbolism of waves in wistfully lyrical shots of the sea after Tony and his gang have whacked Big Pussy, their friend-turned-FBI-informer, it is worth noting that a further reminder of Big Pussy appears comically in the guise of one of those Billy Bass singing fish novelty items. From the deep modernist meaningfulness of the waves to the kitsch tackiness of the fishy gag gift, *The Sopranos* operates in the register of farcical deflation, reiterating that there may be something both sad and laughable about the destiny of seriousness in ironic times.

We might well remember Tony's reply to Melfi when she asserts that it would be good to "confront these moral ambiguities" in their therapy sessions: "English?" In other words, what in the world do those words mean, and what do they have to do with a life as it is lived out here and now? Or, as Tony puts it when Melfi quotes Yeats's "The center cannot hold, the falcon cannot hear the falconer" to offer up her own modernist image of a late world where all moral verities have vanished, "What the fuck are you talking about?"

6 Gaming *The Sopranos*

The Sopranos traffics in big issues, but it also toys with the spectator in using the big issues as tantalizing entryways into its complicated universe. HBO set out to win over the "quality" demographic, but *The Sopranos* also plays with—and even mocks—the values of the members of that demographic. Not for nothing are urban and suburban sophisticates—academics, professionals, intellectuals—frequently shown to be unbearably sanctimonious and patronizing creeps in the narrative universe of *The Sopranos*: the series weaves a complicated game of love-hate around its viewers, toying with them, playing with them, defying them, and subjecting their seeming superiority over kitsch culture to the ebbs and flows of endless irony. The love-hate, then, may not only be that of the show toward its spectators but of those spectators toward themselves, caught between the will to be socially responsible and politically correct *and* the illicit desire to participate in narratives of sex, sleaze, violence, venality, and overblown conspicuous consumption.

For all the seriousness of theme that some critics and TV scholars— most of whom speak from and for the quality demographic—have attributed to the show, *The Sopranos* works fundamentally, perhaps, as a bold challenge played out between the industry of creative workers who constructed the series and the audience that consumes it. In this way, the show can seem to have been testing how far it can go in toying with the very demographic that makes up its preferred fan base. *The Sopranos* serves as an experiment in which one fundamental question has to do with the extent to which the viewer may be willing to follow the show in its every twist and turn, even at its most critical or most subversive of upscale lifestyles and of the very values of personal pleasure that the stratum of the urban professional holds dear. In the original broadcasts, that testing of the spectators endured until the last moment of the controversial ending.

Whatever else goes into our experience of *The Sopranos*, it is at the very least about following an ever-changing fictional universe and working to keep the connections between its various pieces in mind. In many ways, this is like a game: learning, for instance, how to shift allegiances, how to accept momentary defeats, how to care about little but the passing thrills in an unfolding narrative that will meander and deviate, and how to assemble the data of a vast fictional universe that requires one to remember plot details and character interrelation across vast stretches of episodic narrativity.

At the very least, the game of *The Sopranos* can be quite fun. In an age of multitasking and unstable alliances (for example, the many workers in the creative and information industries who will move—or be moved—from company to company), where there is often the sense that no higher morality gives deep purpose to one's actions of the moment, following a show that is itself about playing the game for the thrill and victory of the moment, meandering in and out of this story or that, going in and out of identification with this character or that, and shifting and adapting according to immediate circumstances and situations can be quite appealing.

There's even been a direct attempt in the literature of gaming and computation to connect *The Sopranos* to the world of online play. In an essay entitled "*The Sopranos* Meets EverQuest: Social Networking in Massively Multiplayer Online Games," two scholars of new media technology, Mikael Jakobsson and T. L. Taylor, recount how the game world of the very popular EverQuest made most sense when thought of as a space of social interaction along the lines of a Mafia organization, rather than as a narrative of heroic individualism in which a single player strives to triumph over resistant forces.[1] As the authors recount, one of them (Jakobsson) was a newcomer to EverQuest and imagined that it would be about "a lone brave explorer fighting ferocious creatures and perfecting his skills." In fact, he learned, success in the game revolved much more around interconnecting to other players and building up a reputation with them (in both one's game identity *and* one's real-world "out of character" identity) that could lead to alliances, shortcuts, favors, and aid from others. In the authors' analysis, the way in which game advancement depends on separating off one's self from immediate competitors and entering into the clique of those who will offer assistance is like what happens in the family world of the Mafia, where belonging to "this thing of ours" brings favoritism. As the authors put it, "Mikael slowly started to see the importance of the social networks inside the game. He saw that instead of having Gandalf [from Tolkien] as a role model, he would be better off trying to think as Tony Soprano."

Richard Florida, in his best-selling *The Rise of the Creative Class* (2002), a pop-sociological outline of urban professional practice, offers a picture of the new creative worker of the information economy, who dwells in a vibrant city culture in which he or she needs endless visual stimuli and strong experiences, a variety of social interactions, malleable boundaries between work and play, and always wants to be abreast of the next new thing. A show like *The Sopranos* provides much of this (which is not to say that this is the only kind of viewer who gravitates to the show): to know it is to be culturally in the know, to watch it is to learn skills of negotiation requiring allegiance, commitment, interconnection but also readiness to shift one's identification and emotional engagement, to comprehend ever more complicated narrative permutations, to hold incommensurate moral positions and social values, and to mix thrills with moments of uplifting high seriousness.[2]

Thus, when critics compared *The Sopranos* to the works of Zola or Balzac, no doubt the intention was to allude to the French writers' revealing depictions of the social interactions—the intrigues, the power plays, and so on—of French urban culture in the nineteenth century. But it would seem that the comparison appeals, too, insofar as these writers succeeded, in more purely formal or structural terms, in constructing massively complicated sprawling works, with multiple plot lines, vast casts of characters, and complex interweavings of past and present that thereby call on the reader to become active in the reading process. The reader then becomes someone who takes up the challenge of the expansive text and tries to plot a rewarding path through it by following clues, making connections, and being willing to move from one character to the next, one plot to the next.

Indeed, *The Sopranos* is a central test case for Steven Johnson's argument that, as the title and subtitle of his attention-grabbing book claim, "Everything Bad is Good for You" and "Today's Popular Culture Is Actually Making Us Smarter." For Johnson, contemporary popular culture offers a formal complexity so extreme that attending to its play and permutations strongly hones viewers' cognitive skills and makes them intensely adept at establishing connections, remembering complex links, parsing massive flows of data, and juggling multiple bits of information. Johnson asserts that the series,

> the most ambitious show on TV to date . . . routinely follows a dozen distinct threads over the course of an episode, with more than twenty recurring characters. . . . The total number of active threads equals the number of multiple plots of *Hill Street* [*Blues*], but here each thread is more substantial. . . . A single scene in *The Sopranos* will often connect to three different threads at the same time, layering one plot atop another. And every single thread . . . builds on events from previous episodes, and continues on through the rest of the season and beyond. Almost every sequence in the show connects to information that exists outside the frame of the current episode. For a show that spends as much time as it does on the analyst's couch, *The Sopranos* doesn't waste a lot of energy with closure.[3]

Eschewing interpretation—"The work of the critic," he says, "is to diagram . . . forces, not decode them" (1)—Johnson argues that complexity and complication in contemporary popular culture aspire to the condition of the game—what he terms "the cultural dominance of games in this moment of pop culture history" (92).

To the extent, though, that a game involves the interaction of a player with a constructed field of options and outcomes, a fictional television show like *The Sopranos* would seem only ambiguously to approximate the purely formal world of game culture. The metaphor of the game seems much more apt for the *Sopranos*-branded pinball machine or the *Sopranos* board game. The latter indeed seems to take gaming to a reductio ad absurdum degree of minimalism: a big tin box is opened to reveal lots of packing material and little more than a simplified foldout felt playing board, a bunch of chips, a score pad, and cards with trivia questions. You make bets as to whether or not opponents will guess correctly (for example, "True/False: Tony went to college for a short period." "Answer: True, he had a semester-and-a-half of college"). Perhaps, if we wish to maintain the game metaphor for the popular-culture narratives we *watch*—rather than those we *play* at with varying degrees of interactivity—we might do well to think of their spectators as what Internet lingo refers to as a "lurker": that is, someone who watches the efforts of active participants (in an online game or a chat room) from the obscurity of relative anonymity and relative passivity.[4] No doubt, there are feedback loops and circuits of influence from viewers to the television shows and other narrative forms they watch. For example, some producers and writers regularly check in on chat groups about their shows, and this may give them ideas (even if minor ones), but this is still an indirect form of interactivity at best, and in the case of *The Sopranos* the "interactive" power of the spectator over creative directions of the show would appear to be excessively limited.

An essay by Mary Beth Haralovich, a media scholar, and Michael W. Trosset, a mathematician, is specifically useful for our discussion here. In it the authors set out to theorize gaming aspects of popular television in particular and, toward that end, contrast the more classically formalized aspects of play in reality TV versus fictional narrative television programs and their much more metaphorical status as games.[5] In particular, Haralovich and Trosset examine the ways in which the *Survivor* reality TV show relies on a particular kind of uncertainty over outcome that is quite distinct from the suspense that is generated over endings in fictional works on TV. The reality TV competition begins from a position of general unpredictability: there is at the beginning a large group of competitors and no statistical assurance as to the identity of the ultimate victor, since strong figures are as likely to be eliminated by their rivals (for example, through acts of sabotage) as to survive until the end. While, in this respect, both *Survivor* and *The Sopranos* represent situations in which alliances are fraught and where trust can easily turn into betrayal, the fact that *The Sopranos* is not unambiguously about elimination (some rivals, such as Johnny Sack, remain over several seasons, even though it is always possible they'll get whacked at some point) means that its form of uncertainty is quite different than that of the game show. On the one hand, episodes of *The Sopranos* make it clear that seemingly essential characters can disappear (for example, Ralphie or Richie or Adriana), and it is fully within the realm of possibility that a character who appears essential can be eliminated before his or her time. On the other hand, nothing guarantees that such central characters will, in fact, be eliminated. Even in the last episodes of the last season, the compression of the show to a few key characters gives no indication that any of the remaining ones won't survive (conversely, there's no indication that they all *will*). To the last moment, the show is not necessarily about a rule-driven game's inexorable whittling down of a core group of figures.

Second, while there is unpredictability about the content of the specific outcome in a reality TV game since it is not clear who among the survivors will be the finalist, there is no doubt that there will be some outcome and that it is one in which there will be a winner. Unless a reality TV show of this sort were to be cancelled midstream, it has to end with a winner. In contrast, there are no game rules to dictate that the narrative fictional work must end in one single way. There can even be that metareflexive ending where the screen simply goes black. Interestingly, for a long stretch of television's history, many episodic fictional narrative series didn't have endings: the cancelled show would simply fade away. One would never know if Ben Cartwright ever would remarry or if a Man Called Shenandoah would ever regain his memory, or if Captain Jason McCord, "marked with a coward's shame" (*Branded*), would ever clear his name. In fact, ABC's show *The Fugitive* created quite a stir in 1967 when it brought its long-running narrative (118 installments) to resolution in a two-part episode that had Richard Kimble helping bring to justice the one-armed man who had killed Kimble's wife.

Nothing guaranteed how *The Sopranos* would end on June 10, 2007. Obviously, because of its setting in a gangster world and its debt to the gangster genre, *The Sopranos* might have inherited some possible options for resolution. But as I noted in the prologue, the very presence of the prior tradition of gangster films made a borrowing from them unlikely. Conversely, the alternate-universe subplot of season 6

(Tony in Orange County) suggests that the series didn't even have to adhere to its initial premise of gangsters situated in New Jersey: Tony could have returned to that alternate universe (which, after all, had been shown, at one point, to be Death). For what it's worth, in 2001 David Chase himself had claimed to rule out certain narrative options for the ending at a Q&A at the Museum of Modern Art. As the New Jersey *Star-Ledger* reports, "Asked by interviewer Ken Auletta how he would close out a fourth [eventually, seventh] and possibly final season, Chase avoided specifics, saying only that he hoped to avoid predictability. Tony Soprano wouldn't get killed. 'I don't think he should die,' he said. Nor would Tony consummate his long-simmering patient-psychiatrist relationship with Dr. Jennifer Melfi. 'She's not that kind of woman. She's not an idiot. She's a good psychiatrist.'"[6] Of course, nothing required Chase to stick to his word (assuming, of course, that he was even being truthful at the time), so his comments themselves had no real anticipatory value. Television fiction always maintains an unpredictability of outcome: there is, for instance, always the possibility of an ending that moves into some world other than the one the fiction was founded in, so that, for instance, a series can be claimed to have all been a dream or a fantasy (as with the infamous ending to *Newhart*).

One manifestation of the game-like nature of *The Sopranos* comes, then, in viewers' attempts to figure out the series' conventions to such a degree that plot development could be rendered predictable. Undoubtedly, this would turn out to be an ill-fated exercise. If one looks, for instance, at some of the Internet chat groups that sprang up around the show during its HBO run, it is evident that some spectators took pleasure in second-guessing where the narrative was going and tried to imagine that the show was structured according to rules that could be deduced. Thus, to take a recurrent example, some Internet posters would assert that, while watching the second-to-last episode of season 5, they knew that when gang member Silvio picked up FBI informant Adriana in his car and claimed to be driving her to safety, he was in fact going to kill her, because they had learned from the show's conventions that major figures whose fate was in doubt would die *before* the final episode of the particular season. (Undoubtedly, in the case of Adriana's killing, the probability of her character leaving the narrative universe of the show in some way—whether killed or disappearing into a witness protection program—seemed to have been increased in viewers' expectations by the fact that the actor playing her, Drea de Matteo, had signed to join a network show, *Joey*, the following fall, and it was unlikely that she would be able to be in two shows simultaneously. Ironically, *Joey* was quickly cancelled, and de Matteo would later say jokingly of her bad business decision that first she got whacked and then she committed suicide.)

True, season 2's *last* episode had focused on the killing of another informant, the much-beloved Big Pussy, but the second-to-last episode of that season had included the very unexpected shooting by Janice Soprano of her fiancé, Richie Aprile. We see here the ways the predictive viewers for a television show need to figure out the rules but then render those rules elastic when the show doesn't go as anticipated. The narrative arc of season 3 had been setting Richie up for an all-out, no doubt fatal, confrontation with Tony, and Richie's demise at Janice's hands clearly caught everyone (not only viewers, but also various characters in the show) off guard. It had broken the rules, but then the viewers made that breaking into a new rule: for example, expect that the show would not wait until the last episode of each season to dispose of consequential characters. Season 3, whose last episode ended with the killing of Jackie Junior, might seem to go back to the older model, but now a complex structure that allowed variation—and thereby allowed complicated viewer prediction to always pretend that variation was itself controllable—was already firmly in place. Thus, for example, season 4 went back to the violation-of-the-rule rule and had the despicable Ralphie die much earlier (and in unanticipated fashion) than had been expected. Throughout the seasons, then, there is a complex guessing game going on, and past "behavior" of the show can be interpreted in multiple ways in support of one or more hypotheses.

Haralovich and Trosset note another very specific means by which a reality TV game show like *Survivor* builds unpredictability into its formal universe in ways that aren't typical in fictionalized episodic narratives: namely, by depicting an unscripted competition taking place in a nonstudio-set environment, the reality shows allow for the possibility of violations of the very plans the creators of the show have envisioned for it. Accidents can happen, players can end up not playing the game as expected (for example, one *Survivor* contestant got badly burned and had to be helicoptered away), nature can intervene in unanticipated fashion. Certainly, the creators of reality TV try to control unpredictable reality as much as possible: in the production phase by confining action to setlike locales where there is an attempt to keep all contingencies and accidents at bay, as well in postproduction (where imperfections can be edited out). But there is always the potential for raw reality to refuse to follow plans (one season of *Survivor* had to deal with an unexpected storm) or for contestants to refuse to play according to the rules (in one season a contestant tried to make a mockery of the game in ways that threatened its very concept). Even though there is obviously a great deal of planning to control the environments contestants will be placed into, the reality TV show opens itself up to the unexpected, and this unpredictability is both to its advantage (it can exploit an impression of open-ended liveness) and risky.

Certainly, the scripted fictional show faces its own forms of contingency. The real world bleeds into the fictional space. For example, *The Sopranos* took on some new narrative concerns after the unexpected tragedy of 9/11. There were references to 9/11 in the dialogue, and the Twin Towers were edited out of the opening credits. More importantly, interaction with the FBI involved a new subplot of post-9/11 terrorism surveillance. Furthermore, some critics professed to see a greater emphasis, in the later seasons, on a 9/11-inspired theme of survival and planning for the future. But there are other instances of things not going as originally planned for the scripted show. In the two most famous cases, actor James Gandolfini threatened to leave the series because he felt he wasn't getting paid enough. And even more consequentially, actress Nancy Marchand, who played Livia, passed away after the first season and thereby eliminated one of the show's founding premises—a gangster's fraught relationship to his mother.

Likewise, as series writer Terence Winter explains in his DVD commentary for the episode "The Weight" (season 4), the idea for that fairly stand-alone episode (Johnny Sack almost takes out a hit on Ralphie Cifaretto because of a tasteless joke the latter has recounted about Johnny's wife's weight) came about when actor Tony Sirico was put out of commission because of an ailment and a stand-alone episode planned around his character had to be scrapped. No doubt, the blend of serial structure (ongoing narrative) and stand-alone episodes afforded *The Sopranos* a certain degree of suppleness in the face of the unexpected. While there was always the need to have the aggregate of episodes move forward chronologically, a stand-alone episode could work as a sort of holding pattern, allowing breathing space while the narrative was re-engaged or new narrative lines were opened up for subsequent episodes. Even though many (though not all) of the narratives that had proliferated through a season had to go somewhere, there was still always room for a vignette to be inserted somewhat randomly into the flux of plots. For example, when Michael Imperioli devised a script in which his character, Christopher, had a near-death experience in which he imagined hell (or perhaps purgatory, as Paulie explained to him) as a pub filled with nonstop partying Irishmen, David Chase realized it could complement his own plans for the series design to have Christopher be shot and come close to dying. Imperioli's vignette was moved into an episode that hadn't originally included it. In fact, while Chase had charts that indicated what would happen to characters both across a season and by the end of each episode, the writers he worked with had relative freedom in writing the dialogue and actions that would ensue before those furtive moments of closure occurred. There was thus some openness in the planning process of the show, although its unpredictability played itself out within the limits of a carefully constructed universe whose generic conventions limited how much vulnerability to the vagaries of the outside world there could be.

But in this respect, there is perhaps also a resemblance between reality shows and fictional series, one that separates them off from more fully fabricated and artificial fictions such as the animated film (which has little real-world contingency or accident to deal with). Reality shows and fictions may certainly diverge in their degree of scriptedness and in the ability of the outside world to intrude into the fiction. But they also are alike in using flesh-and-blood, real-life people within their universes; in this respect they may differ from more purely formal types of games that involve mere tokens as playing pieces (although card games have queens, kings, and so on, most of them cease to require the royal-family connotations of these figures; the names have become mere placeholders). The actors who play the characters in a live-action series are vulnerable to contingencies of existence. For example, an actor can die or age or become ill. Unlike a game in its purest state, where the elements at play might have little or no psychological being (for example, the silver ball that courses its way through the *Sopranos* pinball machine), it matters still that the television show works with characters who are not merely structural components of an abstract gaming system. And, in this respect, we might suggest that the fictional show on television gains additional resonance from the fact that it films real-life actors. Unlike a novel, even those that range over a vast period, a television show that extends over a long time frame shows us the actors themselves aging and changing physically. It was no small part of some viewers' emotional investment in *The Sopranos* that its long run (eight years) and increasingly long gap between seasons meant that they would watch the actors grow and develop. This could be particularly affecting in the case of the two adolescents who played the Soprano children—Robert Iler and Jamie-Lynn Sigler—and who were moving into young adulthood by the series' end, but it was also resonant for the viewers' experience of James Gandolfini, whose corporeal heft could be an object of fascination (and of suspense) from season to season.[7]

No doubt, we need not rush to embrace as an unequivocal good the fascination of today's culture with a reduction of experience to the condition of the game. In our neoliberal moment, in which the bottom line becomes self-aggrandizement and financial well-being, it is easy to see how the game becomes an apt metaphor for the way we consumer-citizens wend our way through the world: through the figure of the game, life becomes a veritable sport in which everything is about tactic, calculation, and the means to get ahead and do so before anyone else. Certainly, such competitiveness is a key motif within the fictional universe of *The Sopranos*, and, undoubtedly, it is also a factor in the very success of the show as cultural phenomenon where, starting from the notion that "It's not TV, it's HBO," one's participation in the HBO universe and commitment of funds to a premium cable subscription signals a differentiation of oneself from others who haven't subscribed to that universe.

Additionally, that many viewers have indeed been so tolerant of the games being played out on them by *The Sopranos*' unpredictable and

A. J. (Robert Iler) in his first scene in the very first season.

A. J. (Robert Iler) in his last scene in the very last season.

uncertain fictional world cautions us not to assume that playful challenge to one's dearest values by a cultural product (in this case, the inventive *Sopranos*) is the same as overthrow or subversion of those values.

In postmodern fashion, *The Sopranos* no doubt has gained much of its appeal by playing on a complicated relationship to its target audience. First, the savvy urban professional is encouraged at times to feel superior to this world of overdressed Mafiosi living a life of conspicuous consumption that appears to tip frequently into ostentatious arriviste vulgarity. The show flatters the viewer by, for instance, having characters engage in a series of malapropisms and other errors of speech and phrasing. For example, in a flashback sequence, Tony's dad refers to his wife, Livia, as an "albacore around my neck"; in another example, Tony mangles an old saying as "Revenge is best served with cold cuts." However, the show also mocks that very same urban cable-subscribing sophisticate by including in its narrative universe a number of professionals or intellectuals at the edge of the Mafia world, who peek in on it with voyeuristic desire but also unbearably obnoxious pretension. For example, Tony Soprano's therapist, Jennifer Melfi, tries to remain superior to the Mafia world, but her pat phrases sometimes ring as officious condescension rather than elevated wisdom, and she herself often appears fascinated vicariously by the very Mafia lifestyle she seeks to keep at professional arm's length. Likewise, Melfi's sanctimonious ex-husband, Richard (Richard Romanus), with whom she seems to reconcile only to split up again, mimics the very same sort of condemnation of Italian media representations that some Italian American antidefamation groups have launched against the show, but in the fictional universe he is presented as a veritable creep that audience members no doubt would want to distance themselves from. By extension, the viewers then might also distance themselves from the position of liberal and superior political correctness that urban professionals like Richard and themselves often engage in.

By these means *The Sopranos* satirizes some of the very values the targeted viewer would bring to the show and even assails the very assumptions held dearly in the life world of that viewer. The self-mockery that upscale viewers engage in by watching *The Sopranos* might then connect up with another appeal the show makes to them: through its obscenity, sexuality, violence, and depiction of a world of bad-taste arrivistes, *The Sopranos* enables the urban sophisticate a chance to slum, an opportunity to throw off propriety and flirt thereby with a scandalous and even dangerous world. In this respect, it probably is important that *The Sopranos* offer stereotypes of Italians: the show can thereby engage in political *in*correctness for liberals who want both to feel above such attitudes *and* to find relief in a context in which they are not responsible for the content and are therefore—at least for the time of the show— freed of such proprieties. No doubt, the liberal do-gooder experiences political correctness both as an admirable mission and also as a daunting form of self-discipline (always the need to scrutinize oneself to make sure one is acting properly), and it may be that there is appeal in a work of popular culture that provides a temporary, ludic space to indulge in political *in*correctness. The characters in *The Sopranos* do not merely say what they feel about other sexual, racial, and ethnic communities, but, tellingly, those communities are often shown to act in ways that seem to correspond to the stereotypes. Thus, as noted earlier, this is a show where "unidentified black males," to use the title of one episode, are frequently able to be enlisted as cold-blooded killers seemingly well versed in the byways of urban violence.

HBO works thereby to offer that viewer who possesses disposable income and the initiative to subscribe to cable the opportunity to flirt with taboos and to push the envelope of propriety. Ironically, then, *The Sopranos* became an exemplar of high-quality TV even as it eschewed many of the imputed foundations of such quality in profound drama, moral uplift, deep seriousness, and liberal responsibility.

7 Getting High with *The Sopranos*

Throughout its history, television criticism has been caught up in the search for shows of supposed high value—for what has been termed "Quality TV" (with several scholars recently calling for renewed analysis of the concept).[1] In this respect, it has been a strong aspect of the fate of *The Sopranos* that it was inscribed early on within diverse discourses of uplifting and meaningful aesthetic quality. Perhaps the most quoted evaluation in this respect is Stephen Holden's *New York Times* declaration that *The Sopranos* is the "greatest work of American popular culture of the last quarter century," and indeed the *Times* certainly did its best to impute high quality of the deep and uplifting sort to the series. The desire was to treat *The Sopranos* as a work of serious, high art.[2]

It is a frequent irony of the discourse of television quality, however, that it often declares this or that series to achieve aesthetic value only insofar as the show starts to resemble something other than what the writer understands typical (and, by implication, nonquality) television to be like. The quality show first is distinguished from other shows, but it is then distinguished from the television experience itself, which is assumed to not generally trade in quality. There is no doubt that many of the critics and fans who said that *The Sopranos* was the best thing on television actually watch very little television and approximated this one series to other rare, exceptional works of high drama they had appreciated.

In fact, the discourse of television quality often proceeds by imagining that television achieves its aesthetic value precisely when it starts to look like something other than television—particularly, the established visual narrative arts. For example, for both the critics and its creators, it would seem that *The Sopranos* finds much of its distinctiveness on television in inspiration from film and theater as much as from television.

It is striking how often David Chase, especially in interviews during the beginning of *The Sopranos'* run, offers disdain for television (aside from a few exceptional works that stand out from the morass). Chase puts it this way, for example, in an interview with the *LA Weekly* in an answer to a question about whether he watches television:

> No. I mean I watch MSNBC, CNN, I watch the History Channel. The last TV series I watched regularly was [HBO's] *The Larry Sanders Show*. I don't think much about television at all. . . . TV is in a way a prisoner of the word. . . . In a movie there's something else that happens. . . . In television it's only what people are saying that gets through. The image is pretty small and the sound's not that great. Nobody really concentrates very much on sweeping you away, by your senses. I wanted to do a show in which the senses were engaged, the visual sense and the audio sense.[3]

It's perhaps revealing that Chase talks here of the senses and not, say, of intellect. To the extent that Chase finds a useable tradition in television, it tends to involve works with visual flair and quite palpable stylistic flourish. For example, he frequently lauds *Twin Peaks* for its striking look. But he also gives great importance to *Miami Vice*, and this might at first seem surprising. After all, *Miami Vice*, famously or infamously cited as a key moment in the postmodern triumph of seductive and sleek style over substance, might seem the opposite of *The Sopranos*, which is distinguished by a frequently sober style, a seeming emphasis on deep psychological dilemma, and, for the proponents of high quality, a trenchant and quite unsuperficial probing into questions of the human condition. But Chase's estimation of the importance of *Miami Vice*, which he offered in an interview on the *MacNeil/Lehrer News Hour* on PBS, helps clarify the matter. As he says, "What we're saying [with *The Sopranos*] is open it up . . . try to do a feature every week, try to do a small movie, which means more than just talking heads. And they like that [at HBO] . . . I don't think people cared about the visuals back in the 70s. The first show that I can recall—hour drama—that did care about the visual was 'Miami Vice'—I think that made kind of a sea change. But then nobody seemed to care about it after that."[4]

In other words, *Miami Vice* is valorized for its distinctiveness in visuality, but Chase assimilates that to *cinematic* qualities in a feature-film tradition, where visual design is given its due (in fact *Miami Vice* producer Michael Mann moves back and forth between television and cinema with slick action dramas like *Heat* or *Thief* and a film version of *Miami Vice* itself).

In such instances, everyday television is imagined to be the bad object, a worldly form of nonculture too much in thrall to commercial concerns, while cinema is seen as a realm of aesthetic freedom in which unfettered creativity and open expression can ensue. In fact, in an interview for the HBO coffee-table book on *The Sopranos*, Chase explains that as a young man, he initially hoped to play in a rock-and-roll band but then underwent a conversion to cinematic art when, at college, he went to a Friday-night film festival and saw Fellini's *8½* and then Roman Polanksi's *Cul-de-sac*. As he recounts,

> I didn't understand [*8½*] but I liked it. I saw my family in there. I saw those Italians, I saw those faces looking into the lens. I saw those gestures. I saw those "operatic" men and women and I thought "I'm home, this is where we came from." And then when I transferred to NYU, I continued to be interested in foreign films. . . . The one that really did it was Polanski's *Cul-de-sac*. Not only, "Who was this guy Polanski?" but "Hum, there's a guy named Polanski who did this movie and that other *Repulsion* movie? These movies do not come out of a factory . . . like a Ford. They're personal. That would be interesting to do.[5]

There is, in the aesthetic discourse on television quality, a frequent envy for the other arts. As television scholar John Caughie puts it nicely in his study of the quest for quality on British television, "The desire for the prestige and production values of the art film in television drama is a desire not to be television."[6] To a degree, *The Sopranos* and the evaluative discourse around it tap into this. The debt to the European art-film tradition, which David Chase acknowledges, shows up, for instance, in a fascination with dead time, pregnant pauses, silences, and the way characters calmly cast reflective gazes at others in their lives (Carmela, for instance, is sometimes shown looking through her kitchen window, wistfully perhaps, at Tony in the backyard). Declaring that typical network television drama had characters too easily voice their feelings and resolve their problems with others, in one interview Chase called for a recognition that "communication is not clear. Meaning is not clear," and explained that in conversation scenes he often cuts to people reacting with a blank stare to what had just been uttered. This sort of cut becomes a regular stylistic trait in the series: "Even if an actor shows a reaction, Mr. Chase and his producers will throw away that piece of emotive film and replace it with a blank stare."[7]

From the opening of its first episode, when Jennifer Melfi welcomes Tony Soprano into the confined space of her office (designed as an oval, as if to emphasize the sense of enclosure) and the two begin an ongoing psychodramatic duet and duel, the show works within a framework clearly indebted to the aesthetic look and temporal feel of European cinema. Many of the virtually mythologized elements of that brand of cinema show up in *The Sopranos*: a leisurely pacing that, in this case, takes the form of relatively motionless shots in which nothing transpires and which are held for a long time; a style that thereby simultaneously delays narrative, invites reflection, offers a contrast with the fast pace of much television in the post–music video moment, and focuses attention on the shot's framing and composition (not merely are many of the shots long in duration but they use deep focus and distortion of characters close to the camera in ways that make the image itself a target of aesthetic contemplation; this is television literally to be looked at, not just watched for plot); a fascination—well on display in the first scene which chronicles Tony's bewildered contemplation of the statue of a woman—with the depiction of enigma and activities of interpretation; and a luxuriating in a pregnant but ineffable silence that might seem to hint at depths beyond what is visible on-screen. Later episodes add other elements of the art film: for instance, a fascination with flashbacks and complicated temporality, and a blurring of the boundaries between dream and states of wakefulness (the inspiration, for example,

The first two shots of the show.

for the 23-minute dream sequence in season 5 was Buñuel's *The Discreet Charm of the Bourgeoisie*; nicely, a repair shop in season 1 is named Bunuel Brothers Auto Repair).

Given the frequent violence of its stories and the sometimes garishness of the lifestyles it depicts (for example, the kitsch ornateness of the Sopranos' house), it is perhaps paradoxical but ultimately logical that *The Sopranos* be marked by a visual style of relative sobriety. That is, like much of the elegiac art cinema of the 1950s and 1960s, the show often downplays special effects, frenetic montage, or images layered in painterly fashion. To be sure, the show does exhibit, as we see in the art-cinema elements in the very first scene from the very first season, a concern to focus attention on framing and composition in the image and thereby make its own style visible: *The Sopranos* does not try for a full transparency of style and instead frequently displays its shots as manifest objects of aesthetic contemplation. Sobriety of style, then, entails careful compositions often played out in long duration and focusing attention on the work of actors. The frequent use of deep focus—with sometimes striking contrasts between characters in foreground and background of the frame—also works to this end.[8]

Certainly, within a complicated media landscape there are distinctive attractions to be imagined for this sober style. For the upscale metropolitan viewer, for instance, it can have the virtue of directing attention to the work of actors and emphasizing the show's reliance on a model of theatricality, another of the arts whose virtues so-called quality TV aspires to. Not for nothing has high-class dramatic theater been a centrally defining art for culture-seeking urbanites and a model of quality for popular storytelling arts like film and television; it's significant that a number of *Sopranos* actors emphasize their ongoing investment in theater, whether it be Edie Falco's hit run in *'night, Mother* or Michael Imperioli's desire, eventually fulfilled, to open a cutting-edge theater of his own.[9] Even as television operates from an envy for other media, the actor-driven theatrical model—which is also the model of an actor-centered art cinema, from Antonioni to Fassbinder—enables a show like *The Sopranos* to claim attractions that other works in other mass media seem increasingly unable to deliver. A number of influential critics have begun to rail, for instance, against big-budget, effects-driven,

CGI-dominated films—say, *Sky Captain and the World of Tomorrow*, *Sin City*, or *Star Wars: Episode III—Revenge of the Sith*—with particular opprobrium for the ways in which this sort of cinema seems increasingly to divest itself of acting talent, psychological density, and plot-driven narrative sophistication. In some cases, the failing is seen as specific to a particular director (for example, the mechanical coldness of *Revenge of the Sith* has been attributed to George Lucas's worsening desire to play with technology at the expense of people and emotions), but it is as possible to see effects-driven moviemaking as an endemic tendency of commercial cinema today. In such a context, a large audience constituency—say, the older demographic that wants important blends of drama and psychology rather than explosive but superficial visuality—finds itself unaddressed by dominant cinema and turns elsewhere: either to a wave of seemingly modest independent films that eschew special effects for dramatic and intimate displays of old-style acting and each year win critical acclaim and garner prestigious awards or nominations, especially in the area of acting and writing (for example, *You Can Count On Me* or *Sideways* or *Little Miss Sunshine*) or to that theater-based form of television that still seems to believe in character and story. Not for nothing was there an ongoing Emmy battle between *The Sopranos* and NBC's *The West Wing*, since both could appeal to an older demographic of urban liberals who think of television as a place for actors to play out psychologically complex situations through resonant emotion and pithy dialogue. And as the outing to the cinema multiplex seems increasingly to involve greater expense for what seems the worst aspect of commercial television (for example, advertiser sponsorships, with movie theaters now running twenty-minute ad packages before the films), the dramatic television show offers its depth and uplift in the easy space of domesticity (and without, in the case of *The Sopranos*, any direct hawking of commercial wares).

And in the context of home entertainment, the well-written show that serves as an arena for theatrically rich acting can differentiate itself by the very same sobriety of style. Certainly, there are moments of visual flourish on *The Sopranos*—for example, the striking overhead shot of the gang that looks down on them from a pig statue at Satriale's Pork Store, or the vertiginous twist of the camera as Tony Soprano broods in his bed—but these tend to remain mere touches, moments of excess that can serve as aesthetic bonuses to be noted and relished as they pop across the span of the series. For the most part, *The Sopranos* eschews that particular vibrant style that media scholar John Caldwell termed "televisuality" and that flooded much American television in the 1980s with images overloaded with a surfeit of visual data: electronic effects, mutations of visual space, overlaps and superimpositions, multiplication of graphic effects, and writerly inscriptions of words and verbal scrolls.[10] For Caldwell, the explosion of new media formats that threatened the broadcast networks' domination of home-screen entertainment pushed the networks to try to make their products stand out through an ever-expanding visual complication of the image. Televisuality was, for Caldwell, the increasingly prevalent style for commercial television. Recently, another media scholar, Shawn Shimpach, has extended Caldwell's analysis into the 1990s by examining how the internationally financed and coproduced television series *Highlander* "utilize[s] strategies of stylistic exhibitionism to stand out from other programming, attract viewers, and represent itself as a quality, cosmopolitan production."[11] On the one hand, frenetic and action-filled televisuality is planned to have transnational appeal. On the other hand, the very subject of *Highlander*—a man gifted with immortality who travels throughout the globe and across the centuries—is an apt and seductive rendition of an unfettered cosmopolitanism that seeks home and sanctuary everywhere in the world. In this respect, *The Sopranos* may offer a very different relation to globalism and to its own exportability as a visual experience without borders. *The Sopranos* is much more a local work, rooted in a specific time and place, and even parochial in the attitude of its characters to other worlds, other experiences. Notably, only a very few episodes—most notably, "Commendatori," in which Tony and his crew go to Italy and generally fail to interact well with the old country—involve any direct representation of the movement of Soprano family or gang members to spaces elsewhere (unless we count the trip back to Italy by Soprano gang member Furio [Federico Castelluccio] for his father's death [followed by Furio's full disappearance from the show]) or the hallucination in which Tony imagines himself back in the old country with a dream-goddess as his mother). It's revealing that when Anthony Jr. goes on a class trip to Washington, D.C., all he can recount from his visit is the fact that they had video games at the hotel; he is a veritable "accidental tourist." And even when the world of New Jersey encounters Hollywood (in the "D-Girl" episode), the collision of the two ways of life occurs on home turf, Jon Favreau and his associate Amy having flown in from the West Coast. Often quite detailed in its depictions of a New Jersey geography (and different in this respect from its vague and somewhat generic images of much of Manhattan), *The Sopranos* is about a provincial way of life, and it adopts an un-"televisual" style to depict it.[12] In its representations of place and its own articulation of a restrained visual style for that representation, then, *The Sopranos* eschews that sort of mobile cosmopolitanism that has become so much the appealing subject of much contemporary popular culture. Certainly, the show's glimpse at its geographically restricted way of life might itself have cross-national appeal through its very elaboration of a regionalism and a way of life (the gangsters of New Jersey) that itself may seem exotic to spectators elsewhere. Indeed, with an admittedly limited sampling, U.K. scholar Joanne Lacey conducted interviews with British male television viewers of *The Sopranos* and seemed to find that to the extent they became devotees of the show, their fandom derived from their fascination at witnessing a criminality they imagined endemic to U.S. life: the show was one more glimpse into a mythic America that they had already seen on display in films by Coppola and Scorsese.[13]

The fetishizing of regional parochialism at work in *The Sopranos* has its visual correlate in its sober style, one which refuses to be too slick, too energetic, too televisually overloaded to support the slow-paced broodiness of the sort the show luxuriates in. In *Televisuality*, John Caldwell, as noted, had seen the emergence of the new style of visual density in the 1980s and 1990s as a strategy for networks to sell a new image of their hipness and excitement. After the turn of the century, other strategies become apparent. For example, HBO shows like *Six Feet Under*, *Curb Your Enthusiasm*, and *The Sopranos* would seek distinction in a style of relative restraint that lets actors show themselves off in performances of complex dilemmas that frequently generate ever-greater narrative entanglements. Here, again, the model is that of theater and, even more, of complex art-cinema narratives of interpersonal psychodrama.[14]

No doubt, this reliance on high dramatic theater and on the art-film tradition might encourage that sort of deep interpretation and symbol hunting that would seem inevitably to go along with critical elevation of the show to the supposed region of Quality. But it could also be said that the debt to the art film works best of all to establish the series as aesthetically distinct from much of what David Chase and his associates would consider commercial network television. Beyond any profound meaning that we might want to attribute to art-film borrowings in the show, the art-film influence serves first as a strategy of demarcation by which the show can seem to transcend ordinariness (of television and of its typical subject matter). Think, again, of Chase's tribute to *Miami Vice*: a show that references artsy cinema, but not so much for deep meaning as for distinctive visual style. In like fashion, *The Sopranos'* reworking of the specific cinematic model of European cinema enables the series to distinguish itself from both a dominant style of cinema and a dominant style of television. It also seems that *The Sopranos* could use the trappings of art cinema to make itself special without that specialness manifesting itself in patterns of deep, allegorical meaning. Art cinema offers as much a look and a style as a bundle of themes to be found beneath that look and that style.

Take, for instance, Tony's peyote trip in Las Vegas and then out into the desert late in the final season. Given the resonances that each and every moment of the final season would hold for *Sopranos* fans, a drug scene would have potentially special revelatory status, like perhaps the famous minutes-long dream sequence in season 5. And indeed, there are hints of meanings to be had, elements to be interpreted. For example, as the wide-eyed Tony and his equally stoned girlfriend of the moment, a vivacious dancer, wander through a Las Vegas casino, a shot of a pinball machine's icon is suddenly interjected—a horned, satanic figure but with the cherubic rotundity of Porky Pig—followed by a very quick reaction shot of Tony ambiguously taking note of the image. Might there be the expression here of two sides of Tony: the lovable and the evil, or the childlike and the maturely dangerous? As likely, the image tantalizes and hints at meanings without resolving them. And, in any case, what would it mean to come up with this sort of interpretation of this icon anyway? The show has already quite readily conveyed to us

Symbolic?

the many and often contradictory aspects of Tony's personality, so there is no need to further assert that point.

A drug scene could serve as a moment of privileged insight, but it could also indicate an unreliability of vision. Certainly, when the series employs dream sequences in previous episodes, these do not always offer a clear conduit to higher meanings. For example, in season 2, when the wounded Christopher has a dream of hell as an Irish bar and tells Paulie that the latter was there too, the panicked Paulie can eventually resiliently reinterpret the scene as purgatory, not hell, and thereby remain confident that he is not going to eternal damnation. In like fashion, when Tony and the dancer finish off their peyote experience out in the desert and—as the woman slumbers next to him in a shot posed as if it came from some artsy film scene of studied alienation and moral deadness—Tony rises to his feet, stretches out his arms, and yells "I get it, I get it," the art cinema trappings of deep revelation are all there, but it's worth noting that no details of that revelation are made clear to us in the moment. We don't know what Tony gets. Moreover, when Tony tries later to recount the experience to his gang, they *don't* get it, and

The modernist mystery of the desert.

his memory of the experience falls flat. Whatever the revelation, it is negated in the context of the show.

The silences in the European art film were often taken by critics to point at resonant meanings just below the level of expressibility and waiting for a savvy interpreter to bring them into the light of day. But in its quotation of the art cinema tradition, *The Sopranos* suggests that these enigmatic scenes and situations may hint at meaning but never really deliver it up since their real power lies in their performance of style and look. If *The Sopranos* is a stellar case of "Quality TV," perhaps the very notion of quality needs to be updated in order to better address new and complex ambitions of popular television today.

8 Qualifying "Quality TV"

Not all claims about "quality TV" have to do with a denial of the medium of television per se. Thus, one tradition which is frequently adduced when one wants to attribute high achievements of quality to a television show is that of the high British television drama of manners along the lines of *Masterpiece Theater*. It is indeed the case that *The Sopranos* has been compared to the British quality shows. For example, *New York Times* critic Caryn James asserts that "in its leisurely use of the form [of the classic miniseries], it is strangely like *Brideshead Revisited, The Singing Detective*, and *I, Claudius*."[1] Likewise, some critics or scholars even suggest that the first name of Livia Soprano is a direct reference to *I, Claudius*, and that PBS show's depiction of family as site of political machination.

Peggy Noonan's *Wall Street Journal* postmortem for *The Sopranos* is typical: "There have been shows on television that have been, simply, sublime. In drama there was 'I, Claudius,' a masterpiece of mood and menace . . . And PBS's 'Upstairs, Downstairs.' A few others. 'The Sopranos' is their equal, but also their superior."[2]

Likewise, *The Sopranos* can bear comparison to an important indigenous American tradition of ostensible quality TV: namely, the so-called golden age of serious dramas on television in the 1950s. These were the narrative works of everyday life in the contemporary (usually urban) world written by such legends as Paddy Chayefsky, Reginald Rose, or Rod Serling. Revealingly perhaps, in the very last episode of *The Sopranos*, a scene about a TV writer from Serling's *The Twilight Zone*—a show which some critics see as his abandoning the golden age dramas to accept the constraints of commercial diversion—is playing in the background in the safehouse Tony is hiding out in. There is direct but complicated reference here to the vexed history of so-called quality drama on commercial television and the integrity of the writer within the television process.

Many golden age dramas were actor- and script-driven stories that focused on the ordinariness of a supposed Everyman as he confronted life's quandaries. Frequently, the protagonist of such narratives was pictured as a working stiff trying to juggle demands of domesticity and employment together. From Paddy Chayefsky's *Marty* to Norman Lear's Archie Bunker to David Chase's Tony Soprano, there is, for instance, a continued emphasis on a meaty working guy who from time to time has flashes of enlightenment and visions of self-amelioration and who strives to confront the limits of his own situation. Not for nothing did *The Sopranos* receive most of its Emmy nominations and awards in the areas of writing and acting, since it reinvigorated a tradition that valorizes dramatic and narrative qualities and whose accompanying criticism in such venues as the *New York Times* sees these as central when attributing high value to a television show. (It is perhaps revealing that *The Sopranos* never won in the directing category, but only, in fact, in acting and writing.) Quality television of the sort that garners awards is imagined here to revolve around rich and rounded figures who face moral dilemmas and either grow from the encounter or enable spectators to feel that they themselves have grown.

But even as the narratives of television's golden age no doubt enabled a commentary on drive and success in postwar America, they also served as formal structures by which a vast number of interesting actors could try out their skills on carefully honed material. The proliferation of tele-plays allowed, week after week, for a parade of actors to pass through television and show off their performative potential. It is fascinating, when viewing golden age television drama, to witness the sheer number of famous names in acting—from cinema and from theater—that participated in the form and gave it its energy. And it is clear that *The Sopranos* fits within this lineage of televised dramatic works that emphasize the close interaction of a few characters in ways that demonstrate both individual and ensemble acting skill and also allow for guest turns by a venerable old guard of actors such as, in the specific case of *The Sopranos*, Robert Loggia or Polly Bergen.

Both because there really isn't a clear conceptual vocabulary available and because it appears to enter into the realm of subjective opinion, it is not easy to be precise about this brand of quality acting on television. In her call for more attention to the aesthetic qualities of television, Christine Geraghty points to analysis of acting as one of the underdeveloped areas of television study. However, from the discourse of acclaim for the acting on *The Sopranos*, we can hazard some suggestions as to the valued attributes that typically are associated with quality acting: a degree of realism or plausibility by which the spectator readily imagines that such characters typically would react in comparable fashion to such situations in real life; understatement but also volatility that provides the sense that beneath the calm there lurks a brooding energy that can burst out when provoked; psychological depth and layers of implication to which, in the case of *The Sopranos*, is added a concomitant wryness in which the character suggests that he or she knows this is a performance; a display of imperfection that is itself, for the actor, a controlled form of perfection, as when James Gandolfini's Tony Soprano stumbles for the right words to say; and the ability to range through a gamut of emotions.

At the same time, any argument about quality in popular television needs to take note of a point that John Caughie makes about high-class drama on British TV but which seems to apply, too, to the theatrically derived tradition in U.S. television. Specifically, Caughie notes, the high dramatic tradition in television has often had a somewhat puritanical streak to it, an "ethical seriousness," as he puts it, in which characters are to be defined by commitment (whether to work, to politics, or to depth of interpersonal relationship) rather than by leisure and the pursuit of pleasure.[3] The seriousness of quality TV, in this puritanical approach, has to do with a seriousness of purpose in the characters within the fiction. In particular, in the moment before the youth revolution and the pop and mod explosion of vibrant look and lifestyle in England in the 1960s, quality dramas could only view leisure time and popular culture more generally as sites of waste, alienation, emptiness, and triviality. In the American context, too, it could be argued, the hard-hitting black-and-white quality dramas of the 1950s participated in a suspicion toward mass culture, despite the fact that they themselves were being made available through one of the strongest machines of mass culture of the age. In *Marty*, for instance, the eponymous protagonist makes a step forward when he decides to take responsibility for his own life and distinguish himself from his culturally debased buddies, such as drinking partner Angie, for whom Mickey Spillane is the epitome of artistic achievement. Likewise, in *12 Angry Men*, the upright liberal has to fight not merely against prejudice (which is at least commitment to a principle) but against the mindlessness of mass taste. In one scene, for example, a juror has voted "guilty" simply to finish up the trial and get to a baseball game.

In this respect, it is tempting to employ the term *postmodern* to signal the recognition, in more recent works of popular culture, that an immersion in leisure, game, popular representation, and the trivial pursuits of ubiquitous entertainment culture is integral to the everyday lives of ordinary citizens. Hence, in the British context, the realist dramas of the 1950s and early 1960s, whose high seriousness John Caughie outlines, give way to the magical postmodernism of Dennis Potter and his highly self-reflexive *The Singing Detective*.

In like fashion, in *The Sopranos*, the characters live in a world engulfed by fun and often kitschy popular culture, and it is assumed that the show's spectators share in that world of reference. While the series sometimes takes local cases of mass-culture consumption to be a worrisome thing—for example, Anthony Jr. spending too much time in front of electronic screens or Uncle Junior ignoring Mob business because he has become a TV-addicted couch potato—it also holds as a fundamental assumption that popular culture has become an inextricable part of everyday consciousness in ways that can't be isolated from other aspects of people's existence. While some commentators have tried to attribute to *The Sopranos* its own brand of "ethical seriousness" that would distinguish it from, say, the depthless luxuriating in empty coolness in the films of Quentin Tarantino, the opening sequence in the hip film director's first feature, *Reservoir Dogs*, could easily have fit somewhere in the universe of *The Sopranos*: in a diner, a number of cold criminals dissect the meaning of a Madonna song just before going off to try to make a score. The gangsters of *The Sopranos* also know their popular culture and also dissect it with loving and, for the spectator, funny attention. Some scholars have become enamored of pointing out references to other popular culture in *The Sopranos* (David Lavery's anthology *This Thing of Ours: Investigating The Sopranos* has an appendix on "Intertextual Moments and Allusions in *The Sopranos*" that runs for nearly twenty pages, and which is updated to newer seasons in a sequel volume, *Reading the Sopranos: Hit TV from HBO*), but the relation to the surrounding culture is more than just one of local allusion. Mass culture is an integral, pervasive texture within the structure of feeling of the characters who people *The Sopranos*. Popular culture is the air in which these gangsters, and the spectators watching them, breathe and take sustenance.

The sense that the work of mass culture exists in relation to all other such works, and that each is a reference to all the others—so that to enter into the world of mass culture in midstream, as if such innocence were ever even possible, is to have no ability to understand the terms of the cultural conversation—has been defined as one condition of postmodernity. *The Sopranos* is a show in which characters are intensely aware of the popular culture around them and have made it an essential part of the fabric of their everyday existence. Whereas the mass-cultural environment in, say, *The Godfather* receded into the background and became mere distraction—the Hollywood of Johnny Fontaine that the Corleone family has to exert its force against, the sentimental film (*The Bells of Saint Mary's*) that Michael and Kay see at Radio City Music Hall, only to emerge from the theater to discover from a newspaper that Don Corleone has been shot—such culture is, for the characters of *The Sopranos*, a constitutive part of existence. For instance, the gangsters of the television show live under the shadow of *The Godfather* itself as an icon of popular cinema and offer themselves up as ersatz latecomers to its world of criminal accomplishment.

Interestingly, there is one limit to the immersion of the *Sopranos* characters into a mass-cultural world that the spectator, too, is supposed to share familiarity with. *The Sopranos* pointedly indicates that HBO is available in its narrative universe—in season 5, the increasingly senile Uncle Junior watches *Curb Your Enthusiasm* and confuses that show's Larry David and his manager Jeff for himself and his helper Bobby Bacala and wonders why he (Junior) suddenly is appearing on TV. But it is evident that the fictional universe of *The Sopranos* can't include the possibility of anyone in it watching the hit show *The Sopranos*. (However, *Mad* magazine's parody of HBO's *Sex and the City* astutely ended with the New York quartet of women realizing there really were no eligible men left in the Big Apple and deciding to go across the Hudson to hook up with the gang of *The Sopranos*!)

At the same time as its characters are defined in large degree by their inevitable immersion in popular culture, the sense of irrevocable connection to that popular culture extends beyond the story world of *The Sopranos* to engulf the spectator, who is also assumed to be living a life caught up in such culture. No doubt certain specific allusions to popular culture in *The Sopranos* allow for a complicated play of knowledge between viewer and characters. For example, when Christopher yells out to Martin Scorsese, who is being led as a VIP into a club that Chris can't get into, that he loves the director's film *Kundun*, how can this not be seen as an ironic joke? *Kundun*, about the Dalai Lama, was a meditative work that brought in few spectators and seems to be precisely the sort of non-Mafia, highbrow fare that someone like Christopher would not appreciate Scorsese making.

More often, however, popular culture appears in *The Sopranos* as a force that both viewer and character inevitably share in with equal appreciation (or at least recognition), since it is part of their very make-up as denizens of the modern world. For example, the music that generally plays over the end credits (and sometimes over the initial scenes of season openers, as when season 2 begins with Frank Sinatra's "It was a very good year . . .") works from the assumption that audience members would carry such popular songs as part of their cultural baggage. In this respect, the moments where the music bleeds from the story world to that of the spectator are particularly resonant, as if there is a natural conduit between fictional and extrafictional realities, and as if the spectator directly participates in the appreciation of popular culture that the characters in the show are experiencing. Thus, if an early moment in season 4 has Tony interrupted by Carmela to talk about family issues just as he is about to watch the famous sing-along male-bonding sequence from the Howard Hawks film *Rio Bravo* (Dean Martin and Ricky Nelson together crooning "My pony, my rifle, and me"), an episode later in the season will end with the formerly interrupted song now playing in full for the spectator as end-credit music while Tony hunches in a stall at the stables to nurse a sick racehorse he has become fond of. No doubt there are potentially serious layers of meaning here that one might talk about: Tony's ongoing fascination with a cowboy mythology (and the hardcore postmodernist might even note the irony of the choice *Rio Bravo*, since this was a film made, according to its director, to challenge the mythology of Gary Cooper as "strong silent type" in *High Noon*); the show's fascination with an emotive masculinity, just as the sing-along represents a moment of homosocial bonding in which men croon to each other; the contrast of a domestic realm where Tony has to deal with the responsibilities of being the family provider and the masculine space of Tony alone with his horse, just as the cowboy in the lyrics of the song invokes the mythology of the American male as inveterate loner. But the song also has the function of allusion; Dean Martin, Ricky Nelson, this song, this movie—all are parts of a popular culture that the characters of *The Sopranos* would wish to participate in intently and that is also much of the postmodern context in which we would be watching the show. Cinephiles love the song, love the movie, and no doubt love them showing up on this television show about late versions of American masculinity.

9 "Honey, I'm Home"

For all of David Chase's expressed disdain of television and his valorization of a cinematic ideal, the credit sequence of *The Sopranos* clearly references the basic premise of the domestic sitcom—the patriarch comes home to a domesticity that might spell comfort or chaos equally—even as it updates it to a tougher world of macho men, evident economic divisions, and the frenetic drive to get ahead. Integral to television's cultural history has been the revision and adaptation of classic genres to new social conditions. For example, even as it maintained a laugh track and invoked broad, physical humor (for example, Archie's problems in going to the bathroom), *All in the Family* gave a new pretense of seriousness to the sitcom, elements of which clearly influenced *The Sopranos*: the working-class stiff who is trying to adapt to a changing world of new mores and morals; the manifestation of the difficulties of that adjustment in expressions of racism on his part; the wife who has been relegated to her own private world but who then uses it to reevaluate the ethics of the mode of life her husband has built for the family; the politically liberal daughter who is often dismayed by her dad's retrograde attitudes; the very redefinition of the watchable television actor away from classically attractive figures such as the handsome couple on, to take one example, *The Donna Reed Show*, to the frumpy or schlumpy figure of harried disarray, such as chubby Archie and Tony, who offer a masculinity of frequent slovenliness.

But for *The Sopranos*, the revision of the televisual past centrally involves direct reference to, and reworking of, the founding classics of the medium. In other words, while its debts range over vast pieces of television history—for example, the ensemble structure of its gangster-centered fictions might seem a moral inversion of the law-and-order narrative multiplicities of *Hill Street Blues*—*The Sopranos* returns explicitly to the establishing moment of popular television, as if to settle a score with television's foundational history per se. In an early episode, Tony admonishes Meadow that outside their home it may be the 1990s, but inside it's the 1950s; the very attempt of the patriarch to deal with the unruly daughter has its sitcom overtones, and the reference to the fifties reiterates that while the show comes out of many histories, postwar America and its culture are a decisive one.

"Is Tony Soprano Today's Ward Cleaver?" asks the title of a think piece in the *New York Times*, but it's perhaps Ralph Kramden from *The Honeymooners* who offers the more salient comparison from the years of the classic domestic sitcom.[1] As an article in *Entertainment Weekly* elaborates, "Let us seize upon a recent remark made by star James Gandolfini and run with it. . . . 'Tony's appeal is just like Ralph Kramden's appeal,' Gandolfini told a gathering of TV critics earlier this summer. 'It's like this moron is trying to do the best he can and he just keeps screwing up.' This is good: Gandolfini identifying with Jackie Gleason—oversize yet graceful actors portraying men seething with thwarted ambition and rage, married to women who love them yet also take no you-know-what from them."[2]

Gleason appears to matter a great deal to the gangsters of *The Sopranos*; one of the greatest compliments one can pay to another is to say that he has perfected great Gleason impersonations while in prison, and Tony himself perks up when his dad's mistress, Fran, recounting a Washington party at which she had been seduced by JFK, mentions meeting Gleason (among other celebrities) as one of the guests. In fact, *The Sopranos* explicitly compares its own world to that of *The Honeymooners* in a number of episodes. For example, in a dream sequence, Tony and his mistress Gloria replay Ralph's classic "to the moon" line (a threat of domestic violence masked in comic repartee), and, even more pointedly, in season 5, when Carmela tells Tony, from whom she now is separated, that their son should go live with him, there is a cut from Tony's worried reaction to a famous scene from *The Honeymooners* where Ralph wins a chance to go on a television game show (and thereby

Two successive shots: flummoxed men.

perhaps win enough money to ascend in class status), only to get so consumed by nervousness that he can do nothing but repeat meaningless nonsense sounds.

The sitcom background enables *The Sopranos'* depiction of Mafia "Family" to be tinged with some of the meanings given to the domestic family in American ideology: these gangsters are men who work together on activities that require toughness and terseness, but they also interact with affection and understanding as well as misunderstanding, generational conflict, paternal advice, and so on. Tony Soprano is called upon by his crew to be like *Father Knows Best's* pastoral leader, Jim Anderson, who welcomes members of his flock into his private den and tries to sort out their problems, and it is a source of *The Sopranos'* cynical but comic revision of the sitcom that Tony is not always able to fulfill the role. One central narrative line of the classic domestic sitcom recounts the catastrophes that can happen when parents are absent and the children get into trouble, whether intentionally or not. While *The Sopranos* does show such chaos in the domestic sphere—for example, Anthony Jr.'s endless screw-ups or Meadow's drunken partying—the series also sometimes depicts the *workplace* in similar terms, as a social space that can fall apart in the absence of leadership. For example, the much-acclaimed "Pine Barrens" episode from season 3 is nothing so much as a sitcom in which the grown men Christopher and Paulie are reduced to childish helplessness when they become lost in the woods and need patriarch Tony to come rescue them. At the same time, Tony's own frantic need to deal with his two underlings, as well as a Russian Mob boss who might have it in for him and a mistress who wants to spend time with him, has its own sitcom tone: how can one balance work issues with the demands back at the house—even if, in this case, the "home" is that of the mistress, not spouse?

But if sitcoms frequently investigate the affective bonds within the sphere of work, they also, on the other hand, give close attention to the realm of the family at home and tend, in the classic works, to concentrate on the interactions, sometimes supportive, sometimes fraught, between patriarch and matriarch—especially when either ventures into terrain in which the other is master. Typical in the classic domestic sitcom was the narrative of the male breadwinner who is often harried at work (for example, Darren's boss on *Bewitched* endlessly asks him to develop new ad campaigns) and who seeks solace at home only to find further upheaval, frequently at the hands of his homemaker spouse, especially in those cases where she wants to do more with her life than just uphold domesticity (like Lucy Ricardo, for example, who keeps wreaking havoc by wanting a career of her own in show business, or an income of her own).

Where the cheerful resolution of everyday problems in middle-class sitcoms like *Leave It to Beaver, Father Knows Best,* or *The Donna Reed Show* is often mirrored in the cheerful handsomeness of the characters and the homes they live in, more working-class-centered sitcoms like *The Honeymooners* or *All in the Family* emphasize the relative impoverishment of the domestic space (which often is an apartment rather than a single-family house, as if to emphasize that the main characters have not achieved that central American dream of home ownership) and the relative plainness or even frumpiness or coarseness of the actors. At the same time, given the centrality of myths of mobility within American ideology (especially during the period of the rise of the TV sitcom, the 1950s), any distinction between sitcoms on the basis of class has to acknowledge fuzzy examples centered on characters who are in transition from one social stratum to another or who are in danger of being displaced downward (being fired is a constant fear in classic sitcoms, even as escapist and as light as their laugh tracks might make them appear).

Nouveau-riche Tony Soprano clearly may be living a life of luxury beyond Ralph Kramden's wildest dreams, but Tony is as vulnerable to loss of self-possession as Ralph was, and he additionally faces the risk of having his lifestyle of conspicuous consumption come crashing down around him. In fact, season 5—where Tony has to deal with being thrown out of his house by Carmela in the first episodes and which ends with him scrambling through the underbrush to find his way back home—is very much about Tony being stripped of the signs and accouterments of material success and having to deal with loss of rank and prestige.

The show's opening credits, which depict Tony driving from New York to his house in northern New Jersey, thus echo those "Honey, I'm home" encounters of a seemingly sure masculinity with the potentially unnerving world of domesticity that are so much the premise of the classic sitcom. Interestingly, although it is clear in the traditional sitcom that the husband has returned from the world of work—since there is little for this devoted breadwinner to do outside the home but work—in *The Sopranos* it is ambiguous as to just what activity Tony is returning from. The patriarch of the late 1990s and early twenty-first century is not just beholden to work or family, and Tony conducts his drive home with energetic braggadocio, as if returning from a triumph or conquest of some sort.

In an appendix to his book on *The Sopranos*, Maurice Yacowar notes in passing a similarity of the show's opening to that of *The Simpsons*, although it is ultimately the differences that stand out for him. In particular, *The Simpsons* intercuts Homer's journey home with the activities that the rest of his family are engaged in as they also head for home, while *The Sopranos* singles out the patriarch and his return to the fold.[3] We could, in fact, note a series of resemblances between these two hit shows, both of which clearly attempt to revise the classic sitcom for a more cynical age (although I've suggested that even the seemingly lighthearted classic sitcom was, in fact, often quite bitter about both work and domesticity). In this revised form, the job front is a complicated site lorded over by capricious and all-powerful bosses; the sons are slackers who would prefer to get in trouble or watch television than succeed at school; the daughter is a liberal and intellectually ambitious child who is dismayed by her father's déclassé way of life and political incorrectness but who deep down loves him and looks for moments of conciliation; the wife is a homemaker who often searches for something meaningful to her existence and frequently tries to bring cultural or moral enrichment into the home; the bar is a male sanctuary; and there is an overall tone of postmodern fascination with citation and a general sense of today's life as lived out in an immersion in popular culture and with behaviors frequently modeled on that culture.

That *The Sopranos* can be likened to a cartoon series is itself noteworthy. While the classic sitcoms involved live actors filmed with a relative photographic realism (even *Bewitched* counted on an ordinariness into which the fantasy of Samantha's magic would then come as a supernatural disruption), there have been animated series that clearly take as their model an everyday sitcom world of work and domesticity and re-garb it in the fantasy elements of animation's imaginative transformations: notably, *The Jetsons* and *The Flintstones*. In season 5, an FBI agent refers to Tony using the mocking moniker of Barney Rubble (from *The Flintstones*), and in a complicated bit of postmodernism, the highly self-referential television show *Harvey Birdman*—in which characters from old Hanna-Barbera cartoons go on trial and take the eponymous Birdman as their lawyer—ran an episode in which Fred Flintstone was played as if he were Tony Soprano. The opening merged the classic credit sequence of Fred jumping into his caveman car and driving home with the similar opening from *The Sopranos*, all set to music that put Fred's famous "yabba dabba do" to the pulsating sound of rock group A3's *Sopranos* credit song, "Woke Up This Morning." Instead of the lodge where Fred went to be with the boys, the updated Fred now went to a strip club that resembled a Bada Bing for cavemen.

To a large degree, the assimilation of cartoon and Mob sitcom can work because there is already a cartoonlike element in those sitcoms that deal with working stiffs, from Ralph Kramden to (a little bit higher up on the ladder) Rob Petrie to Darren Stevens to Tony Soprano. Unlike the upper-middle-class sitcoms where characters are firmly installed in their worlds, both professional and personal, and where their stable situation is reflected in their cheerful sense of self-possession, the sitcoms of working stiffs and corporate employees reflect their very insecurity concerning status and social position in an uncertain corporeality of the main actors, which gives them a veritably cartoonish nature. Whether the lanky clumsiness of Rob Petrie, who does pratfalls over a settee in one variant of the opening credits for *The Dick Van Dyke Show*, or the manic and tic-filled elasticity of Darren's face as he tries to handle the pressures of work and the zaniness of marriage to a witch, or Tony's slack-jawed, open-mouthed reaction when he is bested in a verbal joust or learns disturbing news, these sitcom protagonists live out the tensions of modern life in the very malleability and vulnerability and awkwardness of bodily posture, facial expression, and movement.

In this respect, scholarly analysis of the show that seeks to attribute quality to it but only by separating it off from the popular culture and the low comedy that infuses it and whose histories it participates in seems a rearguard action, the quite unintended comedy of an often university-based criticism that still imagines the inviolate specialness of works of art. *The Sopranos*, in fact, is itself quite adept at piercing the pretensions of high art and leavening the puritanical seriousness of quality with the levity of comic deflation.

10 Against Interpretation

The very last episode of *The Sopranos* opens with a tight overhead shot of Tony's face, immobile and eyes closed. Vaguely funereal music plays on the soundtrack. Has Tony died? The previous episode had ended with Tony, hunted by Phil Leotardo's gang, going to sleep in a safehouse where he was hiding, with a few of his henchmen, such as Paulie, there to protect him. But some clues might have been pointing to Paulie as a turncoat, and it could well be likely that Tony would die at his hands. Might the first image of the final episode be a jump forward to a funeral, announcing Tony's death at the hands of Paulie?

And then Tony opens his eyes and, from that bed in the safehouse, gets up and goes about his business. As noted, that business includes, over the course of the episode, brokering a truce with New York, having Phil whacked, setting his son on a proper course of employment, seeing his daughter settle into her compromise life choices, and meeting his family for an evening out at a diner. Maybe *The Sopranos* raises big issues, but it also insists on an anodyne reality of ordinary chores, regular routines, life as usual. And it also emphasizes that to make too much of the meaning of things would be to run the risk of overinterpretation. We could well read the shot of the immobile Tony as a sign of the inevitability of the grave for all of us but, pace Edward Said on the bitter fatalism in late style, we could also appreciate it as a joke of the moment, the show playing with the spectator as it refuses every big and dramatic expectation of what its final episode should be about.

There are now a half dozen or so *academic* books on HBO's *The Sopranos*. With some scattered exceptions (a few isolated essays in sev-

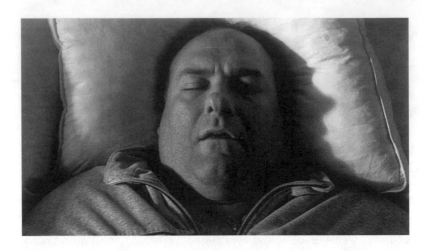

Mother of mercy, is this the end of Tony?

eral anthologies), the bulk of these writings set out to interpret the show and find themes embedded within it. Specifically, such writings treat *The Sopranos* as a vehicle for real-life issues and claim that the show's emotional and intellectual appeal stems from its trafficking in such topics. Popular culture, for these critics, is often a virtually transparent approximation to everyday existence; the television show represents the quandaries we all face as we wend our way through life's trajectory. The title of one such book, *The Sopranos and Philosophy: I Kill, Therefore I Am*, says it all: the show is examined as a parable that stages metaphysical and ethical questions.

Clearly, life issues that the series brings into its narratives and even sometimes has its characters sit down and talk about as if these were PBS-like topics for discussion—topics such as ethnic identity, the value of therapy, sexual orientation, marital fidelity, the very meaning of life in a potentially meaningless universe—are signposts that audiences recognize and can lock into. No doubt, a number of emotionally resonant themes run through *The Sopranos*: the vulnerability of masculinity and patriarchy in the modern moment and some men's desperate need to cling to privilege whenever they can; the concomitant position of women in roles of dependency that they can find both seductive and yet subconsciously limiting; the challenges to whiteness in an age of multi-culturalism; the problems of family and generational conflict; the world of work and its relations of authority, trust, but also exploitation; the nature of evil and our complicated fascination with and sometimes even seduction by it. No doubt, too, that these are themes that many viewers would take as resonant and would find useful to compare (whether con-sciously or not) to their own real-life experiences. *The Sopranos* is very much keyed into concerns of its time and frequently offers trenchant commentary on them. But here, again, many of the resonant moments work best as tantalizing attractions for the spectator: recognizable big issues that bring one into the work but that serve ultimately as free-floating motifs in a playful environment where proper morality is sus-pended and where willful ambiguity is exploited.

In this respect, there are several problems with the standard academic criticism of the show. First of all, the very fact that *The Sopranos* works so clearly within a framework of recognizable issues can make critical interpretation seem redundant in relation to the show's own explicit-ness about its themes. In a sense, *The Sopranos* wears its meanings on its sleeves, and often the academic critics seem to be simply repeating what the show has already said. For example, a number of authors men-tion with an almost breathless thrill their discovery of how Tony, in the "College" episode from season 1, looks up at a motto from Hawthorne on display at Bowdoin College, where he has taken his daughter for a campus visit: "No man can wear one face to himself and another to the multitude without finally getting bewildered as to which may be true." The writers announce that this reveals how Tony is caught in moral dilemma. The problem, quite simply, is that the show already made this obvious (and the episode even emphasizes the theme by cutting point-edly from Tony's face as he reads with bewildered concern, to the motto itself as a way to show his investment in trying to figure out his place in the ethical conundrum). Likewise, any number of commentators will talk about the ways in which *The Sopranos* represents a "crisis of mas-culinity" when this, in fact, has been an explicit topic of the show from its first episode (where Tony talked to his therapist of the loss of an older image of masculinity—Gary Cooper as the "strong, silent type").

Certainly, it's perhaps not so obvious *how* we're supposed to judge the show's raising of such themes. That is, the series traffics in recognizable concerns, but it doesn't necessarily say what it "thinks" about them. For instance, what precisely is its take on the crisis of masculinity? Does it challenge norms of white masculinity, or does it uphold them? Maybe the questions matter more to the texture of the show than any one answer.

Take, for example, an online essay on the sexual politics of *The Sopranos* by Lisa Johnson, a professor of American studies and women's studies. According to her analysis, *The Sopranos* offers an "engaged and embattled representation of contemporary womanhood"—which seems a more than acceptable assertion, since it's part of that discourse of obviousness that the show explicitly participates in. Johnson then goes on to declare more pointedly (and to my mind exorbitantly) that in this investigation of femininity, *Sopranos* creator David Chase "makes a materialist feminist critique of patriarchy worthy of [feminist cultural critic] bell hooks." At the very least, there seem to be some complicated category blurrings going on here, in taking a fictional work produced by a man who has never specifically acknowledged feminism to be as critical and as analytic as the nonfictional argumentative efforts of a well-known feminist theorist.[1]

Johnson's comments come in the context of an analysis of "University," a notoriously violent and sexually rough episode from season 3 that NBC CEO Bob Wright notoriously excerpted from and sent to media figures at NBC and elsewhere to make a case about cable television's immoralities and thereby score points against HBO, his big competitor. Certainly, "University" deals explicitly and extensively with some of the things that being a contemporary woman can mean in a patriarchal culture; the episode weaves together Soprano daughter Meadow having her first sexual relationship (with the sanctimonious college student Noah, who eventually dumps her) and Bada Bing stripper Tracee, who is regularly mistreated sexually (for example, by Silvio, as well as by Ralphie, who eventually kills her). No doubt, the episode says some resonant things about sexual exploitation: whereas in virtually all other episodes the Bada Bing dancers tend to remain in the back of the image as they dance uninspiredly to bored customers, "University" brings one of the dancers into the foreground and grants her voice and identity (to then have it taken away by her brutal murder). At the very least, though, the sexual politics might be seen as only ambiguously progressive, and in fact, the episode could be taken to imply that women will inevitably be punished when they assume a voice and identity. At the same time, there's a uniqueness to the Tracee story (it's a good example of a stand-alone episode) that only ambiguously extends beyond it to a general comment on woman's place in patriarchy. Elsewhere, indeed, the Bada Bing dancers are presented as stereotypical airheads—for example, one of them, in season 1, greets the televised news of Mob boss Jackie Aprile's death with the declaration that she will always remember where she was on this tragic day, an obvious misplaced version of the sentiment that citizens express around national catastrophes like the Kennedy assassination or 9/11. Furthermore, to the extent that Tracee's death has resonances beyond the one stand-alone episode in which she appears, those have to do with the tensions that have now bubbled up between Tony and Ralphie and with Tony's own sense of guilt. Narratively, in a sense, Tracee dies so that Tony can come throughout the course of later seasons to confront the implications of his way of life and the place of femininity within it. Thus, a much later episode has a flash-cut to the memory of Tracee while Tony is gazing at his daughter Meadow; the implication seems to be that Tony is contrasting the life he wants for Meadow with the ill-fated one Tracee had and whose misery and brutality he wants to keep his daughter away from at all costs. It is thus possible to take Tracee as functioning as a mere narrative alibi to get a crisis of masculinity going. The point is not so much that any such reading is the correct one but that the critic needs to be attentive to the complexities of the means by which *The Sopranos* incorporates issues and themes into its plots as ambiguous motifs that can be read and evaluated in numerous ways. The show holds out positions, ethical and otherwise, only to render them ironic in the next moment.

To take another vexed issue the show brushes up against, what precisely is its attitude about ethnic identity? As is well known, *The Sopranos* was the target of vociferous debate—and even legal action—in regard to what antidefamation organizations took to be its dangerous, negative stereotyping of Italian Americans as inevitably and invariably

part of the world of organized crime. In Canada, there was even government investigation of *The Sopranos* after a number of viewers wrote to
the Broadcast Standards Council to claim the show was in violation of
national laws prohibiting hate speech against cultural or social groups
on television. The ruling went in favor of the show, the opinion arguing
that it centered on only one family, that it didn't portray this one family
as representative of all Italians, and that, in any case, the one family was
shown to have a range of values and concerns, not all of them criminal.[2]
More famously, in an incident much reported on in the press, Italian
American pride organizations in New York City objected vociferously
when Mayor Michael Bloomberg invited two *Sopranos* actors, Lorraine
Bracco and Dominic Chianese, to march in the annual Columbus Day
Parade in Manhattan.[3] Claiming, with an evident degree of disingenu-
ousness, that he had invited the two actors not because of their work
on *The Sopranos* but because of past efforts in community activity (for
example, Chianese had, in the Mayor's words, done some public service
announcements "for the city to help the city") and declaring that he
didn't even watch the show, the mayor decided to boycott the parade
and marched instead in the Bronx (although without the actors at his
side).

At the same time, other Italian Americans lauded *The Sopranos*:
for example, working-class citizens cited in New York and New Jersey newspapers as dreaming of being cast on the show (and coming en
masse to an out-of-control audition in Harrison, New Jersey, where it
was clear that many participants viewed the show as the occasion for a
lark, not a consequential defamation of Italian American identity) or an
energized group of Italian American academics who came together to
produce a scholarly anthology in defense of the show—*A Sitdown with
the Sopranos: Watching Italian American Culture on T.V.'s Most Talked-
About Series.*

Both sides in the debate seem able to marshal evidence from the show
in support of their cause, and the contretemps appears irresolvable. The
show's defenders, for instance, can point to the key role of nongangster
Italian Americans in its narrative (such as Jennifer Melfi) or can offer a
series of diverse aesthetic arguments (for example, the show parodies its
stereotypes too much to be taken seriously, or the show only uses Italian

Americans to represent something deeper). The detractors can point to a long history of persuasive stereotyping of social groups and argue the show is simply the most recent manifestation of the ethnic slur decked out in comic form.[4]

The difficulty of pinning the show down—or rather the ease of pinning it down but then finding that other interpreters could offer completely opposed, and yet no less assured, readings—has also to do with the particular nature of a contemporary work of popular culture like *The Sopranos*. *Postmodernism* describes a cultural condition in which such popular culture frustrates easy judgment by incorporating a multiplicity of critical positions into the text so that it becomes unclear to what extent there is one overall moral or thematic attitude that governs the work. In this respect, *The Sopranos* is a work that is part of its particular cultural moment, insofar as its meanings and morality are frequently indeterminate.

Take, for instance, the issue of stereotyping. The series itself displays awareness of the issue when various characters themselves debate the stereotyping of Italian identity. Thus, one running motif is daughter Meadow's vexed relationship to her father's way of life: she will at times refuse to entertain criticism of it, but then herself declare it to be evil— sometimes both in the course of a single episode. For example, in the last episode from season 3, "Army of One," Meadow passes through a complicated dialectic of awareness and willed self-ignorance about the killing of her boyfriend Jackie. In season 1, she had explained to her brother about her dad's affiliation with the Mob; now, with a deliberately short memory, she counters to Jackie's sisters that her dad has nothing to do with the death since he is in the waste management business. Meadow serves, at times, as a voice of sharp and supercilious critique of her dad's way of life, pointing out the little and local ways he is not true to his own principles and values. But Meadow's turn to law as a career option in the last episode offers the ultimate ironic turn of the screw for Meadow's endless shifting of position, self-denial, and self-deception. As she explains to her father, she has decided to fight for justice for minorities after seeing him arrested so often and submitted to the powerful tactics of the police—this, after Meadow has so often been upset by the ways Tony mistreats and maligns racial and ethnic minorities. Of course, the series offers its own ultimate, ironic deflation of Meadow's newfound commitment to social justice: when she explains to Tony that she wants to fight against the excesses of the state, he replies, "New Jersey?"

Again, to take another interpretable theme, it is no doubt true that *The Sopranos* taps into some tenaciously resonant concerns about work in America today. Revealingly, the show's success overlapped with bestseller status for Barbara Ehrenreich's *Nickel and Dimed: On (Not) Getting By in America*, which vividly narrated the author's encounters with the inequities of class and the problems of the working-class job market in America.[5] Easily, one could sense that the politics of labor was a topic of both avoidance and fascination for ordinary Americans, and it would seem certainly the case that *The Sopranos'* representations of workplace loyalty and rivalry, of hierarchies of power in worker-boss relations, of corruption and degradation of skills versus pride in craftsmanship, of tensions between leisure time and work time, of the seduction of the quick and violent and illegal path to success all feed into concerns that many ordinary citizens are feeling in their historical moment. However, such topics seem quite near the surface of the show. They aren't secret meanings mysteriously squirreled away, nor are they articulated into a singular and decidable thesis. Perhaps, indeed, if *The Sopranos* speaks in recognizable ways about labor or other issues, it does so by addressing a range of attitudes we hold toward work, even contradictory ones.

The game *The Sopranos* plays with its viewers, then, is as much about the social values we hold dear as about form and aesthetic structure. Thus, if the show keeps spectators wondering about where the narrative is going, it also keeps them guessing about the judgments they should offer on the activities of the often ethically dubious characters that inhabit the show's fictional world.

Most scholarly interpreters of *The Sopranos* have been inclined to seek firm moral lessons in the show (and, no doubt, there are some, from time to time), as if the only way to legitimate serious scholarly attention to the series is to attribute a sort of ethical uplift to it. Yet, working in the realm of irony, the show flirts with moral values but adheres unambiguously to only a few. I do think it would be hard to argue that the show is in any way ironic about the brutality of Jennifer Melfi's rape (although, it must be noted, it is clearly ambiguous about the appropriate response to that act of violence). Likewise, the series depends on us understanding Tony's cold-blooded killing of a onetime FBI informant in the "College" episode as a horrific, brutal act (even though, it must be noted, it qualifies our attitude by identifying the informant as not merely a rat but one scurrilous enough to have been kicked out of a witness protection program and to be dealing in hard drugs under his new identity in seemingly pastoral New England).

The Sopranos makes the viewer take up contradictory moral positions. Take, for instance, those two black guys in the diner in the show's finale. It is likely that the immediacy of menace that a typical spectator would feel here comes not just from narrative conventions of the show—where in earlier episodes pairs of black males had been hired as expendable hit men—but from the spectator's own investment, however unintended, in racial stereotypes about black men and urban violence. The show plays into stereotypes to play on them, to make us feel what it is like to adopt moral positions we wouldn't normally welcome outside the fictional universe of the series. An episode from season 5, aptly titled "Unidentified Black Males," seemingly challenges such stereotypes when it chronicles how whites often use the specter of black male menace when they need to lie about something criminal that's happened—as when a young Tony Soprano made up a story that he missed a heist (for which his cousin had been arrested) because he had been jumped by black muggers, when in fact he had had an embarrassing panic attack after a berating by his shrewish mother Livia. Nevertheless, the finale to the series makes the stereotype take life again. It plays into and demonstrates the facility by which the stereotype may remain subliminally operative even in supposedly politically correct times.

The Sopranos, after all, is a television show that makes a vicious gangster, and the like members of his world, a sometime object of admiration, respect, concern, and general warm feelings of well-being on the part of spectators. And it does so even as it shows the extent to which this gangster is adept at seducing those around him into overlooking his crimes, which often are of a most heinous and horrible sort. Revealingly, when, a few episodes before the finale, Jennifer Melfi decides to discontinue Tony as a patient because she has come to realize he is a sociopath who will use charm and other wiles of seduction to mislead others, her termination of the analysis comes precisely when Tony's son has tried to commit suicide and Tony desperately needs her help. In this way, the show manipulates the viewer into feeling that Melfi is being unprofessional in abandoning a patient at a crucial juncture. Over the seasons of the show, Melfi had waffled about taking the high moral ground with this dangerous, criminal patient, and now that she is finally deciding on the correct path, it seems improper, wrong even.[6]

Or, as another example, take, again, the series finale. Over the years, we had seen Tony Soprano do horrible things, and yet it is so easy to worry about him in that diner. Hasn't he been through enough? Isn't it good that, whatever else, there is family? The suspense of the scene—created formally by cuts between Tony and his family and those potentially menacing figures all around—is also a final demonstration of the show's ability to make the viewer feel with Tony *and* feel for Tony.

Moreover, beyond how it makes us run through complicated identifications with and distancings from Tony, the series insistently offers a roller coaster of reversals around the viewer's emotional relationship to any number of the vicious mobsters in its fictional world. Thus, although Ralph Cifaretto has brutally murdered a Bada Bing stripper and is a sexual sicko and a disturbingly unpredictable loose cannon, he can nonetheless suddenly accrue sympathy when his young son is gravely hurt during games with a friend and suffers what will probably amount to irreversible neurological damage. Further, it adds to the pity for Ralphie that, at precisely the moment when he needs the emotional support of others, his ex-wife attacks him for his seeming negligence with their son. But, then, the show still has other tricks up its sleeve: just as we may be starting to allow ourselves some positive feeling toward Ralphie in this time of tribulation, Tony discovers that he has burned the race horse Pie-o-My to death for the insurance money and Ralphie's potential for cruel violence is revealed anew. Conversely, another Soprano henchman, Vito, accrues a great deal of sympathy when his homosexuality is found out by the Mob and his life put in danger. Long scenes of Vito trying awkwardly to build a new life in pastoral New England but struggling to negotiate his future desires with the pressures of his past identity add to the resonant emotions (although all of this might already be nuanced if the viewer were to remember that it was Vito who had been the killer of young Jackie Jr., Meadow's boyfriend in season 3, who tragically had gone wrong and whose death was a dismal affair). Again, the series builds up sympathy (and also plays on the viewer's likely liberal dislike of homophobia) only to undercut it in a flash: driving back to New Jersey, Vito has a fender bender with an ordinary New Englander and coldly kills him to avoid the police being called in.

The moral questioning in *The Sopranos* manifests itself in strategies of irony by which the spectator is encouraged to glide in and out of a series of ethical positions and to see, perhaps, the facility by which shifts of moral attitude can be constructed and deconstructed. The point, then, is not that *The Sopranos* doesn't deal with the sorts of issues that scholars claim to find in it. It does, indeed, constantly raise them, but not in a way that can be readily resolved.

In an essay on the ways critics have written about *The Sopranos*, literary scholar Sandra Gilbert notes the persistence of a discourse of recognizability—what she jokingly terms "The Sopranos R Us"—making the point that the series offers issues that resonate because they are like issues we recognize that we deal with in our own everyday lives. Such criticism then takes as its task to approximate the fiction of the series to real life and interpret it for its probing reflections on aspects of the human condition.[7]

Tellingly, however, it is not just the professionally trained critic who sets out to analyze the series in terms of its real-life pertinence. Amusingly, actual gangsters appear themselves to have been active interpreters of the show's representations and to have, in their own fashion, debated the show's degree of recognizability. Thus, as *New Yorker* writer David Remnick recounts in an essay that itself employs the terms of recognition—for example, "The conventions of the Mob [in *The Sopranos*] heighten the conventions and contradictions of a modern family"— actual New Jersey Mafiosi were caught on wiretaps discussing the show and trying to figure out who its real points of reference were.[8] For example, when Joseph (Tin Ear) Sclafani wondered in bewilderment— "Hey, what's this fucking thing, 'Sopranos'? . . . Is that supposed to be us?" one Mafia capo, Anthony Rotondo, responded like any good parser of symbols with the argument that repeated contact with the work of culture revealed new aspects of it: "What characters. Great acting. Every show you watch, more and more you pick up somebody. One week it was Corky, one week it was, well, from the beginning it was Albert G." And if for many professional critics the show matters as a reflection on machismo and masculinity, it turns out that real-life gangsters also were as concerned to figure out just what it meant to be a man in an age of gender troubles. Hence, an article in the U.K. paper *The Guardian* bears the headline "Mafia boss rubbed out 'for being gay'" and recounts that "The boss of the Mafia family on which the Sopranos series is believed to be based was executed by one of his own soldiers because he was gay and they feared that if news got out the family would be ridiculed by the rest of the underworld."[9] Later, obviously, the series would make a similar story part of its fiction through the woeful tale of the outed gay gangster Vito; life and art endlessly imitate each other as the viewer lurks on the sidelines and tries to make critical sense of it all.[10]

Instead of standing as deeply interpretable themes, the resonant topics of *The Sopranos* would serve as tantalizing elements to mix into the narratives and to work complex permutations on. It does seem, indeed, to be a talent of postmodern cultural works both to sense that interpreters will always try to fix ambiguous works within the limits of closed readings *and* to seek to disarm those readings in advance by incorporating satiric renditions of them within the very body of the work. That is, postmodern works not only are about the difficulties of final meanings, but they often directly represent the ill-fated encounter between interpreter and text by staging scenes where interpreters fail at making meaning. If the critic tries to stand as a "savant" who pierces the secrets of complex culture and delivers up its meanings, the postmodern work is itself "savvy"—wise in a crafty fashion. For me, the revelatory case was the 1978 film *The Eyes of Laura Mars*. Three years after film theorist Laura Mulvey's own breakthrough analysis of the ways in which the camera's gaze helped objectify women, here was a film that dealt with a photographer who took erotic photographs of women and then had to deal, among other things, with a feminist theorist who kept arguing that the photographs objectified women. A few years later, when academics were beginning to discern in MTV's music videos a form of popular postmodernism, the channel started to include between clips the mocking image of a professor whom the channel termed "postmodern" and who offered stereotypically extravagant and jargony psychoanalytic interpretations of the clips one was about to see.

In this respect, within the culture of postmodernity, *The Sopranos* is particularly noteworthy for the very ways it incorporates scenes that show the pretense of interpretation at work and that generally gently mock the activity. Interpreters and the interpretations they come up with are frequent objects of derision in the series. Endlessly, the series stages acts of interpretation and hints at the fallibility of the enterprise.

From its very first scene in its very first season—in which Tony Soprano stares at the statue of a woman in Dr. Melfi's waiting room as if he were trying to come to grips with the secret of femininity—*The Sopranos* flings seeming symbols at the viewer but then disarms the act of interpretation by making the symbols reveal nothing (in a later episode, Carmela is also in Melfi's waiting room looking at the sculpture of the enigmatic woman and concludes, "That statue is not my favorite") and mocking characters in their attempts to find meaning. The opening scene may hold Tony up for ridicule in this regard, just as he will later be guilty of reading too much into a painting also in Melfi's waiting room. But soon it becomes clear that any number of figures in the *Sopranos* universe take themselves to be decoders who look with curiosity at objects and experiences they feel have some deeper meaning behind them. (When, in season 3, Meadow somewhat condescendingly interprets a painting at the Met to her mother, she tells her she got her talents as a reader of the visual from her Introduction to Semiotics class at Columbia.) *The Sopranos* itself tantalizes with suggestions of hidden significance, only to show the quest for profound understanding as more than a bit ridiculous and pretentious. A passing moment from the second season can be taken as this show's self-reflexive comment on overinterpretation: visiting the set of an action film, Christopher watches a cheesy shoot-out scene between two women, only to be told by his host, the somewhat superior Hollywood development girl Amy, that their "silencers underscore their voiceless place in society."

Seductive hints of meaning abound in *The Sopranos*. For example, the series is rich in dream sequences, and anyone who's taken a college literature class knows to jump to interpretive alert when dreams appear in an artwork. But *The Sopranos* doesn't make the job of meaning-making easy. Dreams are frequently entered into with little or no preamble to demarcate them from wakeful states of reality. Conversely, once the dream sequence became a convention of the series, the show could make it look like one was about to develop, only to remain in everyday reality—thereby performing a joke on the viewer's expectations. Thus, in the opener to season 7, a downbeat Tony sits by the water, deep in introspection. The song "This Magic Moment" by the Drifters comes wafting up, and one waits for a dream, or at least a meaningful flashback. But then a cut reveals another character standing near Tony, fiddling with a radio.

Obviously, the most famous example of the seemingly symbol-laden dream is the lengthy oneiric sequence in a late episode of season 5, one which even involves dreams-within-dreams, as Tony seems to keep waking up only to find himself at another level of his dream. Such intrusions of the dream into the texture of the show stand as enticing displays of seeming symbolic depth, but it is likely the case that many spectators watch them passively, as weird moments, rather than actively trying to fix a meaning to them. In fact, it is not clear that interpreting these dreams would lead anywhere consequential; it is more probable that one watches, recognizing bits and pieces from Tony's waking experience but not knowing what those pieces really mean (and not necessarily caring). Ironically, Tony himself frequently wakes up knowing exactly what a dream of his has meant. Thus, a dream in season 2 appeared to show him that Big Pussy was an informant, while the extended dream in season 5 convinced him that he needed to kill his cousin Tony B., who had gone against orders and brought down the wrath of the New York Mob on the Soprano crew. There is a gap here between what the spectator sees on screen and what Tony is able immediately to make of his dream as it transpired in his unconscious.

In this respect, in an interview with the Museum of Television and Radio, David Chase declares the legendary work of postmodern television, *Twin Peaks*, to have been a decisive influence on his own interest in television dreams. *Twin Peaks,* says Chase, had television's "best dream sequences" and became, for him, "something to try to emulate." It is noteworthy that David Lynch's postmodern show also involved dreams that would simply appear weird to the spectator but that characters like FBI agent Dale Cooper could take simply to represent direct clues about everyday life.[11] Despite David Chase's professed love of 1950s and 1960s art cinema—where there was often a propensity for symbolically alluring dream or dreamlike sequences that did encourage close readings by interpretive scholars—it is perhaps revealing that his reference for dreams is to television and that he seems most indebted to experimental efforts in that medium, such as Lynch's show, that replace extended interpretation with a mysterious uncanniness that remains on the surface and has no depth behind it. For Chase, as he elaborates in his Museum of Television and Radio interview, there is "something so similar between television and dreams—stuff that's like weird or pushes the envelope." This could serve as an apt description of the *Sopranos'* season 5 dream sequence: more than any meaning it may convey, it serves, first of all, to push the envelope of how much time a plot-driven television show will devote to such a dream, and it is pleasurable for its very weirdness, beyond all signification one might wish to find deep within it.

The ease with which *The Sopranos* accustoms the spectator to the move from one level of reality to another, as in the dreams, perhaps helps explain one of the most enticing moments of seeming symbolism in the series—a moment that the show then quickly punctures. The scene takes place at the very beginning of an episode, "Knight in White Satin Armor," from season 2. In the empty rooms of a nouveau riche–style mansion, two ballet dancers suddenly sweep into view, gracefully following the tones of a bittersweet melody. They themselves make no noise and seem ethereal creatures of the mind. They glide off screen, and in through the front door of the mansion come Tony and his sister Janice, struggling to carry a big couch (the mansion, it turns out, is to be hers for her new home life with Richie Aprile). The contrast of the lumbering furniture movers and the elegant evanescent dancers seems symbolic, especially as the latter appear to have vanished into mere traces

Symbolic?

of poetic vision: were the dancers the dreamlike symbol of a beauty that might have been, an echo of a higher aspiration that has been lost in this crass world of New Jersey lowlifes?

Suddenly, however, the dancers glide back into view and are revealed, by conversation with Tony and Janice, to be Richie's son and his dancing partner, who are rehearsing in the open space of the house. No symbolism is at work, then—just the realist representation of two people borrowing the home to practice their dance steps. The seeming symbolism turns out to be mere tease, and all higher meaning turned into another anodyne activity of ordinary characters within the fictional world of the show.

In several episodes from season 5, members of the extended Soprano family try to look at precisely the sort of high symbolic cinematic culture that the likely typical HBO spectator grew up being told represented great achievements in film art, but these ersatz film viewers within the show don't get it; they can't see what all the fuss about the so-called classics is all about. For example, Uncle Junior attempts to watch Fellini's *La Dolce Vita*, since, after all, it's a film from the old country, but he's not able to make heads or tails of it. Likewise, as part of her ongoing drive for cultural uplift, Carmela organizes screenings of the American Film Institute Top 100 list with her friends, only to have the group bewildered by the critical esteem for the film that tops the list, *Citizen Kane*. An underwhelmed Adriana wonders why Charles Foster Kane never mentioned to anyone what "Rosebud" meant. No doubt, the show is mocking a nondegreed populace too obtuse to understand the subtleties of high culture (in season 1, Tony tells Dr. Melfi he understands Freud, since he had a semester-and-a-half of college at Seton Hall). But it would seem the case that the series also is poking fun at the authoritarian sanctimoniousness with which high cultural arbiters set out to tell the people about the culture they either must have (by means of high- or middlebrow lists of must-see works) or are constitutionally unfit to understand (we might remember, in this regard, that respected critic Pauline Kael was also underwhelmed by the Rosebud revelation, which she tended to see as a gimmicky bit coming from a pretentious work of overinflated and excessively grandiose artistry.)

The Sopranos, notably, is rich in sequences where characters directly confront canonic works of culture and try to assign meanings to them with only partial success, through which the show mocks the very assumption that artistic significance can so easily be fixed and closed down in an act of interpretation. For instance, in an episode from season 3, Anthony Jr., doing a homework assignment, is bewildered by an image of whiteness in a poem by Robert Frost. His older sister, Meadow, tells him that the symbolic key is to see white as death. When he answers that he thought black symbolized death, Meadow replies that both do, demonstrating unintentionally the very silliness of a fixed catalogue of symbolic forms. Meadow, indeed, may imagine herself superior to her family by virtue of her intellect and college preparedness, but she is often presented as someone who has learned her lessons by rote and who applies them mechanically, without really having the conviction of her opinions. For example, when she notifies her mother that she's spent the summer reading the "canon" and therefore has not sought a summer job, her mother clarifies that it actually is potboiler fiction that Meadow has most been seen spending her time with. Meadow may deride Carmela when the latter comes for a dinner with Meadow's roommates in her college apartment and reveals that she does not know who Leslie Fiedler is and does not accept the critic's interpretation of American high literary texts (in this case, *Billy Budd*) as works of homo-social, if not homoerotic, bonding. But the college students are also being mocked for their mechanical application of interpretative lessons they've learned but have no real emotional attachment to.

Frequently, culture mavens are represented in *The Sopranos* as veritable sanctimonious creeps who use the veneer of enlightened knowledge hypocritically and often cruelly: think, for instance, of guidance counselor Robert Wegler (David Strathairn) from season 5, who keeps *Heloise and Abelard* by his bedside and lectures Carmela on the beauties of *Madame Bovary* but can't sustain a deep relationship with her, or of Noah Tannenbaum, Meadow's college-student boyfriend who smarmily talks of the Columbia film course he's taking but can't sustain a deep relationship with her. Son of a well-to-do, name-dropping entertainment lawyer, Noah plays at being forthright and caring toward others, but he ultimately is self-centered, sanctimonious, and callous. He is given to spouting pretentiously about popular culture—"Cagney *was* modernity," he lectures Tony who mentions that he's a fan of *Public Enemy*—and in many ways it could be seen that Noah serves as a parodic avatar of the very sort of urban intellectual viewer who makes a program like *The Sopranos* an object of cultural veneration and critical elevation. In a caution to any academic who is tempted by overinterpretation of popular culture, Noah tells Tony about a course he's taking on the gangster film with the title "Images of hyper-capitalist self-advancement in the era of the studio system"—the ironic savvy of *The Sopranos* here anticipating books by film scholars such as myself! With a few modifications, something like this could be the title of an analysis of the show—and the critical literature on *The Sopranos* includes a number of essays that indeed sound like that—but for the fact that the show has, with the very character of Noah, already mocked such academic enterprise in advance. High culture, in the clichéd defense of it, is supposed to give one higher qualities of ethics and discernment, but *The Sopranos* portrays cultural capital as something urban professionals flaunt smugly as one more tool of power, influence, scheme-making, and condescension toward others.

More generally, *The Sopranos* may mock the nouveau riche kitschiness of its New Jersey vulgarians, but it is frequently no less dismissive of the urban professional lifestyle beyond the world of the gangsters and their followers. To be sure, not every urban professional saw that they were being mocked: for example, the American Psychoanalytic Association gave a special award to Lorraine Bracco for the ways in which supposedly her portrayal of Dr. Melfi helped create a positive image of psychotherapy (to be fair, there are a number of analysts who wouldn't take Melfi as a clear-cut role model, especially in the last season, when she terminated Tony's therapy).[12]

But it is as possible that the upscale viewer gets the joke and somehow enjoys participating in comic self-denigration. Urban professional lifestyle, as the series pictures it, is filled with formulaic clichés, with a superficiality and predictability all its own, with a pontificating haughtiness, and downright silliness: for example, the upscale espresso bar, obviously modeled on Starbucks, that Paulie and Big Pussy go to in search of car thieves (Paulie renames it "Buttfucks") and where an exoticized free-trade blend of the day is on sale, and from which Paulie steals an espresso maker. Jennifer Melfi may serve a narrative function as a mediating figure who can allow the spectator—perhaps an urban professional like her—to enter voyeuristically into the world of this violent, sexy, raunchy, and frequently politically incorrect show, but it would seem that she is no perfect conduit to that world and comes in for mockery of her own. Not merely is Melfi sanctimonious and superior (Tony has frequently to ask her to put her jargon or stock technical phrases into everyday terms), not merely is she in frequent violation of her own professional ethics (a psychotherapist who drinks between patient visits and reveals one patient's identity to her family), but she also, ironically, is doing wrong when she, good liberal that she no doubt is, tries to do the right thing. In particular, if Melfi were to succeed at an immediate level with Tony—to help him, for example, control his frequent bursts of rage ("anger management," as the therapeutic jargon refers to it) or to pull himself out of funk and self-doubt and make authoritative decisions—she would have failed at the liberal professional's dream of helping society at large. That is, if Melfi enables Tony to master his emotions and be a more efficient boss, she would also thereby aid him in being a better criminal. Certainly, at times Melfi tries to make Tony reflect on the very unworthiness of the immoral life path he has chosen, but more often she ignores the question of the ethical life to focus on that of the adjusted life, not realizing until the end, it seems, that for Tony, adjustment would precisely support him in unethical ventures. As she puts it in season 5, "Putting aside the moral and legal issues, clarity can't be a bad thing," as if the former could indeed be separated from the latter. To take just one example of the ways Melfi's treatment can have effects the reverse of what she may have hoped for, when Tony's gang pushes him to kill his cousin so as to avoid all-out war with another gang, he goes to Melfi and speaks of his love for his cousin. Her advice to him—to stop sentimentalizing his cousin and to realize that his feelings of devotion come not so much out of love but guilt (Tony had a panic attack that prevented him from being there the night of an abortive robbery that got his cousin sent to prison for many years)—virtually gives Tony the green light to go ahead and kill his cousin.

This, perhaps, is the ultimate irony: that liberal do-gooders might end up doing bad. Commentators on the postmodern condition have often said that it has to do with a suspicion or cynicism about Enlightenment notions of amelioration through reason—the world can't always be made better. *The Sopranos*, then, may be sardonically postmodern in its cynicism about progress and the rationalists who believe in it and who want their art and culture to offer uplifting, deeply serious lessons about it.

11 New Jersey Dreaming

"Everything comes to an end," Carmela warned Tony about halfway through *The Sopranos'* seven-year run, and her downbeat sentiment perhaps finds an echo in a somewhat tongue-in-cheek notice in the *New York Times* about one curious side of contemporary New Jersey popular culture. The article, a short piece which appeared in the newspaper's Sunday "New Jersey" section a few months after *The Sopranos* finished its HBO run, chronicles an explosion in the state's Beatles impersonators and Beatles tribute shows but also displays the disquiet of one imitator, Glen Burdick, who had played in the musical "Beatlemania" and was then subbing for a member of a Beatles tribute group, "The Fab Faux." With a seeming suspicion as dire as Carmela's about the extent to which current boom times will endure, Burdick worries, "I kind of wonder when the bottom's going to drop out."[1]

But in contrast to Carmela's generalized anxiety about the future, Burdick quickly rebounds to a position of optimism: "Sometimes there are classic musics that resonate with generations. But Beatles music goes one step further. It keeps regenerating." And from the article's perspective, this buoyant outlook has something to do with New Jersey in particular. Thus Pat DiNizio, lead singer for The Smithereens, a long-lived pop/rock band from New Jersey that covered the entire *Meet the Beatles* album in the guise of their 2007 release *Meet the Smithereens*, is quoted as declaring, "Jersey is definitely Beatle-friendly. It seems like it won't go away." But it also has to do with a general state of mind that looks to popular culture for reassurance. As DiNizio elaborates, "People turn to the music that gives them comfort. Obviously there's a need for this music right now."

This bit of *New York Times* reportage is a relatively minor effort and one shouldn't make too much of it. But even in passing, it works to construct a fantasy world redolent of ersatz entertainment and evasion, a New Jersey of the mind where everything is about the artifice of escapism, even as a darker anxiety lurks below. To a degree, *The Sopranos* invests in a like fantasy: its New Jersey is also about popular culture filling up one's time, about the longing for comfort, about an imitation culture that tries to prolong pleasures through the seductions of the faux. The show even brings out an imitator of its own in an episode from season 2, where an overly chatty Elvis impersonator comes across FBI informant Pussy Bonpensiero meeting in a toy store with his bureau contact; the ersatz Elvis is killed by Pussy, who fears he may unknowingly spill the beans to Pussy's Mafia associates. There is little explanation of why a character might be dressed up like Elvis, and that seems all the more natural for a mass-cultured state like the New Jersey of this television show.

Like the vision in the *New York Times* of a state in which there is always potentially a Beatles imitation show going on someplace, the New Jersey of *The Sopranos* is one in which popular culture is everywhere and ongoing. Perhaps nothing captures this sense of an inescapable, continuous mass culture better than the endless strip malls and shopping centers that seem to populate *The Sopranos'* New Jersey as a sort of ribbon that cars flow along, and from which they are pulled into parking lots for their drivers to make often useless purchases, have furtive meetings, or a combination of both. Despite its official slogan as "The Garden State," and its large rural areas, this representation of New Jersey is one in which any resplendent nature is marked by its absence, or, at best, by a presence that comes across as menace. Not for nothing is one of the most famous of the series' episodes, "Pine Barrens," about how the seemingly in-control Mafia henchmen lose their grip on things when they get lost in the woods of "South Jersey" (a term they pronounce with all the dread of the cocky urbanites discovering the supposed horrors of hillbilly culture in *Deliverance*).

Not a garden, not a regenerative Eden, the New Jersey of *The Sopranos*

Ersatz Elvis.

is a geography of constructed kitsch realities, such as the ticky tack box stores in which the state's denizens fill up on products both useful and not. There is even, for these ersatz gangsters, an ersatz mass-culture version of the old country in the Italianissimo restaurant that awaits them in a strip mall. This is a form of comfort bought through things, through a generalized commodification of everyday life. And like the ever-ongoing New Jersey Beatles shows, there is a seeming endlessness to the ways new commodities show up to fill up one's time and create further fresh potentials for comfort. Carmela, for instance, is caught in a cyclicity of consumerism in which Tony can buy her forgiveness for his sins (sexual and financial philandering, especially) by one more gift, one more glittering, glimmering luxury product—until later seasons, when she awkwardly tries to break free only to give up and give in. Having once had a priest tell her, toward the end of season 3, that the way she should deal with the fact that her luxury lifestyle comes from crime and blood money is to concentrate on the good parts of her life with Tony and separate off the bad, Carmela has come to build her own world of commodified artifice in her nouveau-riche house and in the cultural activities of the housewife (for example, a book group, reunions of girlfriends to work through all the titles on the AFI's 100 top movies list, etc.). It is more than indicative of her buying into—or being brought by Tony into—this way of life that when, in a Christmas dinner she hosts at the very end of season 6, her son A.J.'s inner-city Latina girlfriend tells her "You have a beautiful house," she replies not simply with the expected "thank you" that mere etiquette would demand but with the narcissistic (but to her own mind honest) "Yes, we do."

In *On Late Style*, Edward Said argues that one way in which the belated artworks of modernist discontent and cynicism he is dealing with express their critique of easy escapism comes in their fraught representations of far-from-comforting geographies. Said's example is literary and operatic depictions of Venice, a city which, as he put it, "combines two extremes almost without transition: a glorious, unexampled, and shining creativity, and a history of sordid, labyrinthine corruption and profound degradation." He then quotes a telling phrase from another literary critic, Tony Tanner, who had once written of the ways in which in Venice there is a swift transition from "gorgeousness to garbage."[2]

"Gorgeousness to garbage": that nice turn of phrase could well describe the imaginative geography of *The Sopranos*. But if "late style" modernist art is about fallen, degraded realities, postmodern popular culture takes the step beyond wailing about this and moves into a realm of sardonic laughter. Such popular culture often is itself about a world so overrun by popular culture that everything has become mere surface, mere game, mere relishing of the moment to such a degree that lamentation seems mere misguided nostalgia.

Take, for instance, the idea of an interplay of "gorgeousness" and "garbage." It is a central conceit of *The Sopranos*' imagination of modern life to see garbage as an inevitable underpinning of basic human activities. There is the waste that the body produces, and there is the waste of products and packaging that is cast off from the circulation of commodities through their life cycle. Tony Soprano claims to work in "waste management," and *The Sopranos* is rich (if that's the right word to describe garbage) in images of detritus, refuse, and junk. Typically, for instance, a scene in season 1 has Tony practicing his golf swing at a range right next to a garbage dump; it's apt that a shot of him against a gigantic mass of refuse displays the mountain of plastic bottles and other gar-

A New Jersey aesthetic? Glimmering garbage.

bage items as shimmering with an intensity of (artificial) colors, as if the world of waste were the most vibrant and visually sublime thing in the otherwise gray environment of strip-mall New Jersey.

If, as noted, *The Sopranos* is generally bereft of any representation of nature as inspiring fount of life and beauty, it nevertheless might be said that the show substitutes for the organic rhythms of nature a no less organic conception of human life cycles as inevitably culminating in degradation, garbage, shit. In other words, the show doesn't demonstrate faith in a beneficent Nature, but it has a no less naturalizing bent of its own in its assumption of waste as an integral, inevitable moment in human and social life cycles. In an unintended witticism from the very beginning of the series, Tony declares that "garbage is our bread and butter," and the equation of waste and sustenance well captures how the show intertwines accumulation and consumption *and* the production of by-products of refuse and rot.

This means, then, that any notion of a nostalgic gorgeousness that would be opposed to garbage, and not inevitably caught up in it, is an impossibility in the world of *The Sopranos*. Whatever gorgeousness appears there is generally an ersatz, farcical one. Tony Tanner's words no doubt intended to describe an aspect of glorious glamour in Venice, an Old Europe destination city for visitors wanting to luxuriate in a resplendent geography that would blend sublime nature and tasteful built environments. But the New Jersey of *The Sopranos* offers few glimpses of either a natural or built world that could, in any way, be termed "gorgeous." There is no "there" there. "Gorgeous" is, in fact, a word sometimes used by the ill-fated Adriana, and she generally employs the term to categorize some pricey, overblown commodity that Christopher is giving her in exchange for her devotion, or that others around her possess and that she envies. For example, in a season 5 episode, Adriana admires the fox coat of a friend, Tina (whom she will later turn in to the FBI for illegal bookkeeping practices at her job when Tina starts hitting on Christopher), with the awed declaration, "You know I love animals, but this thing is so gorgeous." Across the seasons of *The Sopranos*, Adriana stands as an object of some pity on the part of the spectator for the ways she is coerced into becoming an FBI informant (and eventually killed by the Mafia for that), but from the start she is also rendered pitiful as well as pitiable insofar as she is presented as a figure of kitsch vulgar taste—her hair swept up in a bouffant hairdo, too much makeup, a somewhat cheesy look, and a love for glitter and ostentation in jewelry. Her vulgar, overdone look is matched to a voice at the edge of an imploring nasality, with that awkward, thick accent that signifies ethnic New Jersey lower-classness. Here, "gorgeous" becomes a nasal "gaw-juss" and serves as one further sign of Adriana's fundamental lack of sophistication, her fundamental low taste.

The New Jersey of *The Sopranos* is a place after the fall, but there is no indication that its fall has not always been taking place—that there ever could have been an Eden which only subsequently gave way to mass-culture ticky-tackiness. At best, there are furtive glimpses of a few last outposts of a venerable and old-fashioned artistry, like the stone church that Tony's grandparents designed and that he proudly visits with each of his children at different moments in the series. Revealingly, when Tony first shows off the church—as he takes Meadow home from soccer in the very first episode of the series—the visit has a certain quality of inspiring uplift, in part because Tony and Meadow seem to happen accidentally on the church and it appears virtually out of nowhere, as if it exists unto itself and has no larger context around it. In contrast, when Tony returns with A. J. to the church, several seasons later, that larger context is sharply, realistically, and saddeningly depicted: the church is one last holdout in a neighborhood that has been taken over by crack and that now is in disarray and dilapidation. Whatever glory the church perhaps once had as a mark of craftsmanship and pride-in-work is at risk of fading in the context of an urbanism of ruins.

In fact, Tony and A. J. visit the old neighborhood within a narrative line about how larger forces at work within New Jersey cities are transforming older ways of life—and for the worse. Tony has entered into a scam with New Jersey State Assemblyman Ron Zellman (Peter Riegert) to use various construction schemes to milk money from the state and federal budget. One such project involves the building of a new upscale esplanade in Newark that will further commercialize the area with high-end restaurants, boutiques, and hotels and contribute anew to the transformation of the city into a venue for commodified trendiness. Another scheme entails a team put in place by Tony to receive Housing and Urban Development (HUD) funding for a promised redevelopment of the run-down houses in the crack-infested neighborhoods that Tony and A. J. are paying a visit to. If the first scheme promises to commodify the city as an artificial, and no doubt tacky, environment for the furtherance of upscale lifestyles, the second threatens to further degrade an already-decrepit inner-city squalor. For instance, not merely will the crack houses be left as they are and the money for their renovation pocketed by Tony and his allies, but Tony instructs his crew to strip the houses of their last valuable assets—copper plumbing—for resale to trendy urban professionals who fetishize an old-fashioned look when renovating their upscale habitations. Even as Tony laments the ways in which the church built by his grandparents represents a craftsmanship that is no more, he himself contributes to the inexorable slide of neighborhoods into postindustrial degradation and decay. Likewise, in a later episode, he sells a building he owns and that has housed one of the last old Italian poultry stores in the neighborhood so that Jamba Juice can move in and continue its branding and standardization of city life.

For what it's worth, if the *New York Times* article on New Jersey Beatles events presents the activities of the impersonators as relatively benign—not a crass attempt to exploit the success of the original group but rather a desire to continue its appeal through loving tributes—the HUD narrative line in *The Sopranos* makes its own reference to the Beatles and commercialism. Here the allusion is much more cynical about the ways in which everything can be put up for sale. In a furtherance of the HUD scheme, Assemblyman Zellman calls upon the aid of his old college friend, African American urban activist Maurice Tiffen (Vondie Curtis-Hall), who, as an ostensible community leader, helps broker the deal by which HUD will provide the funds for the promised (but ultimately unfulfilled) renovation of the crack-besotted neighborhoods. After the scheme pays off and Tony, Zellman, and Maurice all divvy up their share of the spoils, the two former college buddies go off to reminisce about the old times and to wonder about the disappearance of their original, progressive ideals. In response to Zellman's expression of moral uncertainty about what they have been accomplishing with cons like the HUD scam, Maurice justifies their actions with the sort of fatalism and cynicism about progressive change that is typical of *The Sopranos'* ironic outlook on social commitment: "It's like shoveling shit against the tide. . . . If it ain't us [scamming the system, that is], it's gonna be someone else. . . . The revolution got sold. You heard the Beatles for H&R Block."

It's all about shit: everything turns to waste. It's all about money: everything is for sale. These two motifs run through *The Sopranos* and intertwine. It's not just that the money of mob corruption is filthy lucre with so much bloodshed behind it. It's also that the specific work of these New Jersey Mafiosi has particularly to do with extracting profit from waste and squeezing everything for all it's got. At each stage of the cycles that lead from the production of goods to the eventual mountains of detritus left behind, there is a further exploitation in which every last bit of value is eked out of items (and people, as well) that may seem to have long lost their last shred of usefulness. Typical, for instance, is a scam the Soprano Mob is involved in in season 5, scavenging wrecked cars for their airbags, which will then be sold to body shops and car dealerships who will sell them as new and reinstall them in functioning cars.

Money is almost never mentioned in the *New York Times* article on

New Jersey Beatles shows. The mythology constructed here is of entertainment as bountifully infinite, always filling up life with escapist joys engaged in without financial benefit or expenditure. The image is of delights that never stop coming. The imputation that any of the Beatles impersonators might exploitatively be out to squeeze their own bit of profit from a phenomenon they are only a derivative version of is avoided for a celebration of these imitators as giving fans what they want and as tapping into the comfort needs of the historical moment.

Like Carmela's "Everything comes to an end," the promotional tagline for 1977's *Saturday Night Fever*—another story of ethnically marked Italian-Americans caught (in this case in Brooklyn) in the rut of dismal lives lived out across the river from Manhattan—bitterly wondered, "Where do you go when the record's over?" The *New York Times* article on Beatles events in New Jersey wants precisely to not ask such a question: its imagination is of the boundless cornucopia of an entertainment that never ceases and that only vaguely lets real-life worries in (such as the quickly quieted worry by one performer that the bottom for Beatles tributes and impersonations might drop out some day).

In this respect, Carmela's warning that everything ends—which within the fictional universe of *The Sopranos* is about the vulnerabilities she and her family face in the dangerous world they inhabit—is also a commentary on *The Sopranos* itself as an entertainment, a cultural product offered up in a precise time and place. The fantasy of an endless show, of endless performances always filling up time and holding dismal realities at a comforting distance, is no doubt a seductive one, but *The Sopranos* at least recognizes an end to fantasy, recognizes the limits of comfort, recognizes the inadequacies of nonstop consumption. Just as Tony, in one of the very last episodes of the show, violently pulls his son A. J. away from his home entertainment system when he needs him to stop living in denial about the world around him, so too does the show hint at a larger world of issues and responsibilities beyond its fiction, even as it may refuse to offer any clear path through them.

2

The Sopranos

in the Marketplace

The Sopranos has had a phenomenal media career, and it will be interesting to see what its afterlife will be. Perhaps it will remain a point of reference in the culture, and perhaps it will be remembered as the major work of popular culture that it is already being claimed to be. Certainly, media companies will do their best to extend the resonances it has for the individual fan by their own attempts to extend the series beyond its first showing in new multiple markets, from reruns to syndication to DVDs and so on. *The Sopranos* will continue to float through everyday life. And then other shows will emerge to captivate the public, and the process will continue.

Throughout, it is certain that business and culture will intertwine. Significantly, when a *New York Times* article from 2005 reported on the decision to extend *The Sopranos* to a seventh season, it presented the HBO executives connected with the series as offering up a rhetoric of creativity and cultural commitment. They were, the implication was, in it fully for the art and not the money. For example, then–HBO head Chris Albrecht claimed his interest in a seventh season was that of enabling the right rhythm for the show: "Seasons for 'The Sopranos,'" Albrecht asserted, "have always been organic," and he thereby reinvigorated a mythology of the artistic work as something that finds its necessary shape logically, inevitably, naturally. Albrecht then went on to say that David Chase had originally wanted to stop making new seasons of the show because he thought he "was coming to the end of his creative ideas" (the myth, then, of the artist as someone who knows exactly what he has to say and when to say it) but then got reinspired by "the reception the show got last year" (the myth of the artist as working according to creative juices and as responsive to public interest).[1]

The reference to "the reception the show got" is ambiguous. Not merely was season 5 the target of public acclaim, but it was also coincident with the syndication auction of the series to the A&E channel. Was Albrecht referring to critical buzz, to public acclaim, or to the frenzy of media interest in keeping the show going in new platforms like A&E? Revealingly, one worry for those networks that had bid on syndication rights was that there weren't that many episodes of the show—as opposed, say, to *Law & Order*, which has so many episodes under its belt that syndication has resulted in channels that seem endlessly to be playing the show. By making more episodes, HBO increased the attraction of *The Sopranos* as a syndication package.

And money, as the *New York Times* article eventually revealed, was indeed the bottom line for the extra season in another, telling way. It turned out that seasons 6 and 7 would be shot back-to-back, without interruption, not only because this would allow artistically for creative energies to be funneled and focused, but also because in administrative terms the two seasons would be considered one and thereby avoid contract renegotiation for the creative talent. In the words of the *New York Times*, "Keeping the show in continuous production now means that for technical and contractual purposes it will remain the show's sixth season."

A work of culture is never reducible to the economic relations that it participates in, but, as these examples show, neither is it ever apart from those. *The Sopranos* meets up with its fans in specific locales—from bus tours to ivory towers—and each of these gives the show new value. This, as much as the meanings read into it by the critics, is its meaning in society. In its cynicism and its savviness, the show unveils the stakes of critical reading and offers itself up as a game in which meanings resonate but float free from any final depth. In this way, the show allegorizes its own status as media work and perhaps offers its most trenchant comments on the ways the business of culture is conducted today. I now want to look at that conduct both inside the series and in a range of exploitations of the series in the culture at large.

12 Tie-ins and Hangers-on

On Saturday, December 30, 2004, I took the *Sopranos* bus tour. The tour transports visitors to several dozen New Jersey spots that have figured in episodes of the series, but the tour organizers make clear that theirs is in no way an officially sanctioned or sponsored activity. Along the journey through forgotten industrial or postindustrial landscapes, the guide tells hokey jokes, recounts trivia from the show's plot lines or from the real lives of its actors, poses questions about the show for which participants can win prizes (ranging from boxes of pasta to a ticket good for taking the tour again), and offers cannoli fresh from an Italian bakery to all tour passengers. In the pauses between the guide's spiel, loudspeakers strung throughout the bus play the *Sopranos* theme or songs from Italian pop singers (including Jersey's own favorite son, Frank Sinatra).

Taking the bus tour certainly is one means to participate in *The Sopranos* as a cultural phenomenon. And in fact, it quickly becomes obvious that the tour attracts fun-seekers who don't even watch the show (although on the day I went, some promised to start watching now that they had seen the geographical context for it). The journey serves as a weekend diversion, a kitsch activity that enables the tourist to enter into the games of popular culture. For example, on the day I went, one of the other participants was a chubby, geeky teenager, Jay, in a *Sopranos* T-shirt and looking the cliché of the fanboy nerd who has immersed himself in the popular culture of his time. For Jay, it would seem *The Sopranos* did not have to do with trenchant analysis of marriage, ethnic identity, family, work relations, and masculinity in the period of transition into the twenty-first century. Jay appeared far from the stereo-

On the *Sopranos* bus tour: my mother-in-law, Marie Sturken, in the parking lot of the diner where Chris Moltisanti got shot.

type of the standard HBO viewer—the somewhat older, sophisticated urban professional who approaches culture with seriousness and wants the encounter to be meaningful and potentially uplifting. For Jay, *The Sopranos* instead opened up emphatically to a tongue-in-cheek fandom world of game and amusement. With glee, he absorbed each anecdote told by the tour guide, and, with energized rapidity, he beat other tourists to the punch to rack up wins in the bus tour's trivia competition. Clearly, despite the warning before each episode of *The Sopranos* that it was intended for a mature audience, Jay had violated the rules of his own younger demographic and found much to enjoy in the show and in the bus tour devoted to it.

The *Sopranos* bus tour offers a take on the show that very much sees it as comic entertainment (rather than, say, a deep commentary on the human condition): here, the series is treated as a light and somewhat ironic amusement that inspires jokes. Significantly, much of the information the guide provides has to do with biographical anecdotes about the actors in the show and incidents that happened during the shoot (for example, the open casting call held in Harrison, New Jersey, brought out so many people that the police had to be brought in, and the town was virtually shut down for hours).

Where thematic interpretation of the *Sopranos* series often proceeds by forgetting that the show is, in fact, just a show and instead imagines that it presents a recognizable universe of real-life figures (so that, for instance, Tony Soprano can be said to try to confront moral and existential issues we all deal with), the tour emphasizes, in contrast, that it is dealing precisely with a fabricated work. We're given production history, we're allowed to see the locales where scenes of the show were shot. And here, pointedly, there's a particular emphasis on the gap between the fictional appearance of such locales on the show and their banal existence in everyday real life, as if again to remind the participant that *The Sopranos* is all about the wondrous magic and trickery of building up an engrossing fictional world out of everyday origins. Thus, for instance, "Satriale's Pork Store"—which, in the narrative world of the show, Tony Soprano's dad seized from Mr. Satriale for nonpayment of debts and which serves as one place where Tony's gang hangs out—is revealed (in one of the longest stops of the tour) to be a nondescript storefront in Kearny, an empty building which the Sopranos production company leased and which only would get decked out with Satriale signs when the show was actually in production. The tour here takes its delight in presenting the show precisely as show, a quite constructed fabrication whose secrets it is the tour's mission to reveal.

And lest we imagine that it is only in the unofficial and unsanctioned guise of the bus tour that *The Sopranos* is rendered as humorous kitsch, HBO itself appeared to assume also that an eye-winking, ironic knowingness would be one of the best ways to "respect the Bing" (to quote the show's own phrase for the code of ethics its Mafia characters must follow by paying homage to the strip joint that is the center of their operations). Hence, a full-page 2002 *New York Times* ad for the Christmas offering of three seasons of *The Sopranos* on DVD declares it "A Timeless Holiday Classic" with the clarification that it comes "without all the glad tidings and goodwill toward man." The ad presents the show as multilayered—not in its purported depth of theme, but rather insofar as it plays on the knowing and sardonic gap between reverent respectability and unrepentant disreputableness.

HBO's own marketing of *The Sopranos* and its ancillary products thus targeted (and continues to target) a savvy audience which replaces aesthetic refinement and critical depth with a bleeding-edge creativity in which morality and meaning matter only insofar as they remain saleable. That is, HBO assumes that the sophistication of its targeted upscale urban professional audience manifests itself not so much in the desire for earnest thematic depth as in an ironic knowingness that just doesn't take things too seriously. The attraction here is irreverence and playful amorality. In fact, two years later, when the fourth season of *The Sopranos* appeared on DVD, the tone of the full-page *New York Times* ad was even more sardonic: in the center of a vast field of cute snowmen, one stands with its head shot off, and the ad sports the slogan, "Bada Bing, Bada Boom. Your Shopping's Done." Where a discourse of interpretation has to find, in popular culture, ever more profound layers of seriousness that make that culture matter, media industries themselves can now take a more insouciant approach to their products and set out to sell the very fact that they don't matter—that they can be upscale even as they are without resonant moral consequence.

Indeed, the products that HBO itself markets around *The Sopranos* exhibit a range of values, from the most reverent to the most tongue-in-cheek. There's an ever-growing array of sanctioned tie-ins: a best-selling cookbook followed by a broader do-it-yourself manual for Soprano-style entertaining, a coffee-table book that serves as guide to the show, an anthology of scripts from select episodes, a trivial pursuit game, a pinball machine, a video game, as well as box sets of DVDs (with a deluxe all-seasons set out at the end of 2008), and so on (at one point, HBO licensed a line of Sopranos-style clothing, but it didn't do well and has been discontinued).

In this respect, there is, to my mind, no ancillary product more vacuous—and more revealing of the desire to eke out revenue even in the case where little of value appears to be offered for one's monetary outlay—than the HBO tie-in book, *The Tao of Bada Bing! Words of Wis-*

Tie-ins: *Sopranos* baseball bat and booze-bottle cigars.

dom from The Sopranos: after a minimal two-page introduction in which the editors argue that the yin and yang of Taoism posits a universe of flux in ways that parallel the play with moral opposites in *The Sopranos*, *The Tao of Bada Bing!* offers thirty short sections that begin with a brief quotation from the Tao and then excerpt dialogue from the TV series to suggest that each illustrates the other.[1] Strikingly, the publishers of the book (a hitherto minor publishing house that hoped to hit it big when it was licensed to produce this volume for HBO) tried to present the very meagerness of the volume as its virtue. An article in *Publishers Weekly* noted that publishing executive Charles Kim hoped "fans [would] appreciate the absence of sociological conjecture," while HBO's own director of licensing Richard Oren declared the tome superior to the denser HBO volume of collected scripts, since "it's easier to read and digest the dialogue this way, in the context of supporting various themes."[2]

There's a jokiness to the title of the book, with its conjoining of Asian philosophy and gangster language. But there's also more than a hint of the exploitation of exoticism: if HBO, its *Sopranos* show, and the ancillary products marketed around that show all have to do with an upscale lifestyle, there's an extent to which part of such a lifestyle has to do with a turn to philosophies of the East. That the story world of *The Sopranos* made fun of the frequent faddishness of Western appropriations of such philosophies—as in Janice Soprano's inconsistent reliance on yoga, Buddhism, Taoism and so on—adds another level of irony to the exoticism. In fact, HBO is not alone in its marketing of an Orientalist slant on the New Jersey show: when Tony Soprano was advised by his therapist Jennifer Melfi to read Sun Tzu's *The Art of War* and reported back that the book's militaristic advice had been indispensable to him in his affairs, sales of the Oxford University Press edition of the book exploded, eventually pushing it into the middle of the *New York Times* bestseller list and leading the venerable press to run a series of ad campaigns specifically linking the book to the HBO show. In one print ad, the slogan reads "For the head of your family"; in another, it explains, "Tony Soprano fears no enemy. Sun Tzu taught him how."

The tensions of the *Tao* book, as it hovers between empty joke or loving quotation of best moments from the show or vaguely serious offer of Eastern enlightenment, have a hard time coalescing into a singular identity. In contrast, the most noted and most successful HBO-authorized commodity tie-in for *The Sopranos*, other than the DVDs themselves, is the cookbook; here there's little in the way of high seriousness to get in the way of gag-gift enjoyment. Jokingly attributed on the book's spine to a character from the show, chef Artie Bucco, but actually written by former experimental TV advocate Allen Rucker, who has also authored such ancillary products as the *Sopranos* trivial pursuit board game and the *Sopranos* video game, the cookbook offers a romp through the richness, both cultural and culinary, of homestyle Italian cuisine. With a print run of over half a million copies, *The Sopranos Family Cookbook* has been a huge success and even reached the number-one spot on the miscellany bestsellers list of the *New York Times* (it held that title for six weeks and was in the top five for twenty weeks). It has been translated into eight languages: French, Hungarian, Swedish, Danish, Finnish, Dutch, Norwegian, and Korean.[3] After a fashion, the cookbook does have its own degrees of seriousness: the recipes are real, and there is an earnest attempt to talk of the worthiness of Italian cuisine and to see it as a resonant form of national cultural identity. But the book is also a novelty item that sets out, good-naturedly, to provide relatively mindless fun. It is as much about the vicarious visual enjoyment of thick, rich Italian food as the actual creation of it; indeed, one imagines that many readers have not actually made recipes from the book but simply enjoyed the pictures. The jokiness of the book starts with its inside-cover photo of the show's matriarchal harridan Livia Soprano, helpless in the face of a fire that has erupted in her kitchen. The image comes from a hilarious subplot of the show (Livia as a walking disaster, both for her own self and for others around her), and its emphasis on culinary disaster would seem a wryly cynical way to begin a cookbook.

That the cookbook is not to be taken too seriously is given a bitter nod in the *New York Times*, which otherwise has been often earnest about promoting *The Sopranos* as a resonant work of high culture. Specifically, a Sunday *Book Review* cartoon strip sets out to joke sardonically about the ways in which worthy books sometimes get lost in the glut of the marketplace, while less-respectable tomes succeed through crass selling strategies. The strip talks of the dismal fate of "countless perfectly fine—but hookless—volumes of recipes currently gazing from the depths of remainder row at the heavily hyped ascension to bestsellerdom of one of their kind, whose rationale for existence is arguably less cogent than their own"; it pictures the *Sopranos* cookbook, which is drawn larger than life, with a golden aura around it and with the jealous other cookbooks glaring up at it, as the prime example of the ersatz best seller. One anthropomorphized loser in this rat race, the "Uzbekistani Barbecue Cookbook," grouses, "What's next? The Sopranos Book of Landscaping?"[4]

With the *Sopranos* cookbook, there is no doubt a tongue-in-cheek mockery of a lower-class world that tries to find "taste" in thick sauces, abundant meals centered on fatty meats, an entire panoply of the tacky, the excessive, and the unhealthy. (If once the ethnic word used to describe the thickly laid-on emotions of popular culture was "schmaltz" [a Yiddish word for rendered fat], it may be appropriate that today's word is "cheesy," although the reference is perhaps less to the goo on pizza than to the sense that in modern America, cheese often appears as processed, artificial, ersatz.) In contrast to an Italian cuisine that supposedly combines everything into messy amalgams of noodle, sausage, cheese, and sauce and that serves it up in massive, overflowing bowls, upscale urban professional cuisine has often been about separation of elements (for example, the nouvelle cuisine which dots the plate with little designs of food and lightly traced patterns of sauce dancing around them) and about a lightness of effect (as in the current vogue for tapas-like small-plate meals).

At the very same time, while food has long been a prime site for the articulation of class and status difference, it is also the case that in the hecticness of today's urban culture, there is an urbanite rediscovery of rich, even heavy food—a deliberate wallowing in the crossing of class boundaries of taste. Food culture is still in a moment of ostensible refinement through exoticism (hence, the vogue for Zen-like Asian cuisine), but there is also a strong investment in comfort food which tends to center on the thick, the mushy, the saucy, the soft, and the cheesy. Comfort food is about primal regression—we go back to the food we loved as kids, we go back to food that we've supposedly grown away from in developing good taste and in rising in the class hierarchy. And in this respect, it may well be that *The Sopranos Family Cookbook* attracts attention not only for its mockery of a world of pasta and sausage but for its embrace of it.

That the biggest selling commodity tie-in for the show is a cookbook is also in keeping with cuisine trends of the urban sophisticate. While urban professionals have turned increasingly to upscale versions of fast food to save themselves time but maintain self-image—as in the rise of so-called "casual dining," supposedly a cut above the fast-food options—it has also been the case that food preparation in the home (or urban apartment) has become one of the prime sites for invigoration of the professional lifestyle. After a day's labor at disembodied head work in the information economy, the creative professional can imagine a reconnection to physicality by playing hard in the kitchen. Cooking is "in" and serves as a means to imagining that material and directly physicalized experience is still possible in a society of the spectacle. Like the Food Network's *The Iron Chef*, the *Sopranos* cookbook both jokingly turns everything into media game and yet promises a path through all simulacra to the reality of direct experience of a lost craft of cuisine. No doubt the gag tone of the book *and* its utility as an easy path to comfort food prepared in the home came together in the proliferation of Sunday-night *Sopranos* parties (usually around first or last episodes of a season), where the playful premise was to make baked ziti and other unrefined delights that one normally wouldn't deign to prepare but which were now sought as something to consume while watching the show with friends.

Clearly, then, the unauthorized activity of the *Sopranos* bus tour is not exceptional in its lighthearted attempt to promote *The Sopranos* as a pleasurable lark. Around this show, whose stories are so much about informal, if not illicit, markets that proliferate to create new profit streams wherever possible, there is itself a proliferation of tie-ins and ancillary products, both official and unofficial. These can get goofy as possible but even that—namely, the very fact that the send-up and the tongue-in-cheek take-off become seductive parts of the universe of this resonant show—tells us something serious about the workings of popular culture in the media economies of today. Irony sells, and that matters.

13 Touring Postindustrialism

The *Sopranos* bus tour is—like the cookbook—an act of escapism that doesn't want to treat the show too reverently. At the same time, the tour flirts with tough economic reality in its own way.

Originally, it seems, there were two *Sopranos* bus tours, one run by a former employee of the other. According to news reports, the competition got pretty intense. One of the organizers even accused her rival of getting to her pickup sites early and stealing customers. There were intimations of legal proceedings. Eventually, somebody backed down, and the two tours appear to have merged into one single venture. In some way, it seems appropriate that a TV show about Mafia gangs that often muscle in on each other's territory should have given rise to a tourist enterprise that was itself caught up in internecine battle and energetic turf war.

One can be picked up for the tour in midtown Manhattan, but in my case, since I had been staying with relatives in central New Jersey, it was more convenient to go directly to the second pickup site in front of the Houlihan's chain restaurant at the Secaucus, New Jersey shopping mall. No doubt, the Manhattan departure gives the tourists the bonus of going through the Lincoln Tunnel, thereby mimicking Tony Soprano's first movements out of New York in the credits sequence to the program (although once in New Jersey, his journey becomes geographically inaccurate, as various analyses of the show have noted). But leaving from Manhattan also runs the risk of diluting the outing into another random vacation activity of the tourist to the Big Apple. That is, it can become just one more Manhattan thing-to-do like many others.

Indeed, the company that runs the *Sopranos* tour also advertises in-Manhattan tours of locales from other TV shows—for instance, there's a *Sex and the City* tour—and it would appear that the appeal of the various offerings is not just to the diehard fan but to the casual consumer who wants contact with any famous regional bit of popular culture. It seems evident, for example, that some of the people who get on the bus in Manhattan have learned of the *Sopranos* tour from their hotel's Web site or from fliers in its lobby and participate without even being viewers of the show.[1] Presumably, the New Jersey pickup avoids some of the more casual tourism of out-of-towners just in for the weekend and looking for any local tour, especially one caught up in contemporary popular culture.

The Secaucus shopping center is a site that clearly has seen better days. Some stores have gone bankrupt, others are bereft of customers, and some have obviously been converted into medical offices and government agencies (for example, a Medicare filing center). There's a bad bit of cold and alienating public sculpture in the center, and a conference hotel that appears most distinguished by its lack of activity. It seems part of the appropriateness that a tour for the *Sopranos* TV show should have its New Jersey pickup spot in such a locale. The Secaucus pickup reiterates the way in which *The Sopranos* so often depicted a New Jersey that has lived the ravages of industrialization and deindustrialization alike. The Manhattan departure eases one, perhaps, into the tough world on the other side of the Hudson, but the New Jersey departure site plunks one smack down in the middle of it. Certainly, as was evident in the last images of the show's credit sequence, in which Tony arrived at the large-scale house he had attained as he moved up the road to success, *The Sopranos* also represented a New Jersey of ostentatious nouveau-riche luxury, but one sees little of that on the tour. There is no visit, for instance, to the real house in North Caldwell that stood in as Tony's residence. Instead, the Soprano McMansion hovers over the tour as a spectral sign of unattainability. The tour is about another side of what anthropologist Sherry Ortner has termed "New Jersey Dreaming": in this case, the sense of entrapment in a no-end way of life with glimpses of escape just beyond the horizon (or just across the Hudson River in Manhattan).[2]

Just as *The Sopranos* depicts a world of haves and have-nots, and makes the coveting of what others possess a central topic (for example, Tony's lusting after Ralphie Cifaretto's girlfriend, Valentina), the *Sopranos* tour inevitably gives tourists some special things (a secret glimpse into the world of the show and its production anecdotes, prizes such as a box of uncooked pasta) but also reminds them that they can't have everything. (Yet the envious or curious fan who wants to know more about the Soprano abode can always check out the spread in *Architectural Digest* [September 2002] or could, until recently, order online the actual blueprints for the Soprano house at $599; there's also a long, rewarding sequence inside the house in the *Sopranos Unauthorized* DVD, about which more in a moment.)[3]

The wait for the bus at the Secaucus shopping center easily sets the scene for the image of industrially ravaged northern New Jersey that will then be expanded on in the tour itself. For instance, at the shopping center, the forlorn storefronts of businesses hitting rock bottom and exhibiting taped-up signs that announce "everything must go" have at least one fictional correlate in the show, in the depiction of the bankruptcy of gambler Davie Scatino's sporting goods store, which he loses to Tony Soprano. Tony pillages Davie's business by charging supplies and services (for example, bogus airline tickets) against it, which he then sells elsewhere for the benefit of his Mafia family, with none of the profit going back to Davie and his business. One of the commodities that Tony puts into circulation this way is high-end bottled water, and later we see restaurateur Artie Bucco trying to introduce the brand into his dining establishment. From Davie to Artie, the show thereby makes explicit just how far the life and trajectory of a commodity can extend and how many people can be caught up in its circulation, whether to their eventual profit or not. Davie's descent into penury is thus contrasted to—but also made the ultimate support of—a high-end consumerist lifestyle in which customers will partake of supposedly upscale items without knowing about their somewhat ethically shady provenance. For what it's worth, though, in a fourth-season episode, Artie will also himself risk economic disaster when he gets in too deep in a dubious get-rich-quick scheme. No one, especially in the post-9/11 seasons of the show, which are very much tinged by a worry about economic survival in a time of uncertainty, will ever be permanently sheltered from the unpredictability in capital's circulation through the culture. And even Tony, too, will suffer from the plundering of Davie's business when his mother tries to use the fraudulent airplane tickets and is arrested, creating a trail that leads federal agents back to her son.

When Davie asks Tony why he would ravage the business of an old school chum in this fashion, Tony replies by referring to the fable of the scorpion and the frog: A scorpion reassures a wary frog he's asked to ferry him on his back across the river that he won't sting him, but when they are halfway out he does. As he is dying of the fatal wound, the frog asks the scorpion why he did sting, since the scorpion will now drown and die too. The scorpion explains that it's his nature as a scorpion to kill, no matter the consequences. In the same way, Tony's nature is to pillage and plunder, even when friends and those dear to him may suffer. Tony is caught by a contagious rapaciousness that seems to inhere in acts of exploitation and economic decimation. Ironically, in a strange version of life-imitates-art, the real store that served as locale for the fictional Davie's sporting goods business itself almost faced financial crisis because of the show: when an episode of *The Sopranos* ended with the image of liquidators locking up the business and putting a foreclosure notice on it, some New Jerseyites assumed the actual real-life enterprise had gone bust and stopped patronizing it.

The *Sopranos* bus tour itself toys with a recognition of the theme of economic cycles from the industrial to the postindustrial and their consequences for the everyday citizen, even as the tour resolutely plays itself out as a kitschy form of fun. The tour may function as lightweight fare, an escapist lark, but it is strangely bound to a worldliness that one might have imagined it the mission of escapist entertainment to make us forget. For example, just after the Secaucus pickup, when the tour really seems to be ready to get underway, the bus is caught on a concrete overpass in what seems an inevitable traffic jam, looking out on an industrial landscape of desolate fields, junked objects, scarred telephone poles, cables, razor-wire fences, petroleum tanks, mud and muck, lack of vegetation on all sides. This, jokes the tour guide, as he beckons the passengers to look around, shows why New Jersey is known as the "Garden State." Evidently, recurrent and predictable traffic jams mean that he gets to use this quip a lot. It will, in fact, be one project of the tour to take this barren environment of strip malls and downscale chain stores, grimy businesses, gray warehouses, small-scale factories, and suchlike, and transform it into something radiant and resonant: sites seemingly marked by the banality of everydayness suddenly gain in aura when one realizes they are part of the universe of *The Sopranos*. Thus, for instance, toward the end of the tour (which lasts close to four hours), one can feel the fatigue of the passengers after they've spent so much time in a bus rattling over broken highways crossed by bumpy freight-train railway tracks. Going up Route 17, one of New Jersey's bleakest arrays of mini-malls and big-box businesses, the bus passes an IHOP franchise, the International House of Pancakes, a seeming symbol of bland American mass society. On the bus, the tired indifference in the air is palpable, but then the guide announces that this is not just any IHOP, but the one in which one of the characters from *The Sopranos* met an FBI agent, and that the dumpster outside is not just any dumpster but the one which the body of another character was thrown into (I may be getting the facts a bit wrong; by this time of the tour, I had had my surfeit of site-specific trivia). Suddenly, the tourists are re-energized, and the digital cameras and video recorders start shooting away. The IHOP and its dumpster have become special. This project of the tour—this transfiguration by which the ordinary objects of everyday life come to gain aura and stand out—is a process of *fetishism*: we, the tourists, invest otherwise banal things with virtually magical resonance, we make them into celebrity objects, just like the celebrity actors that have come into contact with them. But the economic bottom line is always ready to insinuate its way into the insouciant space of carefree jokiness. For example, the cheaply printed tour guide that comes with the trip has inserted into it an envelope for gratuities to give to the guide if you've been satisfied with his spiel. You've already bought a ticket to enter into a special, privileged, magical space (the big bus) from which you can watch places (both real and fictional) of deal-making and everyday labor (for example, the body shop that serves as the front for the character Big Pussy's Mafia operations), but you also end the trip with a last reiteration of monetary relations before you go back to your own everyday life. Furthermore, it is likely, if you met the tour at the Secaucus pickup, that you'll be caught in traffic jams on the way home, not unlike the one the bus seemed inevitably to have gotten into as the tour began. The frolicking country lark is inevitably bordered by the frustrations of a world with little country left to go frolicking in (in the show, countryside was where you bury bodies, it was where your crimes always catch up with you, it was a glimpse of verdancy just beyond the overblown McMansions that were ever more encroaching upon it) and with little sense of an open road for one's escapes to be played out on. Revealingly, if the traffic jam is such a frustrating, if banal, part of everyday modern life, *The Sopranos* also had its characters endlessly in cars and sometimes going nowhere. A show about people whose lives are lived out in vehicles is watched by a contemporary audience that increasingly finds some part of its own life wasted in the traffic jams that are ever more endemic to modern life. Tony at least seems to breeze home in the frenetic montage of the show's credit sequence. Elsewhere in *The Sopranos*, however, trying to get somewhere in a car is often a fraught experience. Traffic jams there are unbearable—for example, the highway tie-up that appears to push corrupt police detective Vin Makazian (John Heard) over the edge into suicide or the back-up that Mafioso Bobby Baccalieri is stuck in and hasn't realized was caused by his wife's fatal car accident.

The bus tour promises a transformation of everyday pressures and needs into a special moment (a long, four-hour one) of free time. But the world left behind insinuates itself into the magic. Narratives of success and failure in a world of work hover over the bus tour. For example, the tour guide repeatedly notes that he had had a small role on the show in its first season. It is clear that the tour has become a surrogate acting gig for him, with his jokes about how evanescent his appearance on the show was only partially covering over an evident wistful regret at not playing a larger part in its fictional universe and at not having more of its aura (and reward) rub off on him. Like the cliché that so many Los Angeles waiters are wannabe actors who are honing their skills at personality projection in the restaurant in lieu of at the studio set, the tour guide has turned the tour into an ersatz profession of performance, and there is something mournful in his carny-like banter and cheesy antics. For example, at the site of the diner where there was a hit on Soprano nephew Christopher Moltisanti, the guide surprises everyone by suddenly shooting off blanks from a revolver he had hidden on his person; strikingly, he does the gag in desultory fashion, as if he knows he is just going through the motions of something his heart might not be into.

Around the show, then, there's a market of wannabe parasitism: the tour that profits from the show's very existence; the guide who keeps joking, but with sadness beneath it, about the career that could have been; the tourists themselves who gain ersatz contact with trade secrets and celebrity aura. Again, this seems particularly appropriate to a tour about *The Sopranos* as a privileged object for tourist exploitation. Just as the show depicts in its story world both the profitable activity of the Mafia (and the Mafia housewives) *and* the envy of those who have a fascination with that activity and want to glom onto it, such as Davie, who longed to get into the high-stakes card game Tony Soprano's Mob runs, so too does the show itself, as economic and cultural fact, captivate onlookers and encourage hangers-on to want to profit from it. For instance, it seems that the *Sopranos* bus tour used to include a stop at a parking lot where one of the actors from the show would actually be waiting with signed T-shirts and other paraphernalia that he would sell from the back of his car, though it was, again, insisted on that this was not an official activity of HBO. Once more, this surreptitious salesmanship seems appropriate to a show that is so much about desires to make a profit, even at the lowest levels of economic activity.

14 Cashing In on the Game

To say it again, everybody wants a piece of *Sopranos* action. There has even been an ongoing lawsuit, thrown out several times by the courts, by a state prosecutor who claims he gave David Chase the story ideas for the show.[1] Numerous *Sopranos* actors, both in important roles and secondary ones, have written books to cash in on the show's success, whether autobiographical accounts of their Italian upbringing and how their lineage prepared them for triumph on the show (for example, *Who's Sorry Now: The True Story of a Stand-Up Guy*, by Joe Pantoliano, who played Ralphie Cifaretto in seasons 3 and 4) or lifestyle how-to books (such as *A Goombah's Guide to Life*, by Steve Schirripa [Bobby Bacala on the show]) and general meditations on life's problems and purposes (for example, Jamie-Lynn Sigler's *Wise Girl: What I've Learned about Life, Love, and Loss*, which recounts her battles with eating disorders during the first seasons of *The Sopranos*, or Lorraine Bracco's *On the Couch*, in which she says her role as therapist Jennifer Melfi encouraged her to write "about telling the truth—about being straight with ourselves").[2] The actors then will advertise these books, along with other unofficial *Sopranos* tie-ins, on their personal Web sites, which seem to exist in large part as promotional tools rather than as blogs geared to personal expression. Additionally, and seemingly appropriate for a show whose title alludes to musical identity, several *Sopranos* actors who had been hoping over the years for musical careers (for example, Dominic Chianese, Jamie-Lynn Sigler, and Aida Turturro) have clearly tried to gain new attention for their efforts by their association with the show: thus, to take just two examples, Dominic Chianese's CD is entitled *Hits*, to play off the Mafia lingo, and confirms the pun by a picture of him next to a violin case (the place, as we all know, to keep one's machine gun), while Aida Turturro has had a run on Broadway in the gangster-themed *Chicago*, along with Vincent Pastore, who played Big Pussy in *The Sopranos.*

Ironically, Pastore originally criticized the merchandising of the show—"I think it's garbage. It cheapens everything. It makes it like Coney Island"—and he evinced particular disdain for the bus tour. But that did not prevent him, as *USA Today* notes, from using his own image as tough guy to appear in TV commercials and on the cover of *Cigar Aficionado* for a line of cigars he was promoting.[3]

Within the story world of *The Sopranos*, commodities move through circuits of thievery and exploitation, and capital changes hands. The last shot of the opening episode for season 4, the first after the terrorist attacks of September 11, is a slow zoom into a twenty-dollar bill that comes to fill up the screen, suggesting the extent to which money lords over this world as one of its biggest obsessions. But as a commodity itself—a product from a cable and original-programming production subsidiary of the big media giant Time Warner—*The Sopranos* itself is part of this circulation of entertainment capital, and here too there have been ambitions, both official and informal, to participate in its success. Sometimes, in fact, it's hard to know which activities are sanctioned and which are not, and, if official, which ones were part of the show's actual production efforts and which ones were simply marketing ploys. For instance, as noted, there was some minor controversy in 2000 when HBO held a casting call for *Sopranos* extras in the working-class community of Harrison, New Jersey (a town the bus tour passes through, since a number of locations for the show are there, such as Anthony Jr.'s high school). On the one hand, many more people than expected showed up (20,000 by most estimates) and overextended the local resources: there were traffic jams, police were overwhelmed, and HBO eventually had to cancel the casting call early in the day, leading to veritable threats of crowd violence. On the other hand, many of the people who showed up (including quite a number who knew of the series only by hearsay) took the event as a sort of kitsch, comic outing and came in overdone versions of Italian Mob or moll garb. For example, there were sightings of wannabes who appeared with handcuffs dangling from their wrists. Quickly, Italian-American antidefamation organizations condemned the fact that the event had incited ordinary citizens into playing into the worst stereotypes of Italian identity. And just as quickly they encouraged rumors that HBO had never really planned to cast extras this way and cynically intended for the event to get out of control, since that would focus attention on the next season of its show. In fact, HBO did end up making some minor casting decisions based on the Harrison audition, but the sentiment that this had all been a put-up job for publicity purposes lingered.

One venue that reported in great detail on all this energetic activity, in which production and promotion appeared to blur (the original event plus the rumors about its impurity of purpose), was the New Jersey *Star-Ledger*.[4] In another mixture of fiction and reality and of formal and informal participation in the celebrification of *The Sopranos*, the *Star-Ledger* is the paper that awaits Tony at the end of his driveway at the beginning of each season (and, in season 5, in which he has moved out of the house, it is run over by a car as it waits forlornly on the ground) and that in the show is often depicted as reporting on Soprano Mob activity. But the actual newspaper also devoted itself in its real life to reporting extensively on activities and events surrounding *The Sopranos*. The show became a way for the paper to laud cultural and economic life in New Jersey, and it followed each new turn in the series and its production history with great relish. The *Star-Ledger* talked endlessly about the content of the show (there were short reflections and analyses of each episode as it appeared, and then compendium assessments of overall seasons), but it was also fascinated by the show as an economic phenomenon, a good one for the state's revenues. Significantly, the reportage on *The Sopranos* in the *Star-Ledger* often took the narrative form of depicting a problem (for example, after the chaos of Harrison, and in fear of promulgating negative stereotypes, one New Jersey county refused to give a license for an on-location shoot) and then recounting a triumph over that setback (other communities in the state rushed in and affirmed their support of *The Sopranos* and of the revenues it could bring in if the show was shot in their vicinity). With great relish and great pride, the *Star-Ledger* presented the coming of *The Sopranos* to New Jersey as a regional success story, and it linked itself inexorably to the show and its accomplishment. The show's cultural rewards rebounded to the newspaper, too.

Across the river, a *New York Times* article from January 23, 2000, reported on the large number of business people and New Jersey residents who had written HBO to offer up their homes and stores to *The Sopranos*.[5] The article is particularly revealing, as it demonstrates the extent to which everyday citizens seemed to show themselves willing to do almost anything to share in the success of *The Sopranos*, even to degrees that might seem ghoulish: thus, the marketing director from a New Jersey branch of the fairly yuppie-ish lifestyle-cum-hardware-store Brookstone is reported to have written to the show's producers to encourage them in a bit of product placement, in which Tony Soprano would "stab someone in the eyes with a BBQ fork." Ultimately, the purveyor of upscale home items had to be content with a simpler placement: Tony used a Brookstone bathroom scale, although not to hit anybody with, but just to check his weight. In such a context of ordinary bystanders looking for revenue streams everywhere, and with regard to a show that was so often about schemes and scams, it seems appropriate that some of these attempts to pull benefit from a show about the economically parasitical world of the Mafia appear themselves to have been cons. The *New York Times* article ends by noting how the informal economy of ordinary citizens benefiting from the show tipped quickly and easily into illegality: as the *Times* explains, "Several people paid 'fees' to a man who posed as an agent registering locations for the show. As truth imitates television, it turns out it was a scam. The crew of 'The Sopranos' and the police are on the man's case. Maybe they just ought to put him in the show."

The Sopranos itself dramatizes the influences and byways of money's flow, both licit and illicit, and the ways it can make or break the fortunes of those who would hope to participate in it. Money forms a lattice of complicated interconnection, with success for some dependent on failure for others. For example, I've noted how the depiction of compulsive gambler Davie's descent into ruin is accompanied by an allusion to the ways that at another point in the food chain (pun intended), restaurateur Artie benefits indirectly from the process, albeit only for a while.

Even more ambitiously, a montage from the last episode of season 2—in which a high school graduation party for Meadow Soprano is intercut with scenes that vary from money pouring in for the Soprano gang, to a heroin addict being shooed out of the lobby of a motel Tony had seized partial control of in the previous season, to a man hawking fake telephone cards for another scam Tony's involved in—dramatizes economics as an ever-expanding network that eventually will draw everyone into its sphere of influence for better or for worse, for economic advancement or decline. And the reference to an incident back in the *first* season shows that the networks of economic insinuation extend themselves in great measure both spatially *and* temporally. The consequences of Tony's takeover of the motel are followed out to their bitter conclusion months later.

No doubt, the montage has other functions than just to reveal the spread of money's influence, both positive and negative. For example, the intercutting of a family celebration with scenes of Mafia growth and self-aggrandizement harkens back to a similar kind of montage at the end of Coppola's *Godfather* films—scenes of crime interwoven with family rites of passage, usually religious—even as *The Sopranos'* version concentrates not on the rise to power but on a less assured and somewhat bittersweet attempt to hold on to what one already has. As Tony recounts to therapist Jennifer Melfi in the pilot episode of the series, he has the feeling of having come in at the downwardly spiraling end of something. The *Godfather* films, especially the first two, are about consolidation of power, whereas *The Sopranos* is often concerned with the desperate, even fraught, maintenance of the economic power one has already achieved.

But one curious detail from the montage that ends season 2 hints that *The Sopranos* might be getting at something other than just a postmodern allusion to the Coppola films: the *Sopranos* montage begins with an anonymous figure, who figures nowhere else in the story, paying his money and walking into a porn theater in a seedy part of a city.

Every other part of the montage shows someone, usually identifiable from his or her role in the story, who elsewhere has been seen to have a direct connection to Tony Soprano's activities. Where the *Godfather*

The anonymous spectator in the big city.

films had used their montages to depict immediate actions undertaken by the Michael Corleone Mob against those particular figures who stood directly in the way of its ascent to power, *The Sopranos* suggests here, in the image of anonymity, a more expansive image of control, one which can go beyond direct influence on identified figures in the immediate orbit of Tony's power to impact ordinary citizens so removed from a direct sphere of action and influence that they remain unidentified in the scene. "I believe in America," the first voice-over in *The Godfather* had declared, and the fact that the assertion came from a man paying court on Don Corleone (asking him, in particular, for vengeance against the violators of his daughter) had already hinted at the entanglements of criminality and America's foundational identity. But *The Sopranos* goes further, to offer the image of an everyday life where nothing would not be influenced by market and exploitation. And not just in its criminal moments: when Tony talks, in the famous episode "College," with his daughter Meadow about his being in the Mafia, she replies that it isn't the worst thing, contrasting him favorably with advertisers for the big tobacco companies and with morally dubious corporate lawyers. Endlessly, too, the show depicts hucksters and hawkers of all sorts of products, as if to insist on a world where everything is marketed all the time: for example, there is, in the background of the show—literally in the background, since it is often on a television screen playing unwatched behind the mobsters—the running motif of the commercials for the miraculous penile-enhancement procedure of Dr. Fried, who elsewise helps Tony in various schemes and plays in his big poker game.

Certainly, both an unofficial tie-in like the *Sopranos* bus tour and the *Sopranos* television show itself are something more than just a dire and desperate depiction of the ravages of avaricious capital. Earlier in this book, I invoked the jokester funniness of the series. We need to recognize the values of game, playfulness, and aesthetic adventure in such a show. But it undoubtedly also is the case that the relation between the offer of aesthetic playfulness and participation in economic relations is not one of full opposition so much as complicated interaction. Aesthetic playfulness becomes precisely a marketable commodity. The common rejoinder to serious analysis of light popular culture is that such culture is "just entertainment," but then it becomes all the more compelling to wonder why we would invest—monetarily, psychically, emotionally—so much in something "just" that. As Silvio Dante clarifies, right after Tony gives a speech to his gang about the pyramidal flow of money and shit (the former should flow up to them, the latter flows down to all the losers), two businesses have been particularly recession-proof across historical time: entertainment and crime. That, in the case of entertainment, money would flow so strongly to something we claim to take so lightly is itself a potential paradox worthy of explanation. At the beginning of *TV Living*, their study of the habits of television viewers, British television scholars Annette Hill and David Gauntlett note that television serves no basic necessity for humans' survival, yet fans of this or that show often talk nonetheless as if it did: for example, they may claim that they will "die" if their preferred program is taken away from them.[6] This, then, is the question of the commodity's secret and our fetishizing of it: why do we commit an often substantial part of our lives to something that is just entertainment? Why do we need the culture that we gravitate to (or that gravitates toward us)? There is no natural and inevitable fashion by which the television show *The*

Sopranos meets its audiences—both its original HBO one and the ones that come to it in other guises—and is consumed.

The Sopranos and its tie-ins, both official and not, at least render the cash relationship that subtends this consumption an explicit part of their subject matter. For example, the bus tour even makes the spending of cash a seductive part of the game itself and coats it with a thrill of surreptitiousness not unlike the frisson that so many of the characters in the show gain from the flow of money gotten by illegal means. Hence, the tour ends with a visit to the real-life strip club that serves as the infamous Bada Bing on the show, but before the weary tourists are allowed in, the tour guide goes through a complicated story about how he has to go in first and talk things over with the owner to make sure that it's a good moment for the tour to be showing up. Perhaps his warnings are true, but they also create the dramatic setup for a sense of entrance into an illicit, shadowy world where secret arrangements and covert codes apply. There's the frisson of the taboo here, which makes the investment in the tour seem eminently worthwhile.

Once the go-ahead for the tourists to enter the morally murky site of the strip joint has been given, there are further ploys of seduction, ones more directly tied to monetary expenditure. For example, there's the ATM whose presence is signaled at several reprises by the guide and which gives only one-dollar bills (since that's what regular customers stuff in the G-strings of the dancers—a sad reminder of just how meager the regular profits of the women must be). Even more a part of the game of seductive economics is the use of a pool table at the back of the club—near the back rooms where, on the show, one might imagine Tony and his cronies would be plotting their schemes of illegality—as a display where one can buy Bada Bing products (such as shot glasses, branded bottles of wine, and T-shirts) and other *Sopranos* tie-ins, once again all declared to have no official connection to or recognition by HBO. One of the purchasable items that, to my mind, sums up this informal economy and its connection to a jokey theatricality that enables one to play with popular culture is a DVD entitled *Sopranos Unauthorized*, which sports an additional reiteration on both front and back that it is "not authorized by HBO" (again, the frisson of the illicit). A review of the DVD at amazon.com fairly accurately sums up this offering:

The Bing doing its thing.

Cheesier than a double-thick slice from Pizzaland, Sopranos Unauthorized lives up to its title as a goombah's tour of New Jersey filming locations for HBO's hugely popular Mafia series. With no obligations to discretion or production values, this homespun documentary takes the low road of a tacky wiseguy, following host John Fiore ("Gigi Cestone" from two seasons of *The Sopranos*) and his mock-bimbo girlfriend (Marie Ruffalo) as they limousine around Jersey, visiting nearly every *Sopranos* location, from the aforementioned Pizzaland, to Vic and Patti Recchia's plush mansion (a.k.a. Tony Soprano's house) in North Caldwell, to the infamous Satin Dolls club, better known to *Sopranos* fans as the Bada-Bing. Good-natured and sporadically amusing, the tour is laced with behind-the-scenes video of *Sopranos* filming, and interviews with some of the show's whacked co-stars, like Vincent Pastore ("Big Pussy") and David Proval ("Richie Aprile"). It's all about as tasteful as leopard-skin pants at a funeral, but hey . . . it's Jersey!

The unauthorized DVD tie-in pulls together a number of aspects of *The Sopranos'* open-ended circulation as cultural commodity: the actor who is no longer part of *The Sopranos* (Fiore's character ignominiously died on the toilet) but who still hopes to profit informally from it; the jokey take on the show (the approach here is definitely not one of high seriousness!); the illicit appeal of entry into a morally dubious world (we are being offered surreptitious glimpses of behind-the-scenes activity and doing so in "unauthorized" fashion); the seductive display of things (the limo, the bimbo sidekick, the Bada Bing dancers, even the lavish house that the bus tour doesn't take you to but which the DVD spends a lot of time at); and the sheer degree of aesthetic roughness (in contrast to the show itself, the DVD is distinguished by low production values; likewise, many of the personal Web sites by actors from the show have an unhewn amateurishness to them, as if to emphasize they are not the glossy product of slick HBO itself).

Tie-ins that assert their "unauthorized nature" can partake of the economic experience of *The Sopranos* while maintaining an air of independence from the marketplace of the big media firm. Revealingly, for example, some scholarly studies of the series, such as David Simon's *Tony Soprano's America*, Glen O. Gabbard's *The Psychology of The Sopranos*, and Regina Barreca's anthology, *A Sitdown with the Sopranos*, all take pains on their front covers to issue the disclaimer that their book "was not prepared, licensed, approved, or endorsed by any entity involved in creating or producing *The Sopranos* television series." No doubt one should take the publishers at their word and imagine that there is a relative autonomy of academic writing from the objects of media production it addresses. But it's interesting to note that the academic books' disclaimers of economic relationship to the show's production—which are also then declarations of scholarly purity—bear a strong resemblance to the declaration of independence on the Web site for the *Sopranos* bus tour: "The Sopranos and all related characters are the property of Brillstein-Grey Entertainment, Sopranos Productions, Inc., Chase Films and Home Box Office, a Division of Time Warner Entertainment Company, L.P. On Location Tours, Inc. is in no way associated with the aforementioned companies. The sceneontv.com content is assumed to be within the realm of the Public's Right of 'Fair Use' and no copyright infringement is intended."

Each in their own way, the books on *The Sopranos*, the bus tour, and the illicit DVD bought at the "Bada Bing" all participate in the informal economy around the authorized transactions the show engages in. Significantly, at least one article, from the *Star-Ledger*, about the explosion of books on *The Sopranos*, lists the academic titles along with the cookbook, the script collections, and the self-help volumes by the actors, as if they all easily are lumped together in one promotional universe.[7] In some cases, for the academic writer, participation in this informal economy can be nicely profitable: an article in the *New York Times* notes that Open Court Publishing, the publisher of *The Sopranos and Philosophy: I Kill, Therefore I Am*, has hit it quite big with its Popular Culture and Philosophy series, whose *The Simpsons and Philosophy: The D'Oh of Homer* has sold more than 200,000 copies and whose *The Matrix and Philosophy: Welcome to the Desert of the Real* eventually hit the *Times* bestseller list (at the same time, the article notes that series editor William Irwin decided not to pursue volumes on *Friends* and *E.R.* "because they lacked the basic depth and literacy for a thorough philosophical discourse").[8]

In the case of *Sopranos* tie-ins such as the scholarly books, money is

sometimes talked about but in ambiguous ways that don't always acknowledge its sway. Take, for instance, David Simon's sociological book,
Tony Soprano's America, which basically offers a description of the ills
of today's America with interposed comments on the means by which
the television series supposedly reflects those ills.[9] Simon argues that
the show taps into the social concerns of its U.S. viewers because its
images of a power that is voraciously out of control speak to the general
sense today's Americans have of living in morally dubious times. Simon
asserts that in a historical moment both of the consolidation of corporations into vast empires and of the temptation by many corporations into
shady activity (as demonstrated by the very public spectacle of government prosecution of corporate malfeasance), *The Sopranos* can only inevitably be a relevant, resonant show. That may be the case, but it is then
interesting to note that, among Simon's many mentions of the imperial
wielding of increasingly consolidated corporate power, one searches in
vain for any mention of the entertainment industry, and in particular of
Time Warner, the corporation that owns HBO (the latter also remaining
unmentioned). For Simon, the show dramatizes the contradictions and
corruptions of industry in America today, but he can only make it do
so if he disavows its own nature as industrial product, as media object
marketed and sold by a large-scale firm. Within such a perspective, the
show comments on business practices in America, but it is never itself
taken to be a business practice.

Ironically, Simon's approach echoes one way in which media firms
sometimes promote their own products. They will laud their creations
as somehow special and somehow above the mere requirements of the
marketplace. This itself roots the products all the more in the market
by selling their distinction, their "quality." *The Sopranos* matters to its
consumers but it matters no less to its producers. The next pages deal
with the show's function as a product of HBO and even of a larger media
landscape.

15 Cable and the Economics of Experimentation

If, as it moves into the culture at large, *The Sopranos* is endlessly up for grabs, the process of appropriation and exploitation starts with its initial identity as a specialty series on cable TV. For HBO, for instance, *The Sopranos* is no one thing and has no one identity, but is rather a product to be fashioned and refashioned according to the potentials of the market.

In an essay on the fuzzy borders between documentary and reality TV—which includes discussion, particularly pertinent for our purposes, of the ways HBO exploits that fuzziness to market its wares across multiple media platforms and to multiple audiences—television scholar Susan Murray examines how the ambiguity between documentary and reality TV comes not just from objective qualities *in* specific works from the two genres that can make them resemble each other (for example, the use of handheld cameras). There is also a fuzziness in the distribution, promotion, and exhibition of the works that derives from the ways in which sponsoring institutions (the television networks; the conduits of advertising and marketing; the scholars, reviewers, and other arbiters of taste) position the works and create diverse expectations for them. In her words, "There must be characteristics beyond narrative form and aesthetic qualities that help critics define such programs. Indeed, much of our evaluative process is based on the belief that documentaries should be educational or informative, authentic, ethical, socially engaged, independently produced, and serve the public interest, while reality TV programs are commercial, sensational, popular, entertaining, and potentially exploitative and/or manipulative."[1] In like fashion, HBO uses programs like *Real Sex* or *America Undercover*—which promise a direct glimpse into some real activities, albeit frequently taboo or curious ones, of everyday people—as a means to bring in audiences through tantalizing glimpses of daring subject matter given relevance and immediacy through the claim of documentary truth. The upscale spectator who might find a sensationalistic documentation of raunchy sexuality to be unworthy of attention can come to value scandalous sex when it is presented in the guise of valuable insight into a reality of the world.

Freed, as a subscriber cable service, from the FCC constraints around obscenity and not caught up in PBS's public service mandate, HBO can be more explicit around sexuality, and it promotes cultural fare that plays on multiple connotations of "mature": challenging, serious, but also sexually daring and promising entry into illicit worlds. In Murray's words, "The very nature of HBO's premium channel payment structure allows the network to escape the cultural vilification and calls for censorship that plague broadcast and some basic cable stations. Coupled with an audience who wishes to see itself as more capable, responsible, and mature than the average television viewer, this creates an ideal setting for the presentation of 'tasteful,' but possibly lurid nonfictional programming. Over the past decade, HBO has aggressively marketed itself as a quality network for the paying television connoisseur" (42–43). And Murray goes on to note that fictional programming at HBO falls within the same strategies of marketing "mature" culture across a range of qualities: as she puts it, "Through its original programming, such as *The Sopranos*, *Six Feet Under*, and *Sex and the City*, the cable network has refashioned liberal notions of 'quality' television to include 'adult' content" (49). HBO, as Murray suggests, is particularly adept at keeping the identity of its products fuzzy to maintain a variety of appeals across a variety of consumer cultures.

HBO may try to offer its products as alternatives to the supposed crassness of commercially sponsored network television—as in its slogan "It's not TV, it's HBO"—and insist on their cultural distinction from the marketplace, but that very insistence is a way of marketing its products as special and specially desirable. HBO's participation in the marketplace of media starts with the ironic fact that premium cable television actually bears a more direct connection to a consumer's outlay of capital than does advertiser-sponsored broadcast television: after all, a premium cable channel like HBO relies directly on subscription fees, whereas the consumer pays for traditional over-the-air television indirectly, through the purchase of the products that figure in the ads and, increasingly, are placed conspicuously within the shows. It may even be the case that for all its talk of quality and distinction, HBO is potentially more reliant on sheer numbers of spectators than the networks, for whom demographic factors become as important as quantity.

Specifically, what matters to HBO, despite its rhetoric of upscale appeal, is as much to have a large number of subscribers as it is to attract a particular quality of spectator. In a classic analysis of the networks' increasing interest in demographic distinctions, television scholar Jane Feuer studied how in the 1970s the networks came to believe that their goal was less to reach as many viewers as possible than it was to catch the right kind of viewer, one increasingly interested in notions of quality lifestyle through commodities and with the disposable income to follow through on that interest.[2] Clearly, HBO also tries to distinguish a "quality audience" and to claim it is serving that demographic particularly well. HBO's frequent self-representation as a quality service gives the channel cultural capital in the marketplace. For example, Emmy nominations and wins are quite important to the channel for the sort of prestige that brings in new subscribers. The rhetoric of privilege does help it target its preferred consumer, who may buy more than just a subscription to the cable service. For example, HBO heavily pushes its DVD sets and other ancillary items; the company has, for instance, brought out a deluxe DVD set for *The Sopranos* at close to $400. But with no need to please advertisers, HBO can engage in broader-based marketing through sex, sleaze, and violence as much as uplifting quality.

Interestingly, in any number of interviews, HBO and Time Warner executives declare that the direct financial impact of shows like *The Sopranos* is not easily calculable, since revenues for HBO are often interwoven with cable subscription fees that cover many other channels. That the specific influence of particular shows on the consumer's decision to subscribe is difficult to detail is no doubt partially true, but only partially. For example, there would be noticeable upward spikes in subscriber numbers when a season of *The Sopranos* was about to air, and downward spikes when a season finished out and subscribers would cancel the service. In fact, media companies such as HBO can track decisions to subscribe in various ways. For example, they will set up campaigns that tie a new subscription to some gift, such as free installation, which, when asked for, gives the company data on factors that went into the choice to subscribe. In the case of *The Sopranos*, in particular, as an article in *Multichannel News* clarifies, there were numerous subscriber campaigns designed to give HBO feedback on subscribers and their motivations for signing up. Thus, for the third season, HBO had cable companies that carried the show send out close to 40 million pieces of mail about HBO subscription, most of which offered additional benefits that had explicitly to be asked for (and thus could be tracked). For example, in some localities, new subscribers could enter contests that might win them prizes from "Carmela's Kitchen" or a trip to Italy or to New York's Little Italy, while elsewhere the potentially new subscriber could ask for trial months of HBO service to be activated on top of existing cable service. This was the strategy, for instance, of Time Warner Cable in Los Angeles, whose campaign slogan was "We'll Make You an Offer You Can't Refuse" and which obviously had an investment in letting its parent company know how its local cable offering was doing in attracting customers.[3] More recently, HBO has put clips of its new comedy series, *Flight of the Conchords*, on YouTube so it could track the number of plays from visitors of that Web site.

At the same time, HBO executives would frequently adopt a rhetoric that denied that the cultural appeal of a series like *The Sopranos* could be calculated. *The Sopranos* tapped, they appeared to be saying, into public consciousness in a spontaneous fashion, and HBO's own targeting and marketing had little to do with its success. Take, for instance, the stance of former HBO chief Chris Albrecht in an interview he granted to *Multichannel News*:

MCN: Is *The Sopranos* the highest-profile thing that's ever come to HBO, and how has it affected subscriber acquisition and retention? Where does it stack up in HBO's pantheon?

Albrecht: You know when you turn on CNBC and the guys are talking about what happened on *The Sopranos* episode last night, you have something that is invading the culture in a big way. You can't quantify that impact and compare it to anything else. Again, whether positive subscriber growth or retention is a result of that, we actually have no idea. Obviously, we're happy with the show and we hope that it's on HBO for many more years.[4]

Significantly, if the use of advertising has always given the commercial networks the reputation of crass commercialism and enabled a channel like HBO to garner a reputation above that of the marketplace, *The Sopranos* is not bereft of product placement. Quite the contrary, it is filled with named commodities. HBO prided itself on not being paid by manufacturers for such informal advertising of their items, but the show benefited indirectly by saving money on props, including the luxury cars which were offered by the companies for product placement. Predictably, companies flocked to the opportunity to have their items show up in the episodes, although some advertisers desisted because of the show's violence and/or sexuality. Predictably, too, some of these product placements are accompanied by dialogue that directly sings the virtues of the product. For instance, Tony attributes his ability to emerge unscathed from his car accident while out with Adriana to the solidity of the brand of vehicle he was driving.[5]

In its television broadcasts, *The Sopranos'* mutable identity can go beyond its initial mooring at HBO. It's revealing that David Chase originally tried to market the show to network television, with Fox nibbling at a spec script but then demurring when they decided the show was too rough. Certainly, if *The Sopranos* had aired on a commercial network, it would have had to be something other than what it ended up being on HBO. For example, Chase has noted in numerous interviews that network executives had asked the show to be shot on the West Coast, with generic neighborhoods and sets standing in for New Jersey. There was also the suggestion that the lead needed to be played by a classically handsome actor, and Anthony LaPaglia was evidently a network preference. While Chase bridles at the idea of such accommodations to the networks' needs for broad-based appeal, it is interesting to speculate on the very fact that it was ever imagined, by him and others, that *The*

Sopranos might have ended up as a network show. It's tempting to think about what it would have been like had *The Sopranos* had been called *The Family Man*—as was once bandied about—or if "Tony" had ended up "Tommy" Soprano (from David Chase's love of the James Cagney character in *Public Enemy*), or if Steven Van Zandt or David Proval, who ended up as Richie, had tested well in their auditions for the role of Tony (these what-if stories are unconfirmed). The show's identity, like so many cultural works, is perfected from a string of compromises and revisions.

But beyond speculation about *The Sopranos* that might have been, we can also wonder about cable *futures* for the show. It is not clear, for instance, if the show is having the same resonance following its move into syndication on the basic cable channel A&E. In the spring of 2004, there had been heated battles among cablers (as the industry trade journal *Variety* refers to cable companies) for the syndication rights to the show, and A&E won the bid by proposing more money than had ever been offered for the syndication of a television show.[6] The strongest competitor had been TNT, and if that subsidiary of Time Warner had landed syndication rights, it might well have been the case that more of the connotations of the HBO brand would have stayed with the show in its new manifestation, especially since a multimedia company like Time Warner has been particularly effective in using various of its subsidiaries to cross-promote one another's products (so that the HBO/TNT connection might have been insisted on in ways that gave to the latter some of the quality aura of the former). In the case of A&E, there were potentially new connotations: originally a somewhat high-arts channel—for which *Masterpiece Theatre* is one model and for which a framing of *The Sopranos* as high-class moral parable might have then been appropriate—A&E increasingly is reshaping itself as a hip purveyor of classy entertainment for a younger, urban audience, rather than the older, established working professional in a prestige job.

One change to the syndicated version of *The Sopranos* comes from the fact that, although a basic cable offering such as A&E is not beholden to FCC decency regulations, the channel is advertiser-supported and does have to worry about violence, nudity, and obscenity. Evidently, HBO had all along been shooting a version of *The Sopranos* that was not as explicit as the one that ran on premium cable, and A&E chose to play that expurgated version, jokingly referred to as *Sopranos*-lite. In this respect, it is also worth noting, as *Star-Ledger* reporter Alan Sepinwall points out, that "most 'Sopranos' episodes run 50–60 minutes, while advertiser-supported dramas [such as those that a channel like A&E would typically play] run 43 minutes or less," which leads to a cut-down version of *The Sopranos* for basic cable.[7] Again, one can speculate on the ways a doctored version of *The Sopranos* on A&E would resonate differently than in the broadcasts of it on HBO. There are, in fact, several hilarious pastiches of a *Sopranos*-lite in circulation on the Web in such venues as YouTube. One has the mobsters trying to use the f-word, only to find that innocuous words like "fugalicious" or "fairy dust" come lilting out of their mouths.

But even on HBO, *The Sopranos* had no one stable identity.[8] Indeed, despite the fact that it is this one series that in many ways has now come to define the HBO brand and that set the standard that other HBO offerings now have to strive after,[9] one can find common mention in industry trade papers of the assumption that the series only somewhat arbitrarily or accidentally came to be associated with HBO and was never really the quintessential or representative product of the HBO brand. Thus, in the hiatus between season 5 and season 6, newspapers and trade journals were spilling lots of ink over the fact that HBO seemed to have committed itself in the meantime to the anthropology of a very different world than that of the Mafia—namely, Hollywood, and the entertainment business more generally, to which it was devoting new series such as *Unscripted, Entourage, The Comeback*, and an import from the U.K., *Extras*, about the unsung rank of secondary actors in media production. While some of the talk about HBO's fascination with the behind-the-scenes side of the entertainment business asserted that the channel had lost its way by becoming so navel-gazing, it was as common for critics and media analysts to argue that Hollywood self-reflection and self-scrutiny were perhaps more defining of HBO's content than the uniqueness of *The Sopranos*. For example, an article in the "On TV" column of the *Los Angeles Times*, by columnist Paul Brownfield, bore the pointed title "At HBO, the bonfire of the vanity projects" and argued

Afterlives: A&E *Sopranos*.

that the newest crop of Hollywood navel-gazing shows at the channel actually had a longer lineage at HBO and a stronger role in defining the channel than did *The Sopranos*; this history started with an earlier HBO entertainment industry–focused series, *The Larry Sanders Show*, and the more recent *Curb Your Enthusiasm*. In Brownfield's estimation, the success of these series about the entertainment business provided HBO with resonant subject matter but also, and even more, with an attractively simple mode of production that made it easy to generate new shows: as Brownfield put it, "Because [*Curb Your Enthusiasm*'s Larry] David, seemingly just by virtue of being himself, made it all look so easy and self-evident and, most especially, creatively rewarding, he made getting a semi-autobiographical show on HBO feel like the ultimate expression of the freedom to do what you wanted to do."[10] In this respect, Brownfield could argue that Larry David indeed sums up the dominant trend of HBO programming: "The ultimate model for the HBO auteur is not David Chase, a respected series creator but not at the top of anyone's list before HBO picked up his oft-rejected pilot of 'The Sopranos'; it's Larry David, who was fabulously wealthy after the success of 'Seinfeld' [for which he had been a producer-writer] and came to film a little special on his return to stand-up comedy. That little special ended up being a special about the fear of doing a special. The special on the fear of doing a special led to a series, 'Curb Your Enthusiasm,' about being Larry David." In other words, for Brownfield, HBO was obsessed with the image of the media business and let that obsession dominate (dangerously, in his view) its production slate and its content.

To be sure, a number of HBO series have taken a distance from Hollywood self-reflexivity, some by moving into a past long before the rise of media industries (for example, the Western *Deadwood* or the ancient epic *Rome*), others by claiming to represent a gritty real world that possesses a street-tough authenticity far from the falsity and artificiality within Hollywood hypocrisy (for example, *Oz* or *The Wire*). Revealingly, two of HBO's biggest non–entertainment industry hits, *Sex and the City* and *The Sopranos*, offered a sort of symbolic declaration of independence from the Hollywood world by setting their stories on the East Coast, yet including episodes where some of their characters flirted with the seductions of Hollywood lifestyle, only ultimately to reject what they saw as its superficiality, its dishonesty, and its fundamental venality. It's worth recalling that David Chase actually thought for a moment, albeit a very brief one, of setting his story not among Mafiosi but among entertainment business executives. But as he explained sardonically in a public seminar at the Museum of Television and Radio, "If there's anybody that people would have less sympathy for than a mobster, it would be a TV producer."[11]

It might well be that by its setting in New Jersey, rather than in New York, *The Sopranos* was self-reflexively raising issues of its own relative independence from Hollywood. Like some independent producer who has gone off with his team to be relatively free of the influence of the home office, Tony sets out to maintain a site for control and creative management of his crew located away from the big-city seats of power (in this case, New York, the country's other big media metropolis). In its narratives of subservience to the powers that be versus declarations of independence, *The Sopranos* would give voice to its own status as an uncertain object in the dialectic of business and culture.[12]

In this respect, a work like *The Sopranos* is not just a product of a culture industry, but an allegory of it. And the uncertain identity of the series may itself contribute to its circulation in the market of entertainment and culture. We might argue, in fact, that a certain degree of *in*stability in its products is endemic to HBO's operations. Some of this instability no doubt derives from market unpredictability (how to know, for instance, which new show will work or not?) and suggests that HBO is not always in control of things (for example, HBO announced cancellation in 2005 of its Lisa Kudrow behind-the-entertainment-scene show, *The Comeback*, after a mere half-season). But instability can also be a way for a media company like HBO to keep options open by using the ambiguity of identity in its products as a way of trying out and determining marketing strategies and possible fits between its cultural offerings and particular demographics of audience. In this respect, an individual show like *The Sopranos* needs to be understood within the larger context of a media industry that is endlessly testing the waters of social taste at large.

From its start, indeed, HBO has had to be an operation of resilient refashioning, always seeking new means to generate cash flow from culture's flow. In fact, it is possible to think of HBO as an *experimental* arm of Time Warner: experimental not only in the often daring nature of its shows, but also in its economic practices and media operations. A 2003 article in the London *Economist* explains how HBO takes up its special place within the larger context of Time Warner (at that time AOL Time Warner): "To the untrained eye, HBO might look like just another bit of the sprawling AOL Time Warner empire. But it is fiercely independent and has carved out a distinct identity. Employing only 1,770 people, less than 2% of the group total, HBO is physically and operationally removed from even the group's other TV activities, notably Warner Brothers in Los Angeles. That nobody ever suggests merging New York–based HBO into the other TV studios points to its strength as autonomous operation. The secret has been twofold: the creation of a small boutique-like identity within a huge corporation; and the granting of creative independence within a tightly controlled operation."[13]

It is no doubt highly useful and highly rewarding for Time Warner to have a branch that can seem to luxuriate in experimental independence. Consolidation doesn't necessarily lead to branches of large firms all operating in the same fashion and producing a single sort of cultural product. Some of the biggest attempts at converging media across platforms haven't yet seemed to work as planned—we might indeed remember that HBO's parent company, Time Warner, was once "AOL Time Warner"—and big firms may encourage diversity within their fold as much as conformity. Some media giants may give some subsidiaries a relative independence in which they can test products and strategies that it would be risky for the umbrella company as a whole to (as of yet) make its guiding philosophy.

One function of a multiplicity of internally managed branches for a big media company is that it allows a flexibility of operations: if something doesn't work, there can always be a reallocation and new concentration of efforts elsewhere in the firm. And it can enable any one media product to move through the branches and be repurposed and refashioned for each of them (thus, for instance, *The Sopranos* is an HBO show, but it also manifests itself as a set of books published by Time Inc.). In this respect, the dropping of "AOL" from the name of the company doesn't mean an abandonment of a dream of digitalization of all electronic media, and here even a single show like *The Sopranos*, so seemingly unconcerned with new technology in its story world (Christopher, for example, has trouble learning to use a word processor on his laptop), has its role to play as an experiment in furtherance of digital convergence. Even with AOL no longer in its name, Time Warner continues to hold out a dream of convergence through the computer, and its moving-image products such as its television shows are a key component to be experimented on in the working out of that dream. That is, whatever their content and whatever their initial media platform (original film or television series), HBO productions are also intended to serve in a circulation of media into a digital realm. Thus, even AOL, while no longer named as central to the firm, became integral for a while to a new vision of media convergence with announcement of Time Warner plans to develop technologies for carrying Warner Bros. film and television and HBO programming through the AOL portal. The hope was that film and television programming could eventually be streamed and viewed on the Web through AOL as a portal.[14] Here, HBO's own success as a content creator was described as a model for AOL to emulate. In the words of a 2003 *New York Times* article, AOL "has shifted from its original business of selling access to the Internet to concentrate on selling access to a panoply of add-on programming and communication tools like video sports highlights and personalized instant-message cartoons, in search for its own counterpart to an HBO programming hit. 'People are always saying, where is your *Sopranos*?' Mr. Miller [chief executive at AOL] said. 'No one has it yet on the Internet. And we aren't there yet, but we are going in the right direction.'"[15] Ultimately, the plan appears to have petered out—at least for the moment—and the AOL site does not really function as a special entryway to HBO, or Time Warner, product. But the dream of convergence still drives the media industries.

HBO, with its original programming and its complex array of tie-in practices and ancillary marketing, serves as a laboratory in which Time Warner strategies are tested: Which ones enable successful convergence? Which ones work best in relative independence while continuing to generate important revenue streams? For instance, although the producers of *The Sopranos* showed a classical veneration for cinema by shooting their series on celluloid (an aspect, perhaps, of what I analyzed earlier as quality television's envy of other media forms such as art cinema), theirs was also the first HBO series to have its film images transferred into a high-definition digital format in anticipation of the FCC-mandated conversion of television transmission standards to high definition. At the same time, high definition uses a wider aspect ratio than standard television, one much closer to the prevailing aspect ratio of cinema productions, and it thereby enables experiments in complex composition within the image. In other words, although it is a digital format, high-def can seem itself like a form of cinema that is superior to ordinary TV. This helps give *The Sopranos* an aura of cinematic resistance to standard television screen images cut off on both sides by pan-and-scan processes, and this increases the show's reputation with creative craftspeople who continue to hold out a model of cinema's aesthetic superiority over television.[16] Such transfer into the digital realm makes *The Sopranos* a supple commodity that can exist across media and means that its cinematic debt gives it only part of its identity. Likewise, HBO has recently been quite aggressive in pushing cable companies to offer its programming in video-on-demand (VOD) form: here, the imputed limitations of a subscriber model, such as the aforementioned difficulty in knowing why people subscribe and what they're actually watching on HBO, are traded for individual choices made by the viewer to look at this or that program in ways that are readily trackable. Thus, for example, it could be known instantaneously when viewers chose to order up an on-demand showing of a *Sopranos* episode. Media companies like Time Warner are hot to develop VOD, which promises to bring in more revenue when all the individual demands are added up than does monthly subscription which has to be spread across several shows and services. HBO has even encouraged some cable carriers to offer VOD versions free to subscribers to its regular premium cable service. This gives HBO two options: either to eventually start charging customers for their VOD once the free offer of it has seduced them to the service, or to attract new subscribers to premium subscription cable by using VOD as an attractive bonus. In such ways, HBO becomes a site in which a media company like Time Warner can test the waters for convergence and see what is working (and what is not).

Here, it may be to the parent company's advantage to not be stuck owning one of the major commercial networks (ABC, CBS, or NBC). While reports of the imminent demise of network television are no doubt exaggerated, network TV clearly no longer has the field of popular television to itself, and the large-scale media firms that own commercial networks seem willing to cordon them off, if need be, to reduce revenue bleeds and put their real attention elsewhere. Revealing in this respect may have been the move by media giant Viacom to pry its various media units apart rather than to encourage further synergy among them. Decision was made to split Viacom at the end of 2005 into two independent businesses: the one now called Viacom that combines film production (Paramount studio) and the operations of the very valuable and visible hip cable-TV channel MTV, the other carrying the moniker of the CBS Corporation and wedding that network TV company with lesser cable channels UPN (now itself merged into a joint venture with Time Warner's WB network called CW) and Showtime, along with its radio and a billboard-advertisements subsidiary. The official rhetoric at Viacom was that both offspring would still be loved by their parent, but it was clear that the original impetus for the split allowed Viacom to take distance from the weaknesses of network television (now imagined to be comparable to billboard advertising) and to focus attention on media enterprises imagined to be hipper and more youth-oriented (MTV cable and film). For our purposes, it matters that, within this arrangement, chosen to be the new head of Paramount Pictures was Brad Grey, one of the executive producers of *The Sopranos*, who was recruited for his success in putting together successes, like that series, which can move across multiple platforms of media and spectatorship and serve as a model for new media strategies of the twentieth-first century. In fall 2005, in fact, Grey managed to tempt two award-winning *Sopranos* writer-producers to the Paramount stable. And, as noted earlier, Grey recruited David Chase himself, after the end of *The Sopranos*, to develop a film project at Paramount. Grey moves easily from cable to film and works now within a structure that links the two, while finding standard over-the-air, advertiser-supported network television to be a thing apart. The corporate restructuring at Viacom revised the notion that film is an old-fashioned, even outdated, art form bereft of contemporary appeal and instead suggested a mediation of the older art of cinema and the new hip world of electronic media. For all its relative downplay of glitzy special effects and for all its invocation of an older, more tight-knit way of life giving way under the pressures of a new modernity, *The Sopranos*, by mediating cable television, cinema, and new media, while leaving the networks out of the picture, can serve then as a fitting symptom of cutting-edge New Hollywood.[17]

A 2003 article in the trade journal *Variety* noted that, in a number of ways, HBO could be considered "the single most valuable property in the vast AOL Time Warner portfolio" and well clarified how the subsidiary's particular strategies worked to produce special value for its parent company.[18] HBO, it was reported, accounted then for 17 percent of the conglomerate's sales, a very high figure for a single branch within a media giant, and it accomplished this in a number of ways: for example, production of distinctive original programming that could be easily associated with a brand; complementarily, a disinclination to engage in coproduction with other firms so as to not share profits but also, as importantly, to not dilute the brand (such 100 percent self-financing of productions tends to be the case more with HBO television than with its movies, which are indeed sometimes coproduced); and concerted attention to the computer revolution and digitalization of media products (hence, as noted, HBO's strong interest in turning its hit shows into DVD packages and in increasing cable offerings of VOD).

In its early days, HBO worked to achieve brand and product differentiation and spectator fidelity through special offerings primarily in cinema, sports, and sex (as also was the case, with sex especially, of the early efforts of Showtime, its cable competitor).[19] While it has not abandoned any of these, it has increasingly moved into upscale regions of culture through push-the-envelope comedy and artsy original programming in the form of original feature films and episodic series.[20] Sports has come to matter less as sports-specialty channels like ESPN have learned to target that niche audience. Cinema, while still quite central to HBO's schedule, has lost some importance as VCRs and DVD players make frequent replaying of a film title, which was an early staple of HBO, less attractive and as other distribution practices—such as, for example, video-on-demand and DVD-by-mail services such as Netflix—have provided alternative means by which films can enter the domestic space. Sex remains a staple of HBO—especially after the FCC decided, post–Janet Jackson's Super Bowl halftime "wardrobe malfunction," to crack down on nudity on network television—but increasingly it has been centered less in raunchy "reality shows" that purport to give voyeuristic and exoticizing glimpses at weird practices and more in narrativizations of sexuality within ostensible "quality programming." The fact that, predictably perhaps, *The Sopranos* "inspired" a multiepisode porn series on DVD, *The Sopornos*, seems almost beside the point, since the HBO show itself would often push the representation and discussion of randy sex practices in daringly blunt and open-ended directions.

At the very least, sensationalistic HBO shows like *Real Sex* or *The Sopranos* could, each in their own way, play on the promise of a voyeuristic glimpse into curious, taboo, and daring lifestyles. To be sure, not all of the voyeurism has to do with sexuality: the David Lynch–inspired HBO series *Carnivàle* (2003–2005) tried to reach the urban sophisticate audience through a simple weirdness that was supposed to be hip and watchable in and of itself, independent of meaning. But *Carnivàle* failed to generate the audience figures HBO hoped for and was cancelled. Perhaps the HBO audience needs its exoticism tempered by some degree of normalcy that can serve as a jumping-off point into the more outré side of things. *The Sopranos*, for example, would entice with voyeuristic glimpses into a steamy, sleazy, and sexy world, but it did so by introducing recognizable characters in that world and using some of them as conduits to it. Some "normal" characters, for instance, would brush up against the salacious way of life and flee it—for example, Artie Bucco and high school coach Hauser both got invited to the Bada Bing strip club but resisted the blandishments and sexual favors offered there (with the irony that the seemingly upright and stalwart Hauser had actually molested one of his students). At the same time, these scenes at the Bada Bing would tantalize by sometimes slightly out-of-focus images of the strippers in the background.

Other characters, like therapist Jennifer Melfi, clearly were fascinated by the dark side and wanted to peek in on it (as she did when she climbed up on a toilet to get a glimpse of the Sopranos' house from a neighbor's window). Like anthropology, and like some other HBO shows, both fiction and nonfiction, *The Sopranos* would take the viewer to a special community, with its own rites and symbolic practices, and it did so by using figures from the viewer's own world as guides whose voyeuristic desire for the exotic one could identify with.

HBO's success with *The Sopranos* has served as a spur to imitation and innovation at other channels, both cable and network alike. The show has become a target of complicated envy by other media companies, as was most visible in an ongoing feud between NBC and HBO when their most likely Emmy candidates, *The West Wing* and *The Sopranos*, endlessly went up against each other in the award nominations. Clearly, NBC wanted a hit show that would garner a similar reputation as that of *The Sopranos* for sharp dialogue, strong acting, and thematic resonance and that would bring artistic prestige to the network. *The West Wing* met those criteria for so-called quality TV, and it won out in the Emmy race early on, indicating (depending on one's position in regard to media prognostication) either the triumph of the networks or their last gasp in the new media environment. At the same time, however, *The Sopranos* had something that network fare such as *The West Wing* appeared to be lacking: a push-the-envelope, censors-be-damned insouciance and daring.

For one network, Fox, the answer was to try to render its own programming as particularly possessing HBO-like edginess. Thus, an article in the *Wall Street Journal* began with the assertion that "the broadcast networks are suffering from HBO envy" and explained how Fox directly poached from HBO to redo its own brand in a more outré direction: a top marketing expert from HBO, Roberta Mell, was recruited away specifically to make Fox promotional efforts work like HBO's. As the article explains, "Modeled after the movie-trailer style HBO uses for its promos, Fox's spots are quite a bit different from promos on other broadcast networks. They are long, often 60 seconds, an eternity in TV. And they give away much of the show's plots, a strategy called 'saga sell.'" Mell had her staff go on a retreat at the ultra-cool W Hotel in Los Angeles, where she had a room carpeted with grass sod and directed her creative staff to wear flip-flops and imagine they were out at the beach, in an effort to stimulate free creative thinking; one wonders if she had used similar tactics at edgy HBO.[21]

Meanwhile, for NBC itself, there were two opposing options in its rivalry with HBO, and it went for both simultaneously. On the one hand, NBC attacked the very premise that risqué and randy explicitness, such as it claimed HBO wallowed in, was to be equated with a notion of quality that courageously stood out from television blandness. Pushing the envelope could lead to vulgarity and dangerous immorality as much as to quality. Hence, as mentioned earlier, in an (in)famous incident, a tape that excerpted the violent death of the striptease dancer Tracee from a particularly explicit episode of *The Sopranos* went out from NBC CEO Bob Wright to media figures at NBC and elsewhere with a memo saying that there needed to be critical debate on the issue of violence and explicitness on television, for which the clip from HBO's show could serve as exhibit A. Wright claimed to want to clean up television, but most industry pundits suggested that he merely wanted to clear out HBO as a rival. On the other hand, and perhaps confirming Wright's tactic as mere ploy in a war against cable, NBC undertook at the same time to make its own violent, morally ambiguous, sexually daring gangster show: *Kingpin* (2003), which conveyed the tale of a Mexican drug-dealing family from the point of view of the family's patriarch. Even structurally, *The Sopranos* served as enviable model for the show. Thus, a *Wall Street Journal* article noted how *Kingpin* was setting out to emulate *The Sopranos'* concern with a broad tapestry of interrelation: "The pilot stands out for its dense and complicated tale; it is often hard to decipher the relationships among the many characters. This is part of cable-television fashion. Some executives feel such complexities reinforce audience loyalty by making viewers feel part of an exclusive club."[22] However, the project seemed doomed from the start. Where, for instance, David Chase could bring to *The Sopranos* the cultural pedigree of a Stanford University film education, a college diet of European art films, and a literary savvy (in interviews, he will drop names of literati such as Flaubert or Dostoevsky), *Kingpin* producer David Mills seemed to flaunt bad-boy anti-intellectualism. Thus, the same *Wall Street Journal* article described how Mills had pitched the show to executives as "Macbeth in the drug wars," but it went on to clarify that "Mr. Mills didn't actually read the play. 'I went out and bought Cliff Notes,' he says." And where David Chase could be seen to give his show ethnic authenticity through his Italian background (his father's name is DeCesare), Mills appeared to go out of his way to make it appear he was the wrong person to make a show about ethnically identified criminals in an era of multicultural sensitivity. Thus, in an interview with *Hispanic*, which was adopting a wait-and-see attitude toward the question of potentially damaging stereotypes on the show, Mills flaunted his ignorance of cultural specificity even as he tried to deck it out in the garb of deeper commitment to human truth: "I know nothing about Mexican culture, I've never been to Mexico and I don't speak Spanish. I had to make [the show] about universal issues—using Mexico as this big canvas to write about these palace intrigues and make it the modern-day equivalent of a medieval fable."[23] A midseason replacement that aired only six episodes, *Kingpin* was cancelled by the end of its first season.

More successful in the attempt to take away some of HBO's success with *The Sopranos* was ABC's decision to put a risqué nighttime soap opera with a broadly comedic tone and a kitsch sensibility, *Desperate Housewives*, into its Sunday 9 p.m. slot opposite *The Sopranos*. Sunday night has long had a mythic role in the history of American popular television as a prime moment of concerted and resonant domestic viewing. It is, for instance, a last moment before the work week reasserts itself, and it was thus, in the domestic mythology that subtends much of the history of television, a last moment of family, hearth, and home before everyone in the household had the next morning to go their separate ways (to the office, to school, to the invisibility of domestic labor in the home). Beloved classics like *The Ed Sullivan Show* and *Bonanza* still retain, for some older viewers, the memory of Sunday night rituals of communal television consumption. In recent years, HBO had taken to premiering its important new series on Sunday nights (and using its current hits as lead-ins to help viewers flow into the new offering), and there is some anecdotal evidence that *The Sopranos* reinvigorated communal viewing through *Sopranos* dinners rich in Italian food (there was also a rash of restaurants announcing *Sopranos* nights, although several of the establishments were issued "cease and desist" orders from HBO, which felt its branded show was being used for unauthorized profit).[24] HBO was making Sunday night a venue for fare that was hip, cutting-edge, and not always familial in orientation.[25]

But with *Sex and the City* and *Six Feet Under* finishing their runs, *Carnivàle* failing to take off, and *The Sopranos*, *Deadwood*, and *Curb Your Enthusiasm* all on hiatus, ABC's *Desperate Housewives* could insinuate itself, in 2004, into the Sunday-night schedule and become a smash hit of murder, mayhem, sex, and general bawdiness. Bereft of even the veneer of seriousness and artistic prestige that might be attributed to *The Sopranos* or the more staid *West Wing*, *Desperate Housewives* went for populist interest in the lurid and lascivious, and that seemed to resonate for a large viewership. Perhaps the ultimate sign of a changing of the guard was that if John Kerry could cite *The Sopranos* to try to score elitist points against George Bush, the Bush White House would reference *Desperate Housewives* in what some pundits saw as a desperate attempt to suggest that the Bush family had humor and could speak to ordinary people's tastes. Thus, there was a fair amount of press coverage in spring 2005 when First Lady Laura Bush made several jokes about using her Sunday evening to watch the ABC show and feeling like a "desperate housewife" herself, presumably because the early-to-bed George W. wouldn't stay up and engage in earthy hanky-panky with her.

After some middle Americans voiced concerns that the First Lady was being a little too bawdy and vulgar, it was hastily announced by White House staff that she actually didn't watch the salacious show, but knew about it only through hearsay. Whether or not Laura Bush had in fact ever looked at *Desperate Housewives*, it had a resonant reputation and had become conversation fodder (even at the highest political levels), and that too is a form of cultural consumption. In analyzing the circulation of a cultural product such as a television show, we thus need then to deal not only with those who directly consume it, but also those who don't even have direct contact with it but are aware of it—those who know its buzz and make use of it in conversation and other practices of everyday life and who thereby also participate in the circulation of the product through the culture and give it new resonant identities of their own making. Even commanders-in-chief and their spouses want in on the action of popular culture.

16 This Thing of Ours

In this respect, one of the weirdest fallouts from the non-ending ending of *The Sopranos* certainly has to be the video clip that was fabricated to announce the theme song of Hillary Clinton's ultimately doomed presidential campaign. Quickly disseminated across forms of popular new media such as YouTube, the video offered a parody of the *Sopranos* finale in which, in this case, Hillary waits in a diner to have a meal with her family while a disturbing disquiet floats around her (for example, Vince Curatola, the actor who had played Johnny Sack on the show, passes by her table with an air of appreciable menace). Clearly rushed into production to appear only a few weeks after the *Sopranos* nonending had caused such a stir, but also clearly made with care by producers who had rigorously studied the original and were able to reproduce its setups and its editing style, the Clinton clip has Hillary exchanging cutesy banter and domestic banalities with husband Bill while they wait for Chelsea, who is trying (like Meadow) to parallel park outside. Bill asks what song has been chosen for the campaign, and as Hillary starts to answer, the scene cuts to black (with, then, a title that directs the viewer to the Clinton campaign Web site—where it is announced that a Céline Dion song has won).

One of the motifs of *The Sopranos*, I've argued, is belatedness: everything has already been done, and there is no longer space for meaningful action. But, still, everyone wants to have a piece of the action, whatever the game being played is. But it is the power, then, of the show, in its savvy irony, that it also can make references to it in the culture at large often seem themselves belated and farcical, out of time and out of joint.

Of course, with its prescient and preemptive ability to roam through the happenings of the historical moment and incorporate mocking reference to them in its characters' conversations, *The Sopranos* had already somewhat anticipated Hillary Clinton's political ambitions with a scene in season 3 where the Mafia wives had discussed the Monica Lewinsky scandal and concluded that Hillary was a role model, since she had learned how, in their words, to get her own thing going.

The Clinton parody of the finale to *The Sopranos* is perhaps quite amusing, but it is also quite revealing, and even damning, about present-day political culture: Politics can interest the populace only when merged veritably with entertainment. Political salesmanship today can reduce a presidential candidate and a former president to shtick in their quest for political legitimacy. Politics has something shady about it (why, after all, is a *U.S.* presidential candidate opting for a song from a Canadian singer? Is it worth noting that in the opener to season 7, Tony engaged in dirty dealings with Canadian con artists?) and, in this case, might even suggest an identification of Hillary with her model here (Tony Soprano). Trying to prove herself cool and give herself street cred through a knowing pastiche reworking of a popular culture meme, Hillary Clinton may just have demonstrated something larger about the work of politics today and about how bizarre it has become, and also about how a certain kind of popular culture itself makes politics a parody or an act of kitsch or a joke in its own right.

History, a famous saying has it, repeats itself, but as farce. *The Sopranos* can contribute to the elaboration of a farcical world, one that extends beyond the fictions into reality at large. Here, even our leaders appear as ersatz characters living out fallen, cartoon lives in a cartoon land that renders all higher meaning and substance a joke. This is one effect of *The Sopranos* in our culture.

Notes

Prologue

1 "The *Sopranos* Goes Out with a Rating Bang," *New York Times*, June 13, 2007.

2 It's standard practice, when writing about a work of narrative art, to use the present tense, and I will generally follow that convention here. But when it is not awkward to do so, I will sometimes use the past tense to invoke the reality of a show that ended, that in its original form is no more. While *The Sopranos* will have new cultural roles to play, its initial role as a series, new on the landscape of contemporary media, is over. There is now a before and an after to the experience of *The Sopranos*, and my use of the past tense intends to capture that.

3 Nico Hines, "The *Sopranos* Final Episode: Look Away Now," *Times Online*, accessed at http://entertainment.timesonline.co.uk/tol/arts_and_enter tainment/tv_and_radio/article1916261.ece.

4 Robert Warshow, "The Gangster as Tragic Hero," *The Immediate Experience: Movies, Comics, Theatre, and Other Aspects of Popular Culture*, expanded edition (Cambridge, Mass.: Harvard University Press, 2001 [1962]), 97–103.

5 Actually, having a definitive ending in the diner wouldn't necessarily have precluded a sequel. When, while *The Sopranos* was still in its first run on HBO, I asked a scriptwriter for the series if the oft-floated idea of a movie indicated that the last episode would leave some points unresolved—and some characters standing—he replied (while clarifying that his answer should be taken to be revealing nothing about how the show actually would proceed in its final season) that David Chase was capable of using the movie to explore parts of the *Sopranos* world other than those in the last season's narratives: the movie could spin off to concentrate on other

gangsters or on earlier times in the lives of the Sopranos (*The Sopranos– The Early Years?*) in ways that would bear no connection to the ultimate resolution (or nonresolution) of the original television series. However, when it was reported in May 2008 that David Chase had signed with Paramount to write, direct, and produce his first motion picture, the indications were that he didn't want to do a *Sopranos* sequel or even a mafia story of any kind—at least not for the immediate future.

6 Timothy L. O'Brien, "The Rise of the Digital Thugs: They Found Your Secrets and They'll Keep Them, for a Price," *New York Times*, August 7, 2005, section 3.

7 Laura M. Holson, "There Really Is No Business Like Show Business: Michael Ovitz's Hollywood Is a Dismal Dream Factory," *New York Times*, Sunday Business Section, November 7, 2004. Actually, one episode of *The Sopranos*, "D-Girl," in which Tony Soprano's nephew Christopher (Michael Imperioli) has an affair with a Hollywood "development girl," only to have her and her boss, Jon Favreau, steal ideas from him, suggests the lack of fit between the Soprano mobsters and the world of Hollywood. Mafia crime may be more violent and fatal than Hollywood's no more than metaphoric "cut-throat" activities, but the latter's way of life is revealed to be bound to no code of honor and to have no respect for family and deep ties of commitment and community.

8 John Sutherland, "How the Governor of New Jersey Appointed a Radical Poet Laureate—and Immediately Wished He Hadn't," *The Guardian*, January 27, 2003.

9 Walter Mossberg, "A New Way to Record 'The Sopranos': Prices for DVD Recorders Fall But Devices Are Hard to Use; A Remote with 57 Buttons," *Wall Street Journal*, March 10, 2004.

1 Watching *The Sopranos*

1 At various points in this study, I talk of *The Sopranos* in terms of the "postmodern," which I take, in large part, to refer to a quality of many cultural works, especially in recent decades, that renders our experience of them quite ambiguous, quite hard to figure out, and quite hard to evaluate. The difficulty here is not one of depth: it's not that the works have profundities of meaning that we need to work at surfacing and for which we are never sure that we have exhausted all interpretations. Quite to the contrary, it's the case with postmodernist culture that we're not sure if the works are indeed meaningful at all or just teasingly offer us bribes of meaning that don't really add up, that shouldn't be taken seriously, or are just goofs. One

way postmodern works can play with and perform such uncertainty shows up in their use of a seeming awareness—what we can term a savviness—about likely attempts by the viewer or reader or listener to make sense of them and pin them down through acts of interpretation. Postmodern works sometimes appear to have meanings below the surface, but these often slip away, and the works often defeat interpretation and mock interpretative pretensions: for example, by including moments within the works in which someone pretentious tries to interpret and is rendered ridiculous. Postmodernism then has to do with a blurring of levels: high and low, profound and superficial, serious and playful, reflective and self-reflexive, refined and vulgar, good and bad even.

In this respect, it is to my mind an open question whether or not the slackening of narrative, disruption of plot lines, detour and so on that I assume as operative in *The Sopranos* and as contributing to an ironizing effect in the show are all to be seen as intentional—as, in other words, the effect of an overall design on the part of the creators. To put it another way, if it is indeed the case that *The Sopranos* doesn't deliver on tight narrative, how do we know whether that nondelivery was planned or not? How would we even distinguish any such deliberate planning of plot deconstruction from simple narrative inconsistencies and aesthetic failings of a sort that are perhaps inevitable in a series that extends over many seasons? As we watch a work of popular postmodernism like *The Sopranos*, it is hard to know always what works or not, and it is hard to fix the criteria by which we could know that and convince others of it. That is, to the extent to which we can feel that elements of the show work, it's difficult to say what we mean by that. Working how? To what end?

It's important to hold in suspension the question of intentionality and design, since, as a colleague of mine usefully cautions, it can encourage the "belief that all aspects of the series narrative exist due to the willed, calculated design of a creator and that it all fits together according to the creator's master plan." In this respect, while this study of *The Sopranos* will sometimes credit series creator David Chase with specific decisions and inventions (hoping at the same time to acknowledge the creative input of other workers on the show), it is, to my mind, important to distinguish, on the one hand, the ability of an individual like Chase to have contributory ideas and intentions from, on the other hand, any assumption that this implies such virtues as artistic infallibility, control of unconscious impulses that may lie below the reach of conscious intent, the artist's full grasp of the design of his work of art (and of that which is undesigned and unstructured in the work), the artist's independence from the effects of the decisions of other creative workers, the artist's freedom from the constraints of genre, prior tradition, and the weight of cultural conventions, the inevitable and full realization of the artist's best intentions and designs, and all the other magical values that are attributed to the film or television auteur as special and privileged genius.

2 For one example of such possible interpretation, see Cameron Golden, "'You're Annette Bening': Dream and Hollywood as Subtext in *The Sopranos*," in David Lavery, ed., *Reading the Sopranos*.

3 For one discussion of walk-and-talk, see Emily Nelson, "Rapid-Fire Dialogue Increases on Networks," *Detroit News*, November 19, 2002, accessed at http://www.detnews.com/2002/entertainment/0211/21/b05–14143.htm.

2 Eight Million Stories in the Naked City

1 Jeffrey Sconce, "What If? Charting Television's New Textual Boundaries," in Lynn Spigel and Jan Olssen, eds., *Television after TV: Essays on a Medium in Transition* (Durham, N.C.: Duke University Press, 2004), 98.

2 Rachel Moseley, "'Real Lads Do Cook. . . . But Some Things Are Still Hard to Talk About': The Gendering of 8–9," *European Journal of Cultural Studies* 4, no. 1 (2001): 32–39.

4 Living in the Moment

1 Roland Barthes, "The Reality Effect," *The Rustle of Language*, trans. Richard Howard (Berkeley: University of California Press, 1989), 141–48.

5 The Late Style of *The Sopranos*

1 Theodor Adorno, "Late Style in Beethoven," *Essays on Music*, ed. Richard Leppert (Berkeley: University of California Press, 2002), 564–67; Edward W. Said, *On Late Style: Music and Literature Against the Grain* (New York: Pantheon Books, 2006), 7. Further page references in text.

2 Norman Cohn, *The Pursuit of the Millennium* (New York: Harper, 1961).

3 Geoffrey O'Brien, "A Northern New Jersey of the Mind," *New York Review of Books*, 54, no. 13 (August 16, 2007): 20.

4 John Caughie, *Television Drama: Realism, Modernism, and British Culture* (New York: Oxford University Press, 2000), 178.

5 Theodor Adorno, *In Search of Wagner*, trans. Rodney Livingstone (London: New Left Books, 1981), 40.

1 Mikael Jakobsson and T. L. Taylor, "*The Sopranos* Meets EverQuest: Social Networking in Massively Multiplayer Online Games," paper presented at the 5th International Digital Arts and Culture Conference, Melbourne, Australia. Accessed at http://hypertext.rmit.edu.au/dac/papers/Jakobs son.pdf.

2 Richard Florida, *The Rise of the Creative Class, and How It's Transforming Work, Leisure, Community and Everyday Life* (New York: Basic Books, 2002). In all that follows, I should clarify that I find Florida's analysis useful as a description of the *lifestyle* of the creative class but worrisome in its valorization of the political import of that class, which he tends to laud for a creativity defined in the abstract. There is little sense in Florida's study of the specific purposes to which creativity could be applied and of the contexts in which it is applied so that, in the end, all creative workers in all sectors end up resembling each other. It is sobering to realize that everything he says could apply equally to a military researcher developing new scenarios for war as to a worker in the creative media industries.

3 Steven Johnson, *Everything Bad Is Good for You: How Today's Popular Culture Is Actually Making Us Smarter* (New York: Riverhead Books, 2005). Further page references are provided in the text.

I should note that while I generally concur with Johnson's description of the formal complexity of the TV show, I disagree with his larger perspective on popular culture—namely, that such complexity resonates because it stimulates basic and fundamentally biological processes of cognition that can be analyzed and appreciated outside of particularizing contexts of culture, history, and society. For critical discussion of Johnson, see Allison McCracken's "Evaluating TV Smarts in the Public Sphere" and reactions to her piece, posted on the Web site for the online TV and media studies journal *Flow*, http://idg.communication.utexas.edu/flow/?jot=view&id=783.

4 Jan Symons offers an initial theorization of the viewer for filmed entertainment as resembling a Web lurker in his *Playing the Waves: Lars Von Triers's Game Cinema* (Amsterdam: Amsterdam University Press, 2007), 147–52.

5 Mary Beth Haralovich and Michael W. Trosset, "'Expect the Unexpected': Narrative Pleasure and Uncertainty Due to Chance in *Survivor*," in Susan Murray and Laurie Ouellette, eds., *Reality TV: Remaking Television Culture* (New York: New York University Press, 2004), 75–96.

6 Matt Zoller-Seitz, "Leaving the Family," *Star-Ledger*, February 14, 2001, accessed at http://www.nj.com/sopranos/ledger/index.ssf?/sopranos/sto ries021401chase.html.

7 Film scholar Martha P. Nochimson makes a similar point about the ways in which long-running series "leave room for the ravages and blessings caused by changes in the lives and desires of the members of the creative community of the show, the vicissitudes of public taste, and the sudden appearance of new ideas and personnel." See Nochimson, "Tony's Options: *The Sopranos* and the Televisuality of the Gangster Genre," *Senses of Cinema* 29 (November–December 2003), accessed at http://www.sensesofcinema.com/contents/03/29/sopranos_televisuality.html.

7 Getting High with *The Sopranos*

1 See the useful overview in Christine Geraghty, "Aesthetics and Quality in Popular Television Drama," *International Journal of Cultural Studies* 6, no. 1 (2003): 25–45. A more recent summary of the issues, which makes passing reference to HBO and *The Sopranos*, is Robin Nelson, "'Quality Television': '*The Sopranos* Is the Best Television Drama Ever . . . in My Humble Opinion'," *Critical Studies in Television* 1, no. 1 (spring 2006): 58–71.

2 Stephen Holden, "Sympathetic Brutes in a Pop Masterpiece," *New York Times*, June 6, 1999. The love of the *New York Times* for HBO quality was reciprocated in 2008 when editorialist Frank Rich was hired as a consultant to the cable network while maintaining his job at the paper. Press releases asserted that Rich would be recused from any journalistic project that touched on HBO or its parent, Time Warner.

3 Robert Lloyd, "Mob Rules: David Chase on *The Sopranos*, the Small Screen, and Rock and Roll," *LA Weekly* 23, no. 17 (March 16–22, 2001): 28.

4 "Hit Man," Jim Lehrer interview with David Chase, August 8, 2001, accessed at http://www.pbs.org/newshour/bb/entertainment/july-dec01/chase_8-8.html.

5 Allen Rucker, "An Interview with David Chase," *The Sopranos: A Family History.*

6 John Caughie, *Television Drama*, 122.

7 Julie Salamon, "The Waiting Finally Ends, but the Worrying Never Will" (interview with David Chase), *New York Times*, September 8, 2002, section 2.

8 For explanations of the visual style of *The Sopranos*, there are several firsthand accounts by and about the cinematographers for the show: Eric Rudolph, "Memories of the Mob," *American Cinematographer*, October 1998, 107–8; Eric Rudolph, "Mob Psychology," *American Cinematographer*, October 1999, 62–69; Eric Rudolph, "*The Sopranos* Plants Roots

(and Bodies) in the Garden State," *American Cinematographer*, March 2001, 107–8; "An Offer He Could Not Refuse: Phil Abraham Shoots *The Sopranos*," http://www.tiffen.com/tiffen45.pdf; "Mob Hit: Shooting *The Sopranos*," http://www.kodak.com/US/en/motion/newsletters/inCamera/july2000/sopranos.shtml.

9 See, for instance, the interview with Edie Falco by Jesse Green, "Unmarried to the Mob: Anticipating Life without Tony Soprano, Edie Falco Returns to Her First Love with "night, Mother'," *New York Times*, November 7, 2004. As I write these lines, the *New York Times* has just reported on the explosion of a pipe bomb device outside Imperioli's theater. The writer of the article can't resist making allusions to *The Sopranos* and its frequent use of plots where businesses are bombed or otherwise beset with violence. It is as if the sordid world of the television show bleeds beyond its boundaries to infect the higher world of ambitious theatrical experiment.

10 John Caldwell, *Televisuality: Style, Crisis, and Authority in American Television* (New Brunswick, N.J.: Rutgers University Press, 1995).

11 Shawn Shimpach, "The Immortal Cosmopolitan: The International Co-Production and Global Circulation of *Highlander: The Series*," *Cultural Studies* 19, no. 3 (May 2005), 345.

12 One of the DVD commentaries for the show even explains that a shot of the New York waterfront that opens a key sequence taking place in Manhattan actually was stock footage shot much earlier for another scene; "New York" thus becomes a source of endlessly malleable stock images.

13 See Joanne Lacey, "One for the Boys: *The Sopranos* and Its Male, British Audience," in David Lavery, ed., *This Thing of Ours: Investigating "The Sopranos"* (New York: Columbia University Press, 2002), 95–108.

14 Jane Feuer discusses the double debt of HBO so-called quality TV to theater and to art cinema in "HBO and the Concept of Quality TV," in Janet McCabe and Kim Akass, eds., *Quality TV: Contemporary American Television and Beyond* (London: I. B. Tauris & Co. Ltd., 2007), 145–57.

8 Qualifying "Quality TV"

1 Caryn James, "Addicted to a Mob Family Potion," in Stephen Holden, ed., *The New York Times on The Sopranos* (New York: The New York Times, 2000), 50.

2 Peggy Noonan, "Old Jersey Real," *Wall Street Journal*, June 9–10, 2007.

3 Caughie, *Television Drama*, 69–71.

9 "Honey, I'm Home"

1 Terry Teachout, "Is Tony Soprano Today's Ward Cleaver?" *New York Times*, Week in Review, September 15, 2002. A sidebar to another *New York Times* article on *The Sopranos* actually compares and contrasts the characters of *Leave It to Beaver* and *The Sopranos* one-by-one. For example, Eddy Haskell "flatters the grown-ups, double-crosses his peers," while Chris Moltisanti is "duplicitous with the grown-ups, whacks his peers." See "TV Households, Then and Now," sidebar to Bill Carter, "Calibrating Next Step for 'The Sopranos'," *New York Times*, Business Day, October 7, 2002.

2 Ken Tucker, "All in the Family," *Entertainment Weekly* 670 (September 6, 2002), 2.

3 Maurice Yacowar, *The Sopranos on the Couch*, 283. Interestingly, the production team for *The Sopranos* actually shot footage of the Soprano gang outside the set for Satriale's Pork Store so that Tony would pass by his crew on his way home. It was ultimately decided to leave out this material and concentrate on Tony alone on his voyage home.

10 Against Interpretation

1 Lisa Johnson, "The Stripper as Resisting Reader: Stripper Iconography and Sex Worker Feminism on *The Sopranos*," *The Scholar and the Feminist On-Line* 3 no. 1 (fall 2004), special issue on "Feminist Television Studies: The Case of HBO," accessed at http://www.barnard.edu/sfonline/hbo/johnson_01.htm.

2 A condensation of the Canadian government's investigation and elaboration of its verdict is available at the Canadian Broadcast Standard Council's Web site at www.cbsc.ca/english/decisions/decisions/2001/010524.htm.

3 See, for instance, Jennifer Steinhauer, "Object to 'Sopranos' Actors in Parade? What Are You Going to Do?" *New York Times*, October 10, 2002.

4 For an energetic version of the attack on the show, see the C-Span broadcast from May 15, 2001, "Stereotypes: How Harmful Are They?" which concentrates on the show and features denunciations of it by Camille Paglia and others.

5 Barbara Ehrenreich, *Nickel and Dimed: On (Not) Getting By in America* (New York: Metropolitan Books, 2001).

6 Presciently, when, a few days before this episode aired, a *New Yorker* cover (June 4, 2007) tried to sum up what detaching from the last episodes of the series felt like, it did so with an image of Tony walking out of Melfi's

office in a final goodbye. To the extent that *The Sopranos* had ever had a core narrative premise, it was that of the gangster in therapy, and the *New Yorker* cover aptly captured all the emotional (and now sentimental) resonances Tony's encounters with Melfi had stirred up over the years. *The Sopranos* was tailor-made for a journal like the *New Yorker* that wanted to take the pulse of literary, cultural, and artistic life for readers in the orbit of the urban professional. As aptly, the television series itself had, early on (in season 3), noted the publication's importance for that social stratum. When Melfi was shown trying to recuperate after being raped, the scene began with a closeup of a *New Yorker* issue on her bed as a shorthand indication of the lifestyle demographic of which she was clearly supposed by the show to be a member.

7 Sandra M. Gilbert, "Life with (God)father," in Regina Barreca, ed., *A Sitdown with The Sopranos: Watching Italian American Culture on TV's Most Talked-About Series* (New York: Palgrave MacMillan, 2002).

8 David Remnick, "Is This the End of Rico?: With 'The Sopranos,' the Mob Genre Is on the Brink," *New Yorker*, April 2, 2001, 38–44; quotation from 41.

9 Gary Younge, "Mafia Boss Rubbed Out for Being Gay," *The Guardian*, May 2, 2003.

10 Throughout this study, I imply the power of what we might term the "*Sopranos* effect," by which the show entices viewers to reference it in the culture at large and, more generally, to exploit it for their own purposes, even as it itself anticipates these appropriations and frequently holds them up to mockery, gentle or otherwise. It is perhaps a similar effect that manifests itself when some of the creative personnel that work on *The Sopranos* get caught up in criminal activity not unlike that represented in the show. Thus, Robert Iler, who played the confused teenager A. J., was arrested for drug possession during the run of the series, while Lillo Brancato Jr., the actor who played the impetuous young low-level gangster Matt Bevilacqua, impetuously got involved in a heist that led to the murder of an off-duty policeman and is now in prison (where, art-imitates-life, he talks about how great a movie of his life would be). Most notoriously, in the same week in May 2007 that HBO aired an episode of *The Sopranos* that chronicled how dangerous Christopher Moltisanti's drug and alcohol addiction had become, HBO head Chris Albrecht was arrested in Las Vegas for a late-night brutal beating of his girlfriend while he was drunk. When news media found out that Albrecht had had a history of substance abuse and of violence against other girlfriends, HBO was propelled to dismiss him.

11 Museum of Television and Broadcasting, interview with David Chase (catalogue no. 129593).

12 See Sarah Boxer, "Therapists Go Crazy for One in 'Sopranos,'" *New York Times*, December 29, 2001, A13, A15. Psychoanalyst Glen O. Gabbard, who's written a book on the therapeutic process in the show (*The Psychology of The Sopranos: Love, Death, Desire, and Betrayal in America's Favorite Gangster Family* [New York: Basic Books, 2002]), has also hosted an often energetic Internet dialogue at www.slate.com, where psychoanalysts could debate the propriety, purity, and efficiency of Melfi's mode of therapeutic practice.

11 New Jersey Dreaming

1 Tammy La Gorce, "New Brunswick Still Loves the Lads from Liverpool," *New York Times*, New Jersey section, August 12, 2007.

2 Edward W. Said, *On Late Style*, 155. The Tanner phrase is from his *Venice Desired* (Oxford: Blackwell, 1992), 124.

The Sopranos in the Marketplace

1 Bill Carter, "Tony Soprano and Crew Will Return for '07 Season," *New York Times*, August 12, 2005.

12 Tie-ins and Hangers-on

1 John Weber and Chuck Kim, eds., *The Tao of Bada Bing!: Words of Wisdom from The Sopranos* (New York: HBO, 2003).

2 John Michael Maas, "Wide Angle Tie-Ins: Publishers Lure Readers with Unconventional Approaches to Familiar Media Properties," *Publishers Weekly*, April 21, 2003, 17.

3 Allen Rucker, *The Sopranos Family Cookbook: As Compiled by Artie Bucco* (New York: Grand Central Publishing, 2002). Factual information on the cookbook in this paragraph comes from e-mail communication from Rucker, to whom I offer thanks.

4 The cartoon strip is by Mark Alan Stamaty and appeared in the *New York Times Book Review*, November 10, 2002, 27.

13 Touring Postindustrialism

1 For broader analysis of the TV locales tours, see Leshu Torchin, "Location, Location, Location: The Destination of the Manhattan TV Tour," *Tourist Studies* 2, no. 3 (2002): 247–66. A perceptive reflection on the *Sopranos* tour is Nick Couldry, "On the Set of *The Sopranos*: 'Inside' a Fan's Construction of Nearness," in J. Gray, W. Brooker, and C. Sandoss, eds., *Fandom: Identities and Communities in a Mediated World* (New York: New York University Press, 2006), 189–202.

2 Sherry Ortner, *New Jersey Dreaming: Capital, Culture, and the Class of '58* (Durham, N.C.: Duke University Press, 2003).

3 For the *Architectural Digest* spread, see Michael Frank, "Creating a Mobster's Scene: On the Set of HBO's Dramatic Series *The Sopranos*," *Architectural Digest*, September 2002, 98, 104, 106, 112.

14 Cashing In on the Game

1 At the end of 2007, the case went back into the courts yet again and was thrown out yet again—seemingly for the last time. See Robert Strauss, "Jury Rejects Man's Bid for Share of 'Sopranos,'" *New York Times*, December 20, 2007.

2 Bracco, quoted on *The Unofficial Lorraine Bracco Website* at http://www.lbracco.com/onthecouch2006.htm. Bracco has also been hired by pharmaceutical company Pfizer to do television commercials to direct consumers to a Web site for the antidepressant Zoloft. See Stephanie Saul, "More Celebrities Finding Roles as Antidepressant Advocates," *New York Times*, March 21, 2005.

3 Pastore is quoted within a broader discussion of *Sopranos* tie-ins by Michael McCarthy, "'Sopranos' Mania Means Money," http://www.usatoday.com/money/covers/2001–05–17-bcovthu.htm. It might additionally be noted that Pastore has also signed a minimal and meager "foreword" for *The Sopranos and Philosophy: I Kill, Therefore I Am* (Chicago: Open Court, 2004).

4 For one example, see Matt Zoller Seitz, "'Sopranos' Sought Extras, Got the Works," *Star-Ledger*, August 1, 2000, accessed at http://www.nj.com/sopranos/ledger/index.ssf?/sopranos/stories/0801extras.html.

5 Matthew Purdy, "Royal Family of New Jersey: The Sopranos," *New York Times*, January 23, 2000.

6 Annette Hill and David Gauntlett, *TV Living: Television, Culture, and Everyday Life* (New York: Routledge, 1999).

7 Alan Sepinwall, "Book 'Em—Suddenly, It's a Family Full of Authors," *Star-Ledger*, September 13, 2002. Accessed at http://www.nj.com/sopranos/ledger/index.ssf?/sopranos/stories/sopranos091302.html.

8 David Bernstein, "Philosophy Hitches a Ride with 'The Sopranos': Small Publisher Finds Route to Big Numbers," *New York Times*, April 13, 2004.

9 David Simon, *Tony Soprano's America: The Criminal Side of the American Dream*.

15 Cable and the Economics of Experimentation

1 Susan Murray, "'I Think We Need a New Name for It': The Meeting of Documentary and Reality TV," in Susan Murray and Laurie Ouellette, eds., *Reality TV: Remaking Television Culture* (New York: NYU Press, 2004), 42. Further page references are provided in the text.

2 See Feuer's chapters in Feuer, Paul Kerr, and Tise Vahimagi, eds., *MTM: "Quality Television"* (London: British Film Institute, 1984).

3 Monica Hogan, "Ops Exploit New 'Sopranos' to Fullest," *Multichannel News*, February 26, 2001, 10.

4 Mike Reynolds, "A Highly Original Interview with HBO's Albrecht," *Multichannel News*, June 11, 2001, 124.

5 On product placement in *The Sopranos*, see Janet Stilson, "Should Series Success Ad Up to More Coin? (HBO at 30)," *Variety*, November 4, 2002, A10.

6 For a useful summary of the bidding wars and the importance of syndication of *The Sopranos* to A&E, see Denise Martin, "A&E's Mob Mentality: Cabler Pays Top Dollar for 'Sopranos' in Attempt to Break Out of Niche and Build Up Its Ratings," *Variety*, February 7–13, 2005, 24, 26.

7 Alan Sepinwall, "'Sopranos' Gets Down to Basics," *Star-Ledger*, February 1, 2005, accessed at http://www.nj.com/sopranos/ledger/index.ssf?/sopranos/stories/02012005_alltv.html.

8 It is worth noting that the A&E iteration of the show may not have accomplished all it was supposed to do. An article in *Variety* at the beginning of 2008 suggests that the syndicated version of the series has been reaching an audience, but not the one A&E targeted: "One series that's not drawing as many young viewers as hoped is 'The Sopranos,' whose reruns on Wednesdays and Sundays are more popular with adults over 50 than under. . . . In 2007, 'Sopranos' averaged 1.8 million viewers on Wednesdays, a 37% increase over A&E's prime-time average. (Dismayingly, 54% of those viewers were people over 50.)" See John Dempsey, "Reality-Driven A&E Scripting a More Diverse Future," *Variety*, January 28–February 3, 2008, 24.

9 See Deborah Jaramillo, "The Family Racket: AOL Time Warner, HBO, *The Sopranos*, and the Construction of a Quality Brand," *Journal of Communication Inquiry* 26, no. 1 (January 2002): 59–75.

10 Paul Brownfield, "At HBO, the Bonfire of the Vanity Projects," *Los Angeles Times*, July 10, 2005, E25. See also Denise Martin, "HBO Hot for H'wood . . . but Is Cabler's Strategy Too 'Inside'?" *Variety.com*, July 17, 2005, accessed at http://www.variety.com/article/vr1117926079.

11 Museum of Television and Radio Seminar Series, March 30, 1999, "The Sopranos." Accession number B:57488.

12 A symptom of this West Coast/East Coast battle over art and business might then be the suggestion, by some entertainment industry commentators, that *The Sopranos* initially got shut out of Emmy wins for best drama because it was too East Coast and that David Chase had sinned by his desire to *not* "go Hollywood." See, for instance, Linda Moss, "'Sopranos' Aside, Cable Rules at Emmys," *Multichannel News*, September 20, 1999, 22.

13 "Special Report: How to Manage a Dream Factory—The Entertainment Industry," *The Economist*, January 18, 2003.

14 For background, see Joseph Menn, "Microsoft Courts Hollywood Allies," *Los Angeles Times*, July 17, 2005.

15 David D. Kirkpatrick, "In HBO, AOL Sees a Sibling and, Crucially, a Role Model," *New York Times*, May 5, 2003.

16 See Monica Hogan, "HBO's 'Sopranos' Goes High-Definition," *Multichannel News*, January 8, 2001, 38. On the ways in which *The Sopranos* is part of a general aesthetic style marked by shows (others include *The West Wing* and *Angel*) that resist pan-and-scan cutting down of the frame and try instead to emulate widescreen cinematic processes, see Allan Johnson, "Do Not Adjust Your Sets: It's Just Letterbox," *Toronto Star*, March 2, 2002. In fact, while *The Sopranos* is shot in a widescreen format, the cinematographers are asked to compose their shots in ways that keep all salient plot information within a narrower frame that corresponds to pan-and-scan. This enables the show to be syndicated to channels that don't intend widescreen presentation in letterbox format. Even at the level of its basic form and format, *The Sopranos* is an unstable text which literally can be retrofitted for different visual formats.

17 In an analysis of the representation in *The Sopranos* of late capitalist enterprise, scholars Steven Hayward and Andrew Biro argue perceptively that while Tony Soprano claims a nostalgia for an older way of life with simpler work relations, his actual practice is to thrive in a new age of expansive operations by which he can generate new forms of revenue and extrac-

tion of ill-begotten wealth from the world at large. In their words, "Tony's grandfather was engaged in a materially productive kind of labor that produced tangible, lasting results—a kind of productivity that no longer seems possible. . . . The work in which Tony and his contemporaries are involved is instead the more ephemeral production of the service and information economy: waste management and 'pump and dump' stock schemes." See Hayward and Biro, "The Eighteenth Brumaire of Tony Soprano," in David Lavery, ed., *This Thing of Ours: Investigating The Sopranos*.

18 See also Meredith Amdur, "Has Success Spoiled HBO?" *Variety*, August 25–31, 2003, A14.

19 The standard account of HBO is the anecdotal volume by George Mair, *Inside HBO: The Billion Dollar War between HBO, Hollywood, and the Home Video Revolution* (New York: Dodd, Mead & Company, 1988). A more recent and more analytic account appears in Gary R. Edgerton's and Jeffrey P. Jones's anthology, *The Essential HBO Reader*.

20 For sex programming as an intermediate step in the elaboration of modern cable, see Karen Backstein, "Soft Love: The Romantic Vision of Sex on the Showtime Network," *Television & New Media* 2, no. 4 (November 2001): 303–17.

21 See Emily Nelson, "Fox's Shows, Promos Try Recapturing Youth," *Wall Street Journal*, September 9, 2002.

22 Emily Nelson, "Can NBC's 'Kingpin' Settle Score with Tony Soprano?" *Wall Street Journal*, December 9, 2002.

23 Eric Deggans, "Will Crime Pay?" *Hispanic* 16, no. 3 (March 2003), 44.

24 For one such case, listen to National Public Radio, "'Sopranos' Night Eliminated," November 16, 2002, available at http://www.npr.org/templates/story/story.php?storyId=845074.

25 On HBO's hold on Sunday night, see Michael Schneider, "Securing the Sunday Stronghold (HBO at 30)," *Variety*, November 4, 2002, A38; and Scott Collins, "HBO Is Sunday Schooled: Networks' Grip on Sundays Is Loosened," *Los Angeles Times*, March 5, 2004.

Selected Bibliography

Barreca, Regina, ed. *A Sitdown with The Sopranos: Watching Italian American Culture on TV's Most Talked-About Series*. New York: Palgrave Macmillan, 2002.

Bishop, David. *Bright Lights, Baked Ziti: The Unofficial, Unauthorized Guide to The Sopranos*. London: Virgin Books, 2001.

Bondanella, Peter E. *Hollywood Italians: Dagos, Palookas, Romeos, Wise Guys, and Sopranos*. New York: Continuum, 2004.

Chase, David. *The Sopranos: Selected Scripts for Three Seasons*. New York: Warner Books, 2002.

Edgerton, Gary R., and Jeffrey P. Jones, eds. *The Essential HBO Reader*. Lexington: University Press of Kentucky, 2008.

Fahy, Thomas, ed. *Considering David Chase: Essays on* The Rockford Files, Northern Exposure, *and* The Sopranos. Jefferson, N.C.: McFarland & Co., 2008.

Gabbard, Glenn O. *The Psychology of The Sopranos: Love, Death, Desire and Betrayal in America's Favorite Gangster Family*. New York: Basic Books, 2002.

Greene, Richard, and Peter Vernezze, eds. *The Sopranos and Philosophy: I Kill Therefore I Am*. Chicago: Open Court, 2004.

Grieveson, Lee, Esther Sonnet, and Peter Stanfield, eds. *Mob Culture: Hidden Histories of the American Gangster Film*. New Brunswick, N.J.: Rutgers University Press, 2005.

Jaramillo, Deborah L. "The Family Racket: AOL Time Warner, HBO, *The Sopranos*, and the Construction of a Quality Brand," *Journal of Communication Inquiry* 26, no. 1 (January 2002): 59–75.

Lavery, David, ed. *Reading The Sopranos: Hit TV from HBO*. New York: I. B. Tauris, 2006.

———. *This Thing of Ours: Investigating the Sopranos*. London: Wallflower Press, 2002.

Leverette, Marc, Brian L. Ott, and Cara Louise Buckely, eds. *It's Not TV: Watching HBO in the Post-Television Era*. New York: Routledge, 2008.

Longworth, James L. Jr. *TV Creators: Conversations with America's Top Producers of Television Drama*. Syracuse, N.Y.: Syracuse University Press, 2000.

McCabe, Janet, and Kim Akass, eds. *Quality TV: Contemporary American Television and Beyond*. London: I. B. Tauris, 2007.

McCarty, John. *Bullets over Hollywood: The American Gangster Picture from the Silents to "The Sopranos."* Cambridge, Mass.: Da Capo Press, 2004.

Roman, Steven A., ed. *The New York Times on "The Sopranos."* New York: Simon & Schuster, 2002.

Rucker, Allen. *Entertaining with the Sopranos: As Compiled by Carmela Soprano*. New York: Warner Books, 2006.

———. *The Sopranos Family Cookbook As Compiled by Artie Bucco*. New York: Warner Books, 2002.

———. *The Sopranos: A Family History, Updated for the 4th Season*. New York: New American Library, 2003.

Seay, Chris. *The Gospel According to Tony Soprano: An Unauthorized Look into the Soul of TV's Top Mob Boss and His Family*. Lake Mary, Fla.: Relevant Books, 2002.

Simon, David. *Tony Soprano's America: The Criminal Side of the American Dream*. Boulder, Colo.: Westview Press, 2002.

Yacowar, Maurice. *The Sopranos on the Couch: The Ultimate Guide*. New York: Continuum, 2006.

Index

Italicized page numbers refer to illustrations

Dana Polan is a professor of Cinema Studies
at the Tisch School of the Arts, New York University.
He is the author of several books, including *Scenes
of Instruction: The Beginnings of the U.S. Study of Film*;
Pulp Fiction; *Power and Paranoia: History, Narrative,
and the American Cinema, 1940–1950*; and the forth-
coming *The French Chef* (Duke University Press).

*Library of Congress
Cataloging-in-Publication Data*
Polan, Dana B.
The Sopranos / Dana Polan.
p. cm.
Includes bibliographical references and index.
ISBN 978-0-8223-4392-9 (cloth : alk. paper)
ISBN 978-0-8223-4410-0 (pbk. : alk. paper)
1. Sopranos (Television program) I. Title.
PN1992.77.S66P65 2009
791.45'72—dc22
2008048039